Oye Como Va!

Deborah Pacini Hernandez

Oye Como Va!

Hybridity and Identity in
Latino Popular Music

TEMPLE UNIVERSITY PRESS
Philadelphia

Temple University Press
1601 North Broad Street
Philadelphia PA 19122
www.temple.edu/tempress

∞ The paper used in this publication meets the requirements of the
American National Standard for Information Sciences—Permanence of
Paper for Printed Library Materials, ANSI Z39.48-1992

Library of Congress Cataloging-in-Publication Data

Pacini Hernandez, Deborah.
  Oye como va! : hybridity and identity in Latino popular music /
Deborah Pacini Hernandez.
     p.   cm.
  Includes bibliographical references and index.
  ISBN 978-1-4399-0089-5 (cloth : alk. paper) — ISBN 978-1-4399-0090-1
(pbk. : alk. paper)
1. Hispanic Americans—Music—Social aspects.   2. Popular music—Social
aspects—United States.   I. Title.
  ML3917.U6P33 2009
  781.64089′68073—dc22   2009012832

2 4 6 8 9 7 5 3 1

Contents

Preface

Because hybridity—the mixture of two or more dissimilar elements—produces objects or people that are in between and out of place, it is often considered dangerous, inferior, or contaminating. My dual-region ancestry, set down in two areas widely and erroneously perceived to be racially and culturally distinct (Latin America and the United States), has been the source of tensions and anxieties associated with feeling in between and out of place. My father, who was born in Barranquilla, Colombia, was himself of mixed ancestry: the child of a Colombian mother and a third-generation Italian Colombian father, whose extended Colombian-born Italian Colombian family members kept their ties to and identification with the "old country" as active as they could in the days before means of transportation and communication made it easy to do so. Indeed, my paternal grandfather had broken with his parents' generation's standing practice of returning to Italy to find a bride when he married my grandmother, a local Colombian woman, who, family lore has it, may have been of Sephardic ancestry. My mother, who was born and raised in the United States, has maternal ancestors who have resided in the mid-Atlantic and northeastern part of the country for generations. But her father was an immigrant from Canada, the child of German immigrants to the province of Kitchener, who came to the United States as a young man to practice his chosen profession as a Presbyterian minister.

Complicating my ancestral mix is the fact that I lack strong cultural roots in any one place. Because my father's quixotic and peripatetic nature impelled my family to move repeatedly among New York State, Colombia, and various other parts of Latin America, my childhood—and, hence, my deepest sense of self—was indelibly imprinted with the rhythms, sounds, and sights of multiple locations. As an adult, I have spent several years, on and off, in the northern coastal region of Colombia (known locally as *la costa*), where I lived as a child. My first marriage was to a *barranquillero* (whose indigenous ancestry was unclaimed but phenotypically visible), who turned out to be as unstable as my father; thus, for the seven years of our marriage, I continued moving back and forth between Colombia and the United States. As a result, my daughter, Radha, was born in coastal Cartagena, and my son, Tai, was born in New York, and neither one has lived in the place where he or she was born for more than a few months. After I became an anthropologist, I spent several seasons in Colombia doing fieldwork, but now the years I have lived in the United States far outnumber the years I have lived in Colombia. My vivid memories of and family connections and personal attachments to Colombia nevertheless remain integral features of my psyche, alongside those—equally powerful—that I have developed in the United States. Despite my ambiguous identity and the instability connected with my lack of deep roots in a single location, I am grateful for my life of multiplicities and movement. These are the life experiences that have, among other things, honed my sensitivity to hybridity (and its discontents) whenever and wherever I have encountered or observed it.

This book—which explores the simultaneously powerful, vexing, and stimulating relationships between hybridity, music, and identity—grew out of my personal realization of the dangers (as George Lipsitz has phrased it) of living at the crossroads.[1] Growing up with English- *and* Spanish-speaking relatives and friends, listening to rock 'n' roll *and cumbias,* loving corn flakes *and* Colombia's corn *arepas,* I identified with both the United States and Colombia but never felt that I belonged completely in, or to, either one. As a child, I was unsure how to answer when people asked where I was from, and when I got older, I was confounded by the identity boxes on official forms. In the 1980s, I claimed the term "Latina" as a better alternative than "My father is from Colombia, and my mother is from the United States." Even so, I often found myself excluded from the "Latina" category because my profile did not conform to widespread expectations of what that identifier was supposed to encompass: My background included Latin American ancestry and residence, but my parents were both college-educated and middle-class (despite the economically precarious situations we often found ourselves in as a result of my father's instability). Moreover, because of my light skin and its concomitant privileges, I was not a target of the overt racism experienced by darker-skinned Latinos. But since I did not conform to prevailing ideas of who or what it was to be "American" either, I found myself in between and out of place.

In my adolescence, a time when group identity is so important to a young person's developing sense of self, I did not have one. Now, having spent decades as a researcher and educator exploring the diversity of U.S. Latino experiences, I know that many other Latinos and Latinas with mixed ancestries and multiple geographic roots have also had to defend themselves against charges of fraudulently claiming an identity—be it white, black, Puerto Rican, American, Latino, or any other presumably bounded category. Indeed, the effects of ambiguity and dislocation produced by hybridity and border crossings have been well articulated in a vibrant body of literature pioneered by Latino and Latina writers such as Piri Thomas, Gloria Anzaldúa, Cherríe Moraga, and Frances Negrón-Muntaner and subsequently developed further by many others who have similarly experienced the alienation of feeling out of place. Given the pervasiveness of essentialist notions of fixed and unambiguous boundaries (among Latinos and non-Latinos alike), it is perhaps more accurate to locate myself and other similarly hybrid individuals as living not only at the crossroads but also in the crosshairs of U.S. identity politics.

If many Latinos have themselves been quite conscious of their hybridity, in the U.S. popular imagination the styles of music associated with Latinos have often been imagined as the "natural" expressions of communities defined ethnically or racially, as if they were unmixed and disconnected from other musics or, if mixed at all, mixed only with proximate cultures rather than with broader cultural developments on the national (and international) stage. The corollary has been that Latinos who listened to rock 'n' roll, disco, and other contemporary styles of rock and hip-hop were somehow cultural traitors for having abandoned their ancestral identity and culture in order to get ahead by passing as something they were not. Some scholars, in contrast, have demonstrated the analytical power and possibilities of more inclusive approaches to U.S. Latino musical practices—such as Juan Flores in his pioneering work comparing New York Puerto Rican and Chicano identities and exploring the complicated roots of New York Puerto Rican boogaloo, George Lipsitz in his essays on merengue and *banda* in *Footsteps in the Dark,* and Luis Alvarez in his recent call for "relational" Latino studies.[2]

Oye Como Va![3] builds on and extends such comparative, cross-cultural work by placing hybridity itself at the center, examining and validating Latino music making and identity formation that have always taken place at the intersections of (presumably) dissimilar categories. Latinos' relationship to their hybridity has not been unproblematic, as it has often conflicted with equally powerful and valid desires to maintain a cultural identity uncomplicated by mixture or references to other genealogies. Central to the premise of this book, however, is the idea that far from being something abnormal or problematic, hybridity, whether racial, ethnic, cultural, or a combination of these, is one of the signature characteristics of the Latino experience: It is not a question of "either/or," but rather, like hybridity itself, of "both/and." *Oye Como Va!* brings to the surface and into focus the many ways that Latino musicians and their fans have refused to permit prevailing, often essentialist constructions of individual and group identity (no matter who espouses them) to limit their ability to define themselves.

As we move further into the new millennium, all sorts of border crossings have become easier and more commonplace, and even expected. Taking note of these developments, the eclectic, thoroughly transnational Latin Grammy–nominated musician Kevin Johansen—who grew up in and now performs his unique blend of Latin American and U.S. styles in both his mother's Argentina and his father's United States—announces on his Web site, "Mixture is the future."[4] In validating and valorizing Latino hybridity, however, it is important to emphasize that I am aware of the distinctions between cultural and racial hybridity and that I do not confuse racial hybridity with the concept of color-blindness, *blanqueamiento* (whitening), or other similarly veiled ways of erasing and denying the persistence of racial disparities and inequalities, which I discuss at length in Chapter 1.

My approach to the subject of hybridity and identity in Latino popular music is comparative and connective. I draw data from multiple sources in order to contrast the numerous inter- and intracultural strategies for negotiating hybridity (whether personal or musical) adopted over the past century and into the new millennium by Latinos from different ethnic, racial, and national backgrounds in different regions of the United States. Included are the musical practices of the foundational U.S. Latino communities: New York Puerto Ricans and Mexican Americans in California and the Southwest. Because globalization and the multiple diasporas it has set in motion have complicated the U.S. Latino music landscape, however, I add to the analytical mix examples of the musical blendings and layerings being produced by Dominicans and Colombians, recent immigrants whose identities, in a globalizing context, have proven to be even more complex than those of their predecessors. Still, this book is not intended to be comprehensive; some important groups, locations, and styles receive little or no attention. For example, Cuban music and Cuban Americans in the United States (whose locations and trajectories have not been the same) are mentioned but are not central within my narrative.[5] Other significant "urban borderlands" in the U.S. interior, such as Chicago, where the new musical hybrid *duranguense* appeared, are not covered here either. It is my hope that this book will serve as a template and road map for future comparative research into the layerings and mixings that have always characterized the United States and that have been intensified by newer immigrant flows.

My methodology is also hybrid. I draw extensively on my many years of fieldwork in the Spanish Caribbean and among Spanish Caribbean Latinos, but this is not an ethnography. My primary goals are to connect dots, to reveal patterns, and to interpret them through the theoretical lenses of hybridity and identity—or, more precisely, identities: what happens at the intersections of race, class, ethnic, national, gender, and generational identity formation. It is noteworthy that my work would not have been possible as recently as fifteen years ago, since most of the groundbreaking ethnographies and cultural histories of particular Latino communities and their musics had not yet been published. Today, I can see and interpret "the big picture" only because I can stand on the shoulders of Frances Aparicio, Juan Flores, Ruth Glasser, George Lipsitz, Manuel Peña, Raquel Z. Rivera, Helena Simonett, Peter Wade, Lise Waxer, and other scholars too numerous to mention. I am grateful to and thank them all.

Many others contributed to this book more directly by reading and commenting on drafts, answering particular queries, sharing their own work, or leading me to the work of others. They include (in alphabetical order—and my apologies for inadvertent omissions) Jorge Arévalo Mateus, Paul Austerlitz, Boy Wonder (Manuel Alejandro Ruiz), Christian Capellan, Maria Elena Cepeda, Marti Cuevas, Benjamin de Menil, Jorge Duany, Héctor Fernández L'Hoeste, Kai Fikentscher, Juan Flores, Hannah Gill, Jorge Giovanetti, Rubén Guevara, Peggy Levitt, Jeanette Luna, Peter Manuel, Wayne Marshall, Gerard Meraz, Carmen Oquendo, Jorge Oquendo, Juan Otero, Edilio Paredes, Cathy Ragland, Raquel Z. Rivera, Marisol Rodriguez, Giselle Roig, Helen Safa, Dave Sanjek, Helena Simonett, Roberta Singer, Chuy Varela, and Elijah Wald. I also thank the anonymous manuscript readers, whose insightful and knowledgeable comments were extremely helpful. Others contributed to this book in more practical ways: Aldo Marin from Cutting Records, Marika Pavlis from Rhino/Warner Brothers, and Gerard Meraz, who assisted with images and permissions; the deans at Tufts University, who gave me time off from teaching to work on the manuscript; Tufts University's FRAC Committee, which provided publication support; and Paige Johnson, Lynn Wiles, and Susan Ulbrich in the Anthropology Department and Kathy Spagnoli and Lauren Coy in American Studies, who helped in myriad small but important ways. Many thanks also go to those who assisted in the production process: Leslie Cohen, who helped format the original manuscript; Heather Wilcox, who provided copyediting; Carleen Loper, who assisted with proofreading; and Jan Williams, who did the indexing. Last but not least, I want to thank the Editorial, Production, and Marketing staff at Temple University Press, especially Janet Francendese, Joan Vidal, and Gary Kramer.

My most constant and valued source of support, however, has been my husband, best friend, and partner for life, Reebee Garofalo, whose unfaltering love and sense of humor carried me through some truly difficult moments and made the rest of them just plain fun. He also generously shared his extensive knowledge of U.S. popular music while I was thinking through material that intersected with his own work, making connections that I might not have discerned myself and referring me to additional sources. I am particularly grateful to him for reading many drafts of chapters for which—although he was not always familiar with the subject matter—he managed to provide me with a critical (if gentle) eye that greatly strengthened this book. Reebee's genealogy and upbringing, by the way, could not be more different from mine. To begin with, he is 100 percent southern Italian, as were his parents and his grandparents and his close-knit extended family, who still preface their Thanksgiving turkey dinner with a lasagna. (Luckily I had an Italian surname when I first met the family!) In addition, Reebee has spent all but a few years of his life in the northeastern region of the United States—in New Haven, where he grew up, and in Boston, where he has spent nearly forty years putting his interests in popular music and political activism together in socially productive ways. The almost two decades that I have spent with Reebee in the Boston area—after a childhood and young adulthood spent moving every few years—have given me a stability I had not known previously. I am deeply grateful to Reebee for the gift of roots.

I was also fortunate to be surrounded by a warm and generous circle of family and friends whose support deserves acknowledgment. I am particularly grateful to my mother, Betsey Pacini, whose natural curiosity and ability to savor new places and things taught me to make the best of growing up nomadic. Janine, Murray, and Zamawa in Somerville and Boston enriched my social and intellectual life while the book was in progress. I was also fortunate to be on the sidelines of, but close enough to be inspired by, the activities of Reebee's marching band, the Second Line Social Aid and Pleasure Society Brass Band, and the amazing Honk! Festival of activist marching bands they organize every October in Somerville. Most of the book, however, was written not in my adopted hometown, Somerville, but in our cottage on Broad Cove in Onset, on the south shore of Massachusetts, where we spend our summers and as many weekends as we can. My ability to raise my eyes from my computer screen and look out onto Broad Cove's constantly changing colors and textures and its passing wildlife helped me stay centered and sane during the intensely focused work of writing. More importantly, Carleen, Jim, Elliott, Irena, Dan, Rhonda, Dale, Mike, Bridget, Austin, Randy, Doug, Rocky, and Debby welcomed us into the kind of caring neighborhood community that I did not believe still existed.

Developing roots in Boston and southeastern Massachusetts has been made even easier by the blessing of living in close proximity to my daughter, Radha, and my son, Tai (now grown since I acknowledged them in my first book on *bachata* back in 1995), and their respective partners, Doug and Tiffany. I have had the additional joy of being able to bask regularly in that lovely stream of sunshine provided by Radha's daughter, Soleil. Undoubtedly, I delayed working on the manuscript to grab every opportunity to have Soleil stay with us overnight and on weekends, but I know the book is better for it because her youthful energy and insatiable curiosity about the world she is growing up in are contagious and invigorating. Soleil, I should note, whose father is a black Dominican born in Puerto Rico and raised in Cambridge, Massachusetts, has an even more complicated racial, ethnic, and cultural genealogy than mine. But I am confident that she is growing up in a world where she can celebrate and enjoy her hybridity as an asset and a source of strength. Soleil, this book is dedicated to you and to others like you.

Oye Como Va!

Introduction

Hybridity, Identity, and Latino Popular Music

ye Como Va! I selected this phrase as the main title for this book because of its exhortation to pay attention, in this instance, to the sonic spaces that surround us and, in particular, to the rich mixture of sounds produced and consumed by U.S. Latinos. Translated as "Listen to what's going on!" or "Listen to how it goes!"—but more succinctly as "Listen up!"—this phrase is the title of the famous song composed by the Puerto Rican mambo and salsa bandleader/percussionist Tito Puente in 1963. A veteran of New York's glorious Latin music boom in the 1940s and 1950s, Puente borrowed the signature introduction of "Oye Como Va!" from an older piece called "Chanchullo," composed by the Afro-Cuban bassist Israel "Cachao" López; the rest of the composition, a cha-cha, was original. Puente may not have imagined his song as being anything other than Spanish Caribbean, but, despite its stylistic grounding in Cuba, its composer was born in New York City, raised in a multiethnic U.S. metropolis, and surrounded by an array of Latin and non-Latin styles.

In 1970, a rock version of "Oye Como Va!" recorded by Carlos Santana hit number 13 on *Billboard*'s Top 100 chart. Unlike the U.S.-born Puente, Santana was an immigrant, born in Mexico and raised in Tijuana before moving to San Francisco with his parents when he was an adolescent. In reconfiguring Puente's cha-cha, Santana filtered Puente's Spanish Caribbean sensibilities through his own deep knowledge of U.S. rock, which he had become familiar with not in the United States but in his Mexican homeland, where young people had embraced rock since the 1950s.[1] In 2000, National Public Radio's *All Things Considered* named "Oye Como Va!" one of the one hundred most important American songs of the twentieth century, a decision based on its profound influence on musical developments in the United States.[2] Ironically, then, it was an immigrant Mexican rocker who, in pioneering the subgenre of Latin rock, introduced the U.S.-born Puente's Afro-Cuban dance music to mainstream U.S. rock audiences. This single example of multiple origins and intersecting pathways brings into focus a characteristic of U.S. Latino musical practices: Far from being defined by or limited to musical aesthetics associated with particular national groups, Latino music making has always entailed crossing musical, geographic, racial, and ethnic boundaries. The result has been a dazzling variety of musical practices—many of them not usually identified as Latino—each with its own intricate genealogy and each giving voice to the quintessentially blended and layered qualities that characterize the experience of being Latino in the United States. (Throughout this book, I use the term "Latino" for individuals of both genders with some degree of Latin American ancestry who live permanently in the United States. I use the combination "Latin/o American" to refer collectively to U.S. Latinos and Latin Americans and their musics. Only occasionally—where it is necessary to include gender specificity—do I use the term "Latino/a," since consistent gendering of the full term ["Latin/o/a American"] would be likely to confuse rather than to inform.)

As this book demonstrates, if we heed Puente's call to listen up, if we pay close attention to the mix of styles and inflections embedded in the 1963 and 1970 versions of "Oye Como Va!" we can hear not only the tumultuous social and cultural rumblings that characterized the 1960s but also their echoes, which are still resonating in the extraordinary assortment of blended sounds—from Latin freestyle to hip-hop to *reggaeton*—created by U.S.-born Latinos in subsequent decades. More recent waves of immigrants have further enriched the Latino musical mosaic of the United States, adding such Latin American styles as merengue, *bachata, banda, cumbia,* and *vallenato,* which have been resignified and transformed in the United States as their newcomer performers—and now their children—negotiate their lives, identities, and musical practices in an increasingly interconnected transnational world. All these styles produced and consumed in the United States articulate the multiple dimensions of Latinos' constant but ever-shifting engagements with both U.S. mainstream and Latin American culture.

Within the United States, musical dialogues have also been taking place between established U.S. Latinos and their more recently arrived counterparts. These dialogues have been filtered and modulated by a characteristic common to both groups: a shared history of, and openness to, musical (and other sorts of) blending. The musical hybridity characterizing Puente's and Santana's versions of "Oye Como Va!" was, in fact, nothing new: The styles

Puente brought together in this song—mambo and cha-cha—and Santana's rock were themselves hybrid styles, as were their antecedent genres, Afro-Cuban *son* and *danzón* and African American rhythm and blues, respectively. Indeed, the genealogies of all these musics reach back into the post-Columbian period, when native, European, and African cultures first came into contact, initiating processes of musical exchange, blending, and hybridity that are still ongoing. Moreover, as Latinos, Puente and Santana were themselves the products of biological and cultural mixture, which continues to be a hallmark of Latino lives and identities.

It is important to emphasize that nothing is exceptional about Latin/o American hybridity: The United States has a similar history of racial and blending (as do many other nations around the globe), although ness to acknowledge, explore, and celebrate it has been far more ed among Latin/o Americans than among non-Latinos. As I discuss below, because Latinos themselves, as well as their cultural produc- ave so often defied the neatly bounded categories characterizing the States' bipolar racial imaginary, they have sometimes been perceived r non-Latino counterparts with misunderstanding, anxiety, and fear, a combination whose effects have hampered the efforts of Latinos to full cultural citizenship. Collectively, the chapters in this volume illu- e the many ways that hybridity, *mestizaje* (racial and cultural mixture), nationalism, globalization, and border crossings of all sorts have both rpinned and pinned down Latino musical practices.

The Politics of Hybridity and Mestizaje in Historical Perspective

The assertion that racial and cultural mixture has shaped the contours of U.S. Latino musical practices might appear to be obvious and uncontroversial, but, in the context of the United States' racial formations and racial imaginaries, it is not: In the United States, the very *idea* of racial mixing and its consequent ambiguities have a long history of generating deeply rooted anxieties about boundaries, sexuality, and the body. To the colonial British and their descendants, racial mixture was believed to produce physical and cultural degeneracy, and the result was fear, loathing, and a history of well-documented aggression against people of Latin American descent. Latin Americans' mix of Amerindian and African blood was considered to be the primary source of their inferiority, although even their European ancestors— the Spanish—were believed to be similarly afflicted with problematic genetic predispositions to treachery and violence as well as to other vices, such as indolence, irrationality, and sexual promiscuity. Images of Spanish cruelty and ruthlessness became entrenched in the English imagination in the sixteenth century, after Spanish writers such as Bartolomé de las Casas published treatises decrying the abysmal treatment of the natives; these images were perpetuated during England's ongoing rivalry and wars with Spain in subsequent centuries. The Spaniards, who also believed in the inherent inferiority of natives (and Africans), amply deserved the criticism for their treatment of the natives, but the English, who failed to conjure up the same level of outrage when similar and worse treatment decimated the natives in their own colonies, passed these beliefs about the essentially violent and irrational nature of the Spanish temperament down to their post-colonial-era successors. Negative images of the Spanish were only worsened in the aftermath of the racial and cultural mixture taking place between Spaniards, Africans, and natives throughout Latin America in subsequent centuries—especially during the 1898 Spanish-American War. Indeed, these ideas are alive and well in the work of Samuel Huntington and Lawrence Harrison, who continue to argue that Latin Americans are inherently inferior to Anglo-Americans, although they are careful to ascribe this inferiority to Latin American culture rather than genetics.[3]

Racial mixture, of course, is not unique to the American hemisphere: Genetic studies have demonstrated beyond a doubt that no races are "pure" and that racial mixture is universal.[4] The universality of race mixture on a genetic level, however, cannot and should not be interpreted to mean that it should be considered a neutral phenomenon lacking local significance or disconnected from structural hierarchies. On the contrary, in terms of the quality of life of people throughout the Americas, mixed-race individuals have historically had fewer rights and privileges than Continental Spaniards and other Europeans, although they consistently enjoyed higher status than "unmixed" Amerindians and Africans. Moreover, some mixtures have always been more privileged than others, and, as this book demonstrates, these hierarchies are very visible in the ways Latin/o American popular musics have been produced, consumed, and valued in Latin America as well as in the United States.

Beliefs about the nature and meaning of mixing are also deeply embedded in the language used to describe it. In the colonial period, despite official Spanish concerns about maintaining *pureza de sangre* (purity of blood), miscegenation, whether coerced or voluntary, routinely took place between Europeans, natives, and Africans. (And it is worth remembering that each of these commonly used geo-racial categories referred to peoples who were themselves genetically and culturally mixed.) In Latin America, the term "mestizo" emerged to describe people and culture of mixed European and native ancestry; the related term "mestizaje" has commonly been used to refer to the process of cultural mixing that accompanied biological mixing. Because these terms are based on the Spanish verb "mezclar" (to mix), in principle they can refer to people and culture of mixed European and African ancestries as well, but in practice they are generally used to describe European/native hybridity. The analogous term describing the descendants of a European/African mix—"mulatto"—is less commonly used and then only to describe people; references to "mulatto culture" are rare. In the Spanish Caribbean, which received hundreds of thousands of enslaved Africans in the colonial period,[5] African/European cultural hybridity is more often described with the term "creole," which signals the mixtures produced in the Americas in the wake of European conquest, colonization, and slavery, but without explicit reference to race.[6] While by definition the terms "creole" and "creolization" can refer to the same sort of blendings as the terms "mestizo" and "mestizaje," the former are seldom if ever employed in (or for) regions where the European/native mix predominates, and the contrary is also true: The term "mestizo" is seldom used for mixed-race people and their blended cultural forms in regions of Latin America where a European/African mix predominates.[7]

In areas of North America occupied by the English, sexual relations between Europeans and natives did take place and produce progeny, but, with the exception of the derogatory term "half-breed," a named *category* for mixed people and culture analogous to the word "mestizo" did not enter the American English lexicon—indeed, as this chapter demonstrates, the Spanish term continues to be the only one available. (The term "mixed race" is not analogous to the term "mestizo," as it includes mixtures of any racial groups and is not specific to the Americas.) As for people of mixed African and European ancestry in the United States, it was again a Spanish term—"mulatto"—that was adopted, although more specific terms, such as "quadroon" and "octoroon," were generated in order to specify the proportion and type of racial mixture, or "blood quantum mixture," between blacks, whites, and natives. By the beginning of the twentieth century, these distinctions became irrelevant: All children of unions of Europeans and Afrodescendants in the United States were assigned to the "black" category regardless of an individual's degree of white blood and phenotypical characteristics (the "one drop" rule), creating a bipolar construction of race in the United States that is often contrasted with Latin America's more flexible (if still highly problematic) constructions of race and racial identity.[8]

The existence of a large and publicly acknowledged mixed-race category in Spanish America—and its corresponding absence in the United States—underpins a profound cultural difference between the ways Spanish- and

English-speaking Americans have identified themselves. Latin/o Americans recognize themselves and their cultures as the products of the region's history of racial and cultural mixture; in the United States, in contrast, racial and cultural identities have historically been imagined in binary terms—that is, as black or white. Such binary thinking about race has been changing in recent years as a result of immigration as well as the growing population of bi- or multiracial people, including such high-profile individuals as Barack Obama and Tiger Woods, who publicly embrace their hybridity. The steady stream of newspaper articles and television segments asking the question "Is Obama black?" during the 2008 election season, however, demonstrates the depth of discomfort generated by these new challenges to historical paradigms of racial identity.

Unsurprisingly, given these fundamental conceptual differences, discourses regarding cultural hybridity in (and about) the United States have been markedly different from those employed in (and about) Latin America. Scholars and other observers of Latin American music and culture routinely refer to the biological and cultural mixing that originally produced and shaped them, often employing the concept of mestizaje to analyze cultural and musical developments, particularly in areas with predominantly mestizo populations; in areas whose populations are predominantly of African descent, the terms "creolization" or "syncretism" are used. In the United States, in contrast, where anxieties about racial and cultural mixing persist, bipolar racial imaginaries still generate much of the language used to describe popular music, such as the widely (if controversially) used term "black music" to describe the musics associated with African American communities (most, if not all, of which are, to some degree, the product of cultural mixture).[9]

Musics associated with Latinos, however, regardless of the nature and degree of their racial and cultural mixture, have not generated analogous terms capturing the nature and nuances of their hybridity—and, as I have argued elsewhere, the terms "Latin music" and "Latino music" are highly imperfect substitutes.[10] Indeed, the language of mestizaje seems to drop out of the lexicon when musics of Latin American origins arrive in the United States and musical borrowings occur within and across racial and ethnic boundaries. Rather than generating a term allowing for the transformation and blending of both parties involved in a transaction, such terms as "borrowings," "influences," and "tinges" emphasize the degree of discreteness between the cultural domains of donor and receiver. One noticeable exception is the work of George Lipsitz (following the work of anthropologist Michael M. Fisher), which has effectively employed the postmodern concepts of "bifocality or reciprocity of perspectives, juxtaposition of multiple realities—intertextuality, inter-referentiality, and comparisons through families of resemblance" to describe the hybridity of Chicano musical practices.[11] But as Raquel Z. Rivera has noted, many U.S. scholars and other cultural observers still employ the prism of assimilation to interpret Latino musical practices, viewing Puerto Rican rappers, for example, as imitating African American culture but seldom recognizing that African American culture shares with Puerto Ricans a similar diasporic heritage—or that African American culture itself is also similarly hybrid.[12] In short, Latino hybridity has been marked by being linguistically unnamed and thus out of place and profoundly "othered."

As the chapters in this book collectively demonstrate, the disavowal of racial and cultural mixture in the United States has been a powerful challenge to Latinos' popular music practices because it has excluded them from musical domains perceived in binary terms, such as "black" (e.g., R & B, hip-hop) and "white" (e.g., rock or pop). As Rivera has noted, even phenotypically black Latinos have been excluded from the "black" category because they are members of a group—Latinos—recognized as mixed.[13] Mexican mestizos in the United States have similarly found themselves relegated to an unstable position between the "white" and "black" categories.

If the scholarship on racial, cultural, and musical hybridity in Latin America provides those analyzing U.S. Latino musical practices with useful theoretical models, it is also important to keep in mind that the concept of mestizaje is still highly problematic because of its long history of being misused. Indeed, contemporary scholars of race relations in Latin America, such as George Reid Andrews, Helen Safa, Peter Wade, Miriam Jiménez Román, Anani Dzidzienyo, and Suzanne Oboler, have critiqued, if not roundly condemned, the concept of mestizaje because of its veiled implications and noxious consequences.[14] They rightly charge, for example, that the implicit equation of mestizaje's hybridity with equality—that is, "we are all mixed so we are all equal"—has long been used in Latin America to avoid facing (and altering) the social, economic, and political structures responsible for perpetuating race-based "pigmentocracies," in which white-skinned individuals enjoy privileges of every sort; mixed-race people occupy an intermediate space depending on such variables as their phenotypical proximity to whiteness, education, wealth, and so forth; and people of more unambiguously African or native ancestry are subject to subordination and exploitation of all sorts. Wade, for example, has demonstrated how, in the 1940s, Colombia's elites celebrated mestizaje as a strategy for imposing a unified national identity on a country deeply segmented by culturally diverse and highly independent regions. To symbolize national unity amid this diversity, they elevated the tri-ethnic cumbia—whose mixture of African, native, and European sensibilities was heralded as the sonic embodiment of the nation's mestizo identity—although not before "whitening" it by stripping it of its more audible signs of African and Amerindian origins, thereby confirming rather than upending long-standing racial hierarchies.[15] Jiménez Román has also pointed to the pernicious subtext underlying celebrations of mestizaje, which imply that those who are *not* mixed or who choose not to identify as mixed are problematic, "that the parts themselves—and those who embody less than the ideal mixture, are somehow deficient."[16] The insidious relationship between the Latin American concept of mestizaje and the concept of *blanqueamiento,* or whitening—racial mixing whose goal is to "improve" native and Afrodescendant populations and cultures by diluting them with "white" blood—has also been exposed. These concerns have understandably generated fears of slippages between notions of mestizaje and the (more recent) notion of "colorblindness," which similarly uses the realities of racial mixture to deny racism and its structural manifestations. Critical race theorist Ian Haney Lopez, for example, has argued that celebrations of Latinos' mestizaje as (presumably) ushering in a postracial society in which color does not matter perniciously serve to justify efforts to dismantle hard-fought race-sensitive policies designed to rectify long-standing social inequalities.[17]

Having made similar critiques of mestizaje himself, however, Wade has also proposed that, to many Latin Americans, mestizaje is more than an ideological construct whose purpose is to submerge racial and social divisions in the name of nation building or to preserve entrenched privileges. He argues that, for people of varying degrees of racial mixture, mestizaje is a lived experience and an *idea* that offers them different possibilities for self-identification, because by definition the concept depends on the presence of and interactions between its constituent parts—blackness, indigenousness, and whiteness—and therefore creates space for individuals to assert their blackness and/or indigenousness *within* the space of mestizaje. According to Wade, "Nationalist ideologies of mestizaje contain and encompass dynamics not only of homogenization but also of differentiation, maintaining permanent spaces of a particular kind, for blackness and indigenousness, and creating a mosaic image of national identity."[18] Jacques Audinet has similarly recognized the pernicious way "mestizaje" has been used. However, he emphasizes the term's potential for analyzing creative developments, noting that "mestizaje" can be useful for describing and conceptualizing "how encounters between distinct groups and their cultures are brought about"[19] and for understanding how the outcome of such exchanges can produce "a new language, a new experience, a new relation . . . something in which both protagonists will recognize themselves and, at the same time, something totally new compared to each other."[20]

In short, our task is to remain vigilant regarding the racist ways the concept of mestizaje has been used, while at the same time recognizing and celebrating the extent to which the experiences of Latinos living in the United States have been shaped by racial, ethnic, and cultural mixture. Despite—and sometimes because of—their interstitial position within the United States' racial imaginary, Latinos' personal and collective hybrid genealogies have served to facilitate the bridging and crossing of musical borders. Indeed, Latinos have generated an extraordinary variety of innovative blends of Latin American, African American, and Euro-American aesthetics, bringing them into dialogue with each other in multiple overlapping and intersecting ways. Puente's and Santana's versions of "Oye Como Va!" are but two well-known examples; this book examines many others.

Mapping Mestizaje onto Latino Musical Production

If the concepts of hybridity and mestizaje can be useful for thinking about the complexities of U.S. Latino identities and cultural productions, they also present problems, because the concept of mestizaje, as well as its critiques, do not always map neatly onto the domain of music. Jiménez Román, who rightly criticizes mestizaje's role in perpetuating racial inequalities in Latin America, observes that attempts to identify an individual's constituent parts account for the "assiduous attention paid to the phenotypical details that 'expose' African 'genes' and for the elaborate vocabulary that at once confers privilege and derides the subject under scrutiny. The conceptual difference between 'high yellow' and '*grifa*' [both terms for a lighter shade of skin color] is truly insignificant and responds to the same historical privileging of certain physical characteristics over others."[21] Jiménez Román's critique of efforts to identify the specific origins of an individual's phenotype is absolutely valid in the situation she describes, but it does not easily correspond to the domain of culture and to situations in which scholars seek to identify the constituent roots of Latino musical practices. Identifying the origins of African-derived drumming patterns in a particular style of Latino music, for example, does not have the same implications as trying to identify the origins of an individual's particular hue of skin—not to mention that the musicians performing such music may be white or light-skinned (as was Tito Puente). It is also noteworthy that scholarly interest in constituent roots has not been uniform regarding musics of African and native derivation. The contributions of African-derived aesthetics to Latin/o American popular musics, such as merengue and salsa, among others, have been widely recognized and deconstructed, but, as I discuss further in Chapter 6, comparable contributions of native derivation to musics such as cumbia, while implied by the term "mestizaje," have seldom been sought as explicitly or as thoroughly.

Moreover, the constant aesthetic blending that has always characterized

Latin/o American musical practices simply cannot be equated with the racist desires for genetic mixing, whose goal is to "improve the race" through blanqueamiento. This is not to deny that correspondences exist between the problematic concepts of hybridity embedded within nationalist ideologies of mestizaje and the pernicious effects of racism in the domain of popular music. If quintessentially hybrid musics originating in Latin America, such as Cuban son, Dominican merengue, and Colombian cumbia, have become much celebrated symbols of national identity precisely because they are perceived as expressing the (literally and figuratively) harmonious outcome of racial and cultural blending (notwithstanding persistent racially organized social hierarchies), musics of unambiguously African and native origins have never had the same access to and success within the popular music marketplace as their more audibly hybrid counterparts.

Nonetheless, unlike social structures in which proximity to the ideal of phenotypical whiteness and Eurocentric culture that have historically shaped (and improved) an individual's or group's life chances, the most culturally *and* economically significant popular musics have emerged from the poorest, most dispossessed—and often the darkest—social sectors in Latin/o America: Cuban son, New York salsa, and Dominican bachata are but three examples.[22] To be sure, before such grassroots styles could be accepted in more bourgeois settings, they underwent stylistic changes that distanced them from their lower-class (and more racially marked) versions, through a process of musical "whitening" in which musical aesthetics deemed too "black" were reduced or eliminated. But as the extraordinary cultural influence of musics originating in communities of color—such as the Afro-Cuban mambo and contemporary reggaeton—demonstrate, some of the most successful musical blendings have flourished not due to "whitening" but rather to their strongly audible grounding in Afro-Latin aesthetics.

The fact that in the United States most musical styles have been unambiguously associated with one racial category or another, however, has left little space for those multiracial, bicultural Latinos comfortable with and interested in aesthetic bridging rather than having to choose one identity or the other in order to succeed. Historically, Latinos who could "pass" as white could access the mainstream market, although only if they hid their ethnicity by changing their names, as did Andy Russell and Ritchie Valens, respectively born Andrés Rábago Pérez and Ricardo Valenzuela. In contrast, Afrodescendant Latinos who were phenotypically indistinguishable from African Americans had access to the "black" segment of the market, as did, for example, the Puerto Rican singer Herman Santiago in the doo-wop group Frankie Lymon and the Teenagers, which was identified as African American. More recently, Puerto Ricans Fat Joe and Big Pun began their careers in rap at a moment when it was perceived exclusively as a "black" music; only later, in the late 1990s, when hip-hop began to be more widely acknowledged as a "ghettocentric" music that included Puerto Ricans, did these musicians begin to identify themselves as Puerto Ricans by employing Spanish lyrics and cover art iconography such as images of the Puerto Rican flag.[23]

In contrast, Latinos of all racial backgrounds and national origins who would not or could not relinquish their cultural hybridity and layered identities found themselves facing symbolic dangers and practical consequences. The nature and degree of the outcomes have varied according to local conditions and timing, in dialogue with larger national trends; these are the subject of Chapter 3, which compares East and West Coast Latino rock 'n' roll in an era of intensifying cultural nationalism and identity politics, and Chapter 4, which extends the discussion to turntable-based musical practices in the 1980s and beyond. These twinned essays explore the many ways Latinos born and raised in the United States have resisted the boundaries of the country's black and white–only categories, freely choosing musical sources and styles from among the wide array of possibilities offered by the nation's rich cultural demographics and making them their own. Non-Latinos have often perceived such efforts as second-rate imitations by cultural outsiders and interlopers rather than as natural expressions of bicultural Latino identities. Latinos themselves have often rejected such engagements as signs of cultural loss and betrayal. In contrast, for those who have grown up familiar and comfortable with hybridity and who welcome its freedom to create new sounds and images, such blendings articulate essential components of Latinos' rich cultural and musical genealogies.

Border Crossing and Musical Hybridity in the Era of Transnationalism

The hybridity of Latino identities, expressed in an uninterrupted history of musical blending and aesthetic border crossings, has been further complicated by social processes originally set in motion in the 1960s but that coalesced in the 1980s: economic globalization and increasing waves of immigration from throughout Latin America facilitated by the family reunification provisions of the Immigration and Nationality Act of 1965. In contrast to earlier immigrants, the post-1980s arrivals found themselves able, because of improved telecommunications and increasingly globalized economies, to participate simultaneously in their host and homeland cultures, including their musical practices. Scholars of transnationalism have observed that immigrants' adherence to Latin American ways of doing things has been strengthened by their ability to recreate them here, in constant dialogue with developments back home.[24] The ramifications of the new waves of immigration on the U.S. Latino popular music landscape are explored in Chapters 5 and 6, particularly the extent to which the "here and there" patterns of transnational life and identity formation have added additional layers to the already complex hybridity of U.S. Latino musical practices.

Compared to their predecessors, many newer immigrants, especially those living within large ethnic enclaves in cities such as Los Angeles and New York, have been relatively insulated from U.S. mainstream culture.[25] Their musical practices, however, also reveal rich dialogues with well-established bilingual, bicultural Latinos born and raised in the United States, whose musical sensibilities have been shaped less by their connections to Latin America than by their locations within the United States' extraordinarily diverse (if hierarchical) cultural landscape. Indeed, one major difference between the two groups is that the musical exchanges of more well-established Latinos have been particularly active with African American culture—the result of years of sharing the experiences and spaces of social, economic, and political marginality. The Dominican immigrants who are the subjects of Chapter 5 provide a particularly salient case study of how transnational musical practices have intersected with and complicated existing bicultural U.S. Latino musical practices with additional layerings, particularly in the domain of hip-hop. The mixed, layered, and segmented nature of U.S.-based Dominican identities and their musical expressions—merengue, bachata, merengue *típico, palo,* and, more recently, the quintessentially hybrid reggaeton—also illustrate the degree to which transnational cultural fields are sensitive to the nuances of chronology, locality, and racial identity.

The intersections between hybridity, mestizaje, and transnationalism are explored further in Chapter 6, which focuses on Colombians and the musical styles most widely associated with Colombia—cumbia and its close relative, vallenato. Originally an expression of the tri-ethnic culture characterizing the northern coast of Colombia, cumbia has spread throughout Latin/o America, most notably to those regions where mestizos rather than Afrodescendants are predominant, such as Mexico and Peru. Along the way, cumbia has been locally resignified as an expression and symbol of mestizo working-class identity. These changes have become particularly audible in the United States, where Mexican-style cumbia has become the soundtrack for working-class Mexican immigrants' transnational lives but, interestingly, not for Colombian immigrants. Cumbia's recent appearance in trendy dance scenes around the globe, disconnected from any particular immigrant group, represents an additional twist to cumbia's long history of travel and transformation.

Hybridity in the Latin/o
Popular Music Marketplace

Santana enjoyed far greater success with his 1970 rock version of "Oye Como Va!" than Puente had with his 1963 Spanish Caribbean version, demonstrating that not all blends fare equally in the marketplace; location and timing have also been crucial to commercial success. The dynamic blend of Spanish Caribbean sonorities and African American R & B rhythms characteristic of mid-1960s New York boogaloo, for example, might have enjoyed more commercial longevity within that city's Puerto Rican community had it not emerged at the onset of an era defined by cultural nationalism and identity politics that favored the more unambiguously Latin/o American salsa. But by far the most crucial factor determining the commercial success of Latino popular musics in the United States has been their unstable location within an industry that has insisted on defining and containing musicians and audiences within unambiguous racial and ethnic categories. In the United States, musics associated with either whites or blacks have historically been marketed separately;[26] "ethnic" musics, in contrast, were marketed to particular immigrant groups. As long as Latino musics and musicians did not cross the boundaries of these ethnically or racially defined categories, industry personnel, non-Latino and Latino alike, could promote their musics to segments of the population perceived to be their "natural" audience. This was true of both the mainstream English-language popular music business and the Spanish-language "Latin" music business, each of which operated with its own fixed ideas of what U.S. Latino musical practices and preferences should be. In Chapter 2, I survey crucial historical developments in these two sometimes independent, sometimes intersecting sectors of the music business, demonstrating how Latinos' layered identities and musical practices have always rattled an industry loathe to deal with the ambiguity of hybridity.

Chapter 7 extends my analysis of how ethnicity has shaped the Latin/o American music business in the contemporary era, in which new layers have been added to U.S. Latino cultural geography by large-scale immigration from Latin America, further complicating the media's historically imperfect and unstable constructions of what the musical practices of Latinos are or should be. As anthropologist Arlene Dávila has noted, in recent years the mass media have "Latin Americanized" the concept *latinidad* itself—what it means to be Latino/a—by emphasizing Spanish-language and Latin American roots at the expense of the bicultural and bilingual realities of U.S.-born Latinos.[27] Given the power of the media's image-making machinery to define Latino communities, their identities, and their social locations within the nation, the music industry's responses to these shifts in the cultural terrain in the next decades call for even more careful listening and watching.

In summary, although I frame the contents of this book around the theme of hybridity, it is not intended to deny the problematic ways mestizaje and other terms for racial and cultural hybridity have been used in the past or to obscure the ways they can still be misused to mask persistent social inequalities. I do, however, insist that Latino voices be heard and appreciated on their own terms, which means fully understanding their long and rich history of racial and cultural mixture. If we listen up, as Puente and Santana encourage us to do in their own idiomatic ways, we can distinguish in these sounds the rich interplay between the pressures and the pleasures, the conflicts and the celebration of these ongoing musical and cultural dialogues that have been taking place among Latinos as well as with the larger multicultural society in which we live. *Oye Como Va!*

2

Historical Perspectives on Latinos and the Latin Music Industry

If Latinos' racial and cultural hybridity has always been problematic within the United States, it has been particularly vexing for music industry personnel seeking the illusory comforts of neat and impermeable marketing categories. In the United States, a domestic "Latin" music industry specializing in Spanish-language music of Latin American origins has always existed alongside (but secondary in influence to) an English-only mainstream[1] popular music industry that has viewed U.S. Latinos and their musics as Latin American (i.e., foreign). Although the commonly used term "Latin music industry" suggests a monolithic entity, this industry has always included multiple layers and players—some with strong connections to Latin America, some without—whose domains of activity have often overlapped and intersected with each other as well as with the mainstream music industry. Moreover, many of the most influential players in the Latin music industry—even in the case of small domestic independent labels—have *not* themselves been Latino. Some of these non-Latinos whose professional lives revolved around Latin/o musics have been personally engaged with Latino communities, although for others, Latin music has simply been another product that could turn a profit if marketed effectively. All Latin music industry personnel, however, regardless of their own ethnic and racial backgrounds, have had to ply their trade within a complicated network of multiple ethnically, racially, and culturally defined communities and markets whose boundaries have always been porous and unstable.

Keith Negus's elegantly simple but profound axiom that "industry produces culture and culture produces industry" is particularly useful for examining how the Latin music industry and its personnel have influenced the development of Latin/o music in the United States. Negus observes that "industry produces culture" (i.e., the music industry is not simply a machine that records and sells products—in this case, sound recordings), but he suggests that the corollary, "culture produces industry," is equally significant because the culturally constructed predispositions and values of the individuals who carry out the work of the music industry strongly influence (in both positive and negative ways) the range of sounds and images emerging from that industry.[2] This is true whether the industry personnel in question are Latino or not: Recording company personnel's cultural biases inevitably affect the structure of the music industry itself. As Negus notes, "Recording companies distribute their staff, artists, genres, and resources into divisions defined according to social-cultural identity labels, such as black music division, Latin division, domestic division, international department. Such practices can be viewed as a direct intervention into and contribution towards the way in which social life is fragmented and through which different cultural experiences are separated and treated unequally."[3] This chapter explores the early, segmented history of the Latin music industry in order to illuminate the shifting relationships between commercial music production and socially constructed notions of ethnicity, race, and nationality; Chapter 7 extends this narrative into the 1980s and beyond, when immigration and globalization further destabilized the relationships between the industry producing Latin music and the identities of the populations presumed to be consuming it.

Marketing Ethnic Sounds: The Early Years

The phonograph was invented toward the end of the nineteenth century, but the technological, economic, and legal structures necessary for the infant recording business to thrive did not coalesce until the first decades of the twentieth. The Columbia and Victor companies, for example, initially held a monopoly on recording thanks to their patents, but subsequent legal challenges and technological changes opened the doors for smaller companies to enter the business of recording and selling music. In the 1920s, over 150 small companies had sprouted up,[4] and record players, originally a novelty unaffordable to most people, had come down drastically in price, by 1927 selling over a million units per year.[5] Developments in radio broadcasting and reception technology similarly made the dissemination of recorded music accessible to people throughout the nation, even those with very limited resources.

Chronologically paralleling these developments in the recording and broadcast industries was a burgeoning population of immigrants who added a profusion of styles and languages into the pool of sounds that could be recorded and sold. Record companies quickly understood the potential value of this particular segment of the market, as the following letter sent ⎡ Columbia to its dealers in 1909 indicates: "Remember that in all large ⎡ties and in most towns there are sections where people of one nationality ⎡ another congregate in 'colonies.' Most of these people keep up the habits nd prefer to speak the language of the old country. . . . To these people ECORDS IN THEIR OWN LANGUAGE have an irresistible attraction, and they ⎖ill buy them readily."[6] Another piece of correspondence from 1914 reveals he industry's understanding of how it could take advantage of the adjustment ɔrocess immigrants were undergoing:

> With [thousands] of miles between them and the land of their birth, in a country with strange speech and customs, the 35,000,000 for-eigners making their home here are keenly on the alert for anything and everything which will keep alive the memories of their father-land—build them a mental bridge back to their native land. They are literally starving for amusements. With no theatres, except in one or two of the largest cities, few books in their native tongue, it is easy to realize why the talking machine appeals to them so potently, so irresistibly. Their own home music, played or sung by artists whose names are household words in their homeland—these they must have. They are patriotic, these foreigners, and [it is] their own intense desire that their children, brought or born in this *new* country shall share their love of the old.[7]

The first recordings of immigrant musics made in New York were cre-ated by Okeh Records, founded by a German immigrant, Otto Heineman, in 1918.[8] An unexpected 1920 hit recording by African American vaudeville singer Mamie Smith proved that black musicians singing black vernacular music would sell well within the black community (and even beyond). Rec-ognizing the economic potential of vernacular music, Okeh sent out roving recording units throughout the United States in search of undiscovered tal-ent under the direction of Ralph Peer. Peer is justifiably famous as a central figure in the development of U.S. popular music, because, as an executive of Okeh and then Victor, he was responsible for the earliest field recordings of the black, ethnic, and regional musics that coalesced into the blues, gospel, jazz, and "country" styles now considered quintessentially "American." In the process of transforming traditional folk music into a commercially viable art form, he also coined the race-based marketing terms "race music" and "hillbilly" music.[9] While the musicians he worked with represent a veritable who's who of early U.S. popular music, it is less well known (or commented upon by U.S. popular music scholars) that his corpus of early American musical recordings also included the first recordings of Mexican-origin music in the United States, among them performances by Mexican-born singer and first Mexican American recording star Lydia Mendoza. These musicians were paid very modest one-time fees, although most struggling musicians, like Mendoza, welcomed the opportunity to record in order to increase their audience base.

From its very beginning, the music business reflected and reified the prevailing bipolar racial imaginaries and hierarchies characteristic of the U.S. social structure. English-speaking artists were classified by race rather than by genre, and the resources devoted to producing and marketing each category varied accordingly: White musicians and styles received far more resources than the "race music" made by blacks. Region and class also played a part in drawing the boundaries of these categories, resulting in the designation "hillbilly" for the musical styles preferred by rural whites, while music by and for the urban middle classes remained unmarked and was simply referred to as "popular." Non-English-language musics, in contrast, were categorized collectively as "ethnic," with subcategories defined by country of origin or language. It is important to note that while the music industry insisted on coding musics according to race, class, and region for marketing purposes, audiences listening to radio and buying records often ignored these divisions and consumed whatever appealed to them. For example, some African American listeners and dancers enjoyed "white" Tin Pan Alley music as well as "Latin-tinged" Tin Pan Alley and film music, and likewise some white listeners ventured beyond the boundaries of Tin Pan Alley. "Ethnic" Latino/a listeners similarly had eclectic tastes in English-language popular musical genres (both those coded black and white)—and, as other chapters in this book demonstrate, the interest of Latino musicians and audiences in "non-Latino" genres has remained constant to this day.

The early years of the twentieth century, when immigration to the United States was reaching record levels, were extraordinarily fertile times for ethnic music. Columbia and Victor actively sought to record music abroad so they could sell it to particular ethnic and national groups in the United States as well as back to the countries of origin. Music company personnel traveling in Latin America in search of musics to record were typically unfamiliar with local customs, so they depended on middle-class businessmen to identify musicians suitable for recording. (These businessmen were often furniture store owners who sold record players, which were then contained in large furniture-like cabinets.) Given the bourgeois backgrounds of such cultural mediators, the musics recommended to visiting talent scouts tended to be those considered "nice" enough to be listened to by the middle- and upper-class families who were purchasing record players, which at the time were relatively expensive. As a result, the first recordings made in Latin America were of musics with prominent European-derived aesthetics, such as the Puerto Rican *danza* or the Colombian *bambuco*; the vernacular musics associated with the more populous but poorer, lower status, and racially subordinated sectors of Latin American society, such as the *bomba* music favored by Afro–Puerto Ricans or Dominican *palo* music, were not considered material appropriate for recording.[10] Later, after realizing the difficulties of recording in Latin America—for example, in the Caribbean, the tropical heat would sometimes melt the acetate masters—record companies concluded that it was more efficient to bring or attract Latin American musicians to their studios in New York to record, transforming that city into a mecca for ambitious and talented musicians from throughout the hemisphere and, subsequently, into a creative crucible for Latin/o American musical developments throughout the twentieth century.[11]

In the early decades of the U.S. recording industry, fledgling record companies were open to experimentation, willing to record and press even small runs of music for limited audiences. They realized, for example, that most immigrants, being of working-class origins, preferred vernacular styles, such as accordion-based musics, to the more "refined" musics being recorded in Latin America for bourgeois audiences. As had happened in Latin America, U.S. record companies seeking local ethnic talent depended on middle-class businessmen (again, often furniture store owners) who could identify the musicians and styles that would appeal to a particular ethnic or national community. While predisposed to recommend "nice" ethnic music, such as the *canciones mejicanas* sung by Lydia Mendoza, these ethnic businessmen were generally more amenable to the idea of recording vernacular music than their 'n American counterparts. Thus, if the first recordings made in Puerto vere Eurocentric danzas, in New York they were more likely to be the ʽusic and *plenas* loved by working-class Puerto Rican migrants.[12] In th west, Bluebird (a subsidiary of RCA) and Decca were tapping the mar, ʻorking class–oriented Mexican music as early as the mid-1930s, recorą, ʲpular Texas Mexican accordion musicians, such as Narciso Martínez and Santiago Jiménez.[13] By the end of the 1930s, even the poorest migrant worker could hear recordings of vernacular Mexican American music playing on jukeboxes in bars and restaurants located in the *colonias* (ethnic neighborhoods) that had sprung up in and around towns and cities throughout Texas and the Southwest between 1890 and the 1920s.[14] Even during the Depression, the market for vernacular music remained strong, particularly when the price of records dropped by half.

Record companies began recording Mexican American musicians in Los Angeles during these same years and under very similar circumstances. Okeh, Bluebird, Decca, Victor, and Columbia scoured Los Angeles's Mexican barrios (neighborhoods), seeking ethnic talent with the help of Mexican American intermediaries, recording local musicians in makeshift studios (often set up in hotel rooms), and paying the performers a pittance for each recording.[15] Los Angeles's first Mexican recording star was the Mexican-born Pedro J. González, who recorded with his group, Los Madrugadores. Considered to be performers of "high-quality" Mexican music, González and Los Madrugadores benefited from daily exposure on González's pioneering Spanish-language radio program, which was hugely popular among working-class Mexican Angelenos in the 1930s.[16]

Although recording ethnic music was a fairly profitable business in local terms, vernacular music associated with communities considered to be nonwhite did not make it into the U.S. musical mainstream, where the real money was. More cosmopolitan music from urban middle- and upper-class Latin America, in contrast, had a better chance of being accepted by non-Latino audiences and thus was of much greater interest to the major record companies. Owning the publishing rights to Latin American music popular within U.S. Spanish-speaking ethnic communities that could also appeal to mainstream audiences (especially when translated into English by white performers) could be, in fact, quite lucrative; every time a song was performed in the United States, the owner of the rights received a fee, whether it was performed live or on a recording by the original artist or covered by other artists. (Indeed, the voracious appetite for acquiring such rights placed the U.S.-based music industry in the company of businesses such as Standard Oil and United Fruit, who in these same years were similarly scouring Latin America for other resources, such as oil, rubber, and bananas, that could be sold at a premium within the United States.)

One of the most successful U.S. music publishers obtaining rights to Latin American music was E. B. Marks, who developed the industry's largest catalogue of Latin American music, some of which, translated into English and given new arrangements, became mainstream Tin Pan Alley hits.[17] Another successful music publisher who exerted an enormous influence on the circulation of Latin/o American popular music in the United States was Ralph Peer, who, on his first visit to Mexico City in 1928, had an epiphany when he "discovered" Mexican composer Agustín Lara; then, while overnighting in San Antonio on his way back to New York, Peer heard a version of "El Manisero" ("The Peanut Vendor"), a song written by Jewish Cuban composer Moises Simons and sung by Rita Montaner, which had become wildly popular in Havana.[18] Recognizing the potential for Latin America to be "a popular music resource for U.S. listeners,"[19] Peer opened offices in Havana and Mexico City to facilitate the acquisition of his eventually sizable catalogue of Latin American music. In subsequent years, Peer extended his reach throughout Latin America, from Puerto Rico to Argentina, signing major Latin American musicians, such as Lara and Dámaso Pérez Prado. Peer's catalogue of songs eventually contained some of the most well-known Latin American standards, including such chestnuts as "Bésame Mucho," "Granada," and "Perfidia."

Given the profitability of publishing rights, non-Latino music publishers such as Peer and Marks had as many vested interests in widely promoting their musical property as the labels who originally recorded it, and it was in no small part thanks to their efforts that Latin American styles permeated the mainstream popular music landscape in the first half of the twentieth century.[20] When consumed by mainstream audiences in the United States, however, Latin styles were typically performed by musicians who were neither Latin American nor Latino. In the 1910s and 1920s, for example, the Argentine tango was popularized by the theatrical presentations of professional dancers Irene and Vernon Castle, not by local Latino musicians (Argentine or otherwise) residing in New York's thriving Spanish-speaking community.[21] Mexican music was also popular in the mainstream arena in the early decades of the twentieth century, but the music produced by Mexican Americans in the Southwest did not circulate widely beyond the boundaries of these communities. Thus, until the mambo-inspired Latin music boom of the late 1940s and early 1950s, mainstream interest in Latin and Latin-tinged music did not necessarily translate into receptivity to musics performed by U.S. Latinos.

In summary, several characteristics of the Latin/o music industry were established early on. First, if the recording of Spanish-language music initially depended on the recommendations of middle-class ethnic or Latin American nationals who understood local tastes, the mainstream-oriented recording industry that produced, promoted, and profited from them was run primarily by people who were not connected in any organic way to the communities whose musics they were marketing. Second, from the very beginning, the Latin music industry consisted of two "streams" of music that converged in the United States: recordings made in Latin America and "ethnic" recordings made in the United States. Third, music industry personnel have always had to negotiate the sensibilities of separate but overlapping audiences—well-established Latino communities, newer immigrants from Latin America, Latin American nationals, and mainstream English-speaking listeners attracted to exotic ethnic sounds—whose musical practices and preferences, as I discuss below, have been shaped by different imaginaries of race and racial difference.

Latinos Market Themselves: The Latino
Music Industry in the Early Years

As the U.S. music industry expanded, U.S. Latinos were not unaware that they, too, could profit by fulfilling the desires of their coethnics for culturally relevant music—and without being distracted, as was often the case with the major record companies, by trying to produce "Latin" music that would be acceptable to nationwide mainstream audiences. The record business, however, was highly dependent on infrastructural support—access to radio airwaves and related necessities, such as adequate performance venues, distribution outlets, press coverage—most of which was owned or controlled by non-Latinos. With few exceptions, then, Latino-owned/Latino-operated recording ventures did not take root and thrive until sufficiently substantial and economically diversified Latino communities emerged with the capacity to support a parallel infrastructure of radio, theaters, newspapers, and record stores catering to Spanish-speaking consumers.

Not surprisingly, the first Latino forays into the commercial music business took place in New York, the capital of the U.S. recording industry as well as the nation's premier immigrant-receiving city. As small businesses in New York's Puerto Rican community proliferated and a middle class emerged in the 1920s, some astute entrepreneurs, realizing they were in a position to take advantage of their community's rich musical scene began investing some of their capital in the music business. For example, Julio Roqué, a successful dentist, established the city's first Spanish-language radio program, *Revista Roqué,* in 1924, which featured a variety of Latin American music, including that of his own orchestra.[22] Another pioneering entrepreneur—even more remarkable because she was a woman—was Victoria Hernández, the sister of prominent Puerto Rican musician and composer Rafael Hernández. Like her brother, Victoria Hernández, who arrived in New York in 1919, was a classically trained musician, although she never developed ambitions for a career in music performance. After saving money from her jobs in a textile factory and giving piano lessons, in 1927 she was able to open up Almacenes Hernández, the first locally owned music store in the Puerto Rican section of Harlem that came to be known as El Barrio.[23] Recognizing music's centrality to the Spanish-speaking community's social and cultural fabric, other ethnic entrepreneurs followed suit: As Virginia Sánchez Korrol has noted, record stores "spread quickly throughout the *colonia hispana* and came to symbolize the Latin settlements as the candy store had characterized other ethnic immigrant neighborhoods. Emanating from these establishments were the rhythms of *el Son, la Guaracha,* Puerto Rican *plenas* and *aguinaldos,* combined with the romantic *boleros* and *danzas.*"[24]

In her groundbreaking study of Puerto Rican musicians in New York, Ruth Glasser observes that in addition to selling records, these record stores served as meeting places for musicians, where they could listen to new releases and receive tips about opportunities for gigs. Moreover, when record companies, such as Victor and Columbia, sought local ethnic talent, record store owners were among their best sources of referrals. Taking advantage of her connections, Victoria Hernández became her brother Rafael's manager, booking dates and negotiating contracts and recording sessions with Victor, not only for Rafael but for other barrio musicians as well. Around the same time, she also established the country's first Latino-owned record label, Hispano, which recorded the local Puerto Rican groups Las Estrellas Boricuas and Los Diablos de la Plena. Victoria's pioneering recording label collapsed after she lost her capital in the 1929 bank crash, but, since ethnic recordings remained profitable throughout the Depression, her record store survived, and she continued to serve as an intermediary between local musicians and the major record companies.[25]

The second Puerto Rican entrepreneur to venture into the ethnic recording business in New York also did so after gaining experience as a record store owner. Gabriel Oller, born in Puerto Rico to an educated family (his father was a teacher), was brought to New York by his parents in 1917. Deciding he wanted a career in the entertainment industry, he earned a degree in electronics before opening up his record store in El Barrio, a respectful distance away from Victoria Hernandez's store. In 1934, he founded the Dynasonic label and began recording local musicians—trios and quartets—playing Puerto Rican styles; he was particularly successful selling traditional *aguinaldos* around Christmas time. Oller's Dynasonic label was small—he never pressed more than two hundred copies of any recording—but, unlike Victoria Hernández's label, it survived the Depression, releasing records by such well-known musicians as Noro Morales as well as local neighborhood trios and quartets. He later established two other record labels, Coda and SMC (Spanish Music Center), that were active in the 1940s and 1950s.[26] Hernandez's Hispano and Oller's Dynasonic labels were both relatively short lived, and neither had much distribution beyond New York, but they are significant because they were the first Latino-owned/Latino-operated record labels in the United States, predating by some years comparable ventures that emerged in Texas and the Southwest in the 1940s.

During World War II, shortages of the shellac used to manufacture records prompted the major record companies to drop or reduce their ethnic and foreign catalogues in favor of their more lucrative mainstream offerings. After the war ended, the majors renewed their interest in musics produced in Mexico and other Latin American countries, but they did not resume the recording of U.S.-based ethnic musics. Mexican American entrepreneurs

took advantage of the void left by the departure of the majors and the simultaneously expanding Mexican-origin population in the Southwest. Beginning
in the mid-1940s, a slew of Mexican American–owned companies sprang up
in Texas, the most important of which were Ideal (1946) and Falcon (1948),
but which also included Rio (1948), Corona (1947), and other smaller companies, such as Alamo, Gaviota, and Del Valle. In Los Angeles, ethnically
owned companies, such as Azteca, Aguila, Tri-Color, and Taxco, similarly
began springing up in the late 1940s to satisfy the demand for locally produced music.[27] Another small Los Angeles–based company specializing in
ethnic music that was not Mexican American–owned but that played a significant role in promoting Mexican Angeleno music in the postwar period was
Imperial Records, founded by Lew Chudd in the late 1940s. Chudd's Imperial began as a folk music–oriented label with strong interests in Mexican
music and later became one of the most important Mexican Angeleno music
labels in Los Angeles, recording top local groups such as Los Madrugadores
and Lalo Guerrero; Imperial also recorded in Texas.[28]

Non-Latinos in the Postwar Latin Music Industry

In contrast to the Southwest, where the major record companies' interest in
vernacular music diminished during the war, New York's more cosmopolitan
and lucrative Latin music business not only survived but thrived throughout
the 1940s. Latin music's popularity had exploded in the years prior to the
outbreak of World War II and was given an additional boost when Hollywood
was enlisted by the Franklin Roosevelt administration to combat German
influence in Latin America by producing films with friendly images of Latin
Americans. Latin American–themed musicals were among Hollywood's most
popular products, and they supplied mainstream U.S. audiences with a range
of (mostly) Mexican, Cuban, Brazilian, and Argentine styles (and a few stars,
such as Carmen Miranda, as well). Latin music was given another boost
during the 1941 struggle between the publishing company ASCAP and radio
stations regarding broadcast royalties. During the dispute, ASCAP refused
to allow radio stations to play any ASCAP-owned music on the air, but the
extensive catalogue of Latin American music held by Peer's company, Peer
International (associated with ASCAP's rival BMI), helped fill the void, for a
short time giving Latin music unprecedented access to the mainstream radio
airwaves from coast to coast.[29] Even during the war, when the major recording companies dropped Latin music artists from their rosters, New York's
extensive entertainment infrastructure provided alternative venues for live
Latin music and dancing.

In the late 1940s and early 1950s, the mambo craze set in motion in

Mexico by the Cuban bandleader Dámaso Pérez Prado arrived in New York and spilled beyond the boundaries of New York's primarily Puerto Rican and Cuban Spanish-speaking communities. Bands specializing in mambos and other urban-oriented Spanish Caribbean dance musics began performing in ballrooms throughout the city to enthusiastic audiences of diverse ethnic and racial origins—African Americans, Italians, Poles, but especially Jews. Indeed, Jewish engagement with mambo was so extensive that Jewish fans known as "mamboniks" became the subject of numerous pop tunes with such names as "It's a Scream How Levine Does the Mambo." In his seminal article on Jewish and Latino cultural and musical interactions in New York, Josh Kun notes that Jews, Cubans, and Puerto Ricans had been interacting since the early twentieth century, when Puerto Ricans and Cubans first began moving into East Harlem (later El Barrio), then predominantly Jewish.[30] As Jews began moving out of El Barrio in the 1930s and 1940s, many of the performance venues originally constructed by and for the Jewish community were "recycled" into venues catering to the surrounding Puerto Rican community (although often the buildings remained in Jewish hands).[31] Throughout the late 1940s and 1950s, Jewish-owned performance venues, from the legendary Palladium Ballroom located in midtown Manhattan to the Jewish resort hotels in the Catskills, provided steady work and crucial spaces for Spanish Caribbean Latinos to develop their music beyond the boundaries of the Spanish Caribbean community itself.[32]

When the major record companies began dropping Latin music artists from their rosters in the 1940s during the war, some Jewish entrepreneurs seized the opportunity to enter the record business. The most active of the Jewish-owned Latin record company owners were Sidney Siegel, who in 1944 founded Seeco (and later its subsidiary, Tropical Records), and George Goldner, who founded the even more influential Tico Records in 1948. Seeco's Siegel was personally familiar with the Puerto Rican community and its musical tastes, since prior to establishing his label he owned a variety store in El Barrio called Casa Siegel, which sold records, among other household products, to his mostly Puerto Rican clients.[33] Seeco specialized in a wide variety of Mexican, Caribbean, and Latin American musicians recorded in their countries of origin—even if it meant that its recordings were not as polished as Tico's, which were recorded in New York. Goldner, whose wife was Puerto Rican, was more directly engaged in New York Latin music, participating actively in Tico's studios and imprinting a particular sound that defined New York Latin dance music. As the pseudonymous author of an online history of Tico Records notes, "His Tico tracks were bold, sassy, and tailored strictly to the tastes of big city consumers. He and Alan Weintraub often bathed them in a rippling echo, making them sound as if they were being placed in a subway station. Tico Records was about fancy, dressed-up Latin dance music, and the keyword was sophistication."[34]

Seeco's roster was more diverse and far-flung than Tico's, including many of Latin America's most important musicians, from Cuba's legendary Trio Matamoros to Mexico's famous Trio Los Panchos.[35] Nonetheless, throughout its approximately two decades of activity, Siegel's Seeco recorded virtually all of New York's top Latin musicians, from Machito (born Francisco Grillo) and Celia Cruz to Arsenio Rodríguez. When major label interest in Latin music rebounded in the 1950s in the wake of the success of mambo and then cha-cha, Seeco was listed by *Variety* as the second most successful label in Latin music after RCA.[36] Goldner's Tico label, however, managed to lure away musicians made famous by Seeco and eventually compiled the most extensive roster of New York's Latin music stars. Together, Tico and Seeco dominated the New York–based Latin music business throughout the 1940s and 1950s. (As they had done in Latin America, the majors signed U.S.-based Latino musicians only after they had proven successful in the Latin music market—for example, RCA signed Tito Puente away from Tico in 1955.)

As independent labels, neither Tico nor Seeco owned their own pressing or distribution companies, but they did have more access than their Latino counterparts to economic and social capital that allowed them to promote their music beyond the confines of New York's Latino community. Crucial to Goldner's success was his access to English-speaking radio audiences via his personal and business relationships with personnel working on English-language radio shows (e.g., disc jockeys Symphony Sid, Art "Pancho" Levy, Bob "Pedro" Harris), encouraging (or paying) them to play the Latin music he was producing. One example of such synergies was a fifteen-minute radio show hosted by disc jockey host Dick "Ricardo" Sugar, who was hired by Goldner to play Tico's recordings (it was legal to do so then); one of Tico's artists, Puerto Rican bandleader Tito Puente, was catapulted into citywide stardom via this practice.[37] These DJs' willingness to play Latin music produced by local Latin/o American musicians on their radio shows (as opposed to the Tin Pan Alley and Hollywood versions of it) also drew non-Latino dancers to the Palladium; Wednesday nights in particular became known for their appeal to the "gringo crowd," which often included celebrities.[38] Goldner also organized and financed a nationwide tour for his musicians, "Mambo USA"—although it turned out to be a financial disaster in provincial cities and regions of the United States, where mambo's popularity did not, as in New York City, serve as a bridge for crossing racial and ethnic boundaries.

Local Latino entrepreneurs found it difficult to compete with the majors and the better-funded and better-connected independent companies, Tico and Seeco. Nevertheless, what they lacked in connections to the non-Latino world was at least partly compensated for by their solid grounding in New York's Puerto Rican/Latino community. One such entrepreneur was Al Santiago, born in New York into a family of musicians and raised surrounded by musicians active in the Latin music scene; indeed, he himself was a musician until he decided he did not have the talent to make a career in performance. In 1955, Santiago opened up Casalegre, a record store, and, thanks to his adept use of local Spanish-language media to advertise his records, he became so successful that he decided to parlay his knowledge of Latin music into a record company. Since he lacked cash, he founded Alegre Records around 1956 with a partner, Ben Perlman, who owned a store next to Casalegre.[39] With most of the major Latin music stars under contract with the far-better-financed Tico or Seeco, Santiago signed young but up-and-coming Latino artists who the more established labels were not interested in. Santiago's willingness to provide recording opportunities to young musicians paid off with Johnny Pacheco, who scored a major hit with his first *pachanga* recording; Santiago is also credited with being the first to sign future salsa stars Eddie Palmieri and Willie Colón. In the early 1960s, Santiago recorded seminal live music jams by the Alegre All-Stars (imitating a similar Cuban All-Stars format that had been organized and recorded by the Panart label in Havana), a model that would later be successfully replicated by the next Latin music industry powerhouse, Fania Records.

Latin music had been a reasonably profitable business during the height of the mambo craze, but sales of a typical record were generally modest, around five thousand units; a big hit might sell one hundred thousand. A hit in the national pop market, in contrast, could sell millions of records.[40] In 1953, as mainstream interest in Latin music began waning as young people of all races and ethnicities turned their attention toward the dynamic new sounds of R & B and rock 'n' roll, Goldner established two new labels, Rama and Gee, in order to promote doo-wop. Goldner scored several major national hits (including the Crows' "Gee"), whose profits dwarfed what he was earning from Latin music, and in 1957, he sold Tico to Morris Levy, the owner of the Birdland nightclub (and a reputed Mob boss). Goldner remained active in Latin music, however, continuing to produce for Tico. In 1965, he founded a new label, Cotique, to capitalize on boogaloo, a hybrid of Spanish Caribbean aesthetics and African American R & B rhythms that at the time looked like it might gain traction on the national stage.[41] By the end of the 1960s, however, the boogaloo had disappeared from view, displaced by the more roots-oriented salsa that resonated better with the spirit of the cultural nationalism and identity politics that would mark the 1970s.

In summary, during the height of the cross-cultural Latin music boom of the 1940s and 1950s, Latino-owned labels, such as Santiago's Alegre and

Oller's SMC and Coda, played important historical and cultural roles in New York's Latin music industry, but economically they remained minor players. Santiago sold his label to Morris Levy in the early 1960s, but, with the further decline of interest in Latin music on the national stage during that decade (for reasons discussed in Chapter 3), even Tico and Seeco foundered as the Spanish Caribbean Latin music upon which these labels had thrived disappeared from the national stage.

Moving In and Branching Out: Latinos in the Latin Music Business in the Rock 'n' Roll Era

On the West Coast, the lure of rock 'n' roll had a similar effect on non-Latino entrepreneurs. Chudd's Imperial Records, which had been one of the most active and successful labels producing Mexican American artists, abandoned them in the 1950s in order to pursue work with more lucrative rhythm and blues and pop artists (e.g., Fats Domino and Ricky Nelson).[42] With the majors and then Imperial out of the picture, Mexican American labels specializing in music performed by Mexican Americans, whether in California, Texas, or other parts of the Southwest, largely had the domestic field to themselves. They did, however, have to compete with an extraordinarily robust—and geographically proximate—Mexican music industry. To a degree not matched in the domain of Spanish Caribbean music, Mexican music produced in Mexico was actively and effectively supported by Mexico's film industry, which released a steady stream of musicals featuring Mexican music's biggest recording stars (and turned lesser-known musicians into stars). Indeed, Mexico provided most of the Spanish-language films viewed by Spanish-speaking moviegoers throughout the United States, providing invaluable visibility to Mexican styles and stars. In New York, Spanish-speaking Latinos enjoyed the Mexican music promoted in such films as well as touring Mexican artists for whom New York was an indispensable stop, but Mexican music did not seriously compete with the dynamic Spanish Caribbean dance music being performed and recorded locally. In Los Angeles, in contrast, where Hollywood's film and music industries were closely connected to their counterparts in Mexico City, local Mexican American musicians had to compete directly with Mexican musicians. This is not to suggest that interest in local Mexican Angeleno musicians did not exist; Billy Cardenas, for example, who became the most influential producer of Los Angeles Chicano rock in the 1970s, got his start scouting out local mariachi bands to record for Bill Lazarus's Crown Studios.[43] But in a city where top Mexican acts toured regularly and had records produced and distributed by such major record companies as RCA, Mexican American musicians performing Mexican music were at a clear disadvantage.[44] (As I discuss in Chapter 7, this structurally unequal relationship between Mexican and Mexican American record producers remains in place to this day.)

Mexican Angeleno musicians with interests in rock 'n' roll, on the other hand, benefited from Los Angeles's centrality to mainstream U.S. popular music production in the 1950s (and beyond). Most rock 'n' roll–oriented record companies, however, were owned by non-Mexicans. The Del-Fi label that Ritchie Valens helped put on the map, for example, was owned by Bob Keane. Interestingly, Keane had spent part of his childhood in Mexico, where his father worked as a contractor, so he was receptive to Mexican Americans and their Mexican-tinged rock 'n' roll. Known for its successful doo-wop groups, Del-Fi was one of the labels sought by Mexican American rock 'n' roll and R & B artists, such as Chan Romero and the Carlos Brothers.[45] One notable and major exception to the dominance of non-Mexican rock 'n' roll producers was the partnership between Eddie Davis and the Mexican American Billy Cardenas, who in the 1960s and 1970s managed and produced for various record labels virtually every major Chicano rock artist (e.g., Cannibal and the Headhunters, Thee Midniters, the Premiers, the Blendells; see Chapter 3). As David Reyes and Tom Waldman point out, the complementary interests and cultural resources of each partner worked to their advantage: Cardenas, who was responsible for scouting new talent, grew up in the Mexican American community but loved rock 'n' roll; Davis, in contrast, a former altar boy who had grown up fascinated with Mexican music, "used his record company connections to procure studio time and distribution deals."[46]

Texas and other more provincial parts of the Southwest, in contrast, had no equivalent to either Los Angeles's powerful film and music industries, to New York's international Latin music industry, or to both cities' ethnically diverse demographics, which had advantages as well as disadvantages for Mexican American entrepreneurs and musicians. As Manuel Peña has argued, Mexican American–owned companies may have been small and undercapitalized, but their grounding in the local community, and their consistent and unwavering support for regional musics such as conjunto, allowed them to thrive without the interference of larger companies.[47] In New York, in contrast, the hegemony of the commercially profitable big-band style of Latin music actually limited industry access to smaller ensembles specializing in more folk-oriented vernacular musics.

On the other hand, young Texas Mexicans in the 1960s, such as Sunny Ozuna and Little Joe Hernandez, who were seeking careers in rock 'n' roll rather than with vernacular styles, encountered more difficulty finding recording opportunities than their counterparts in Los Angeles, where Mexican American rock 'n' roll was more central to the local musical scene. Most

Texas Mexican–owned music labels were not interested in English-language pop music, and, conversely, non–Mexican American labels were not interested in Mexican American acts.[48] One notable but fleeting exception was the independent Louisiana-born Cajun record producer Huey Meaux, who in the early 1960s signed Sunny Ozuna and his group the Sunglows and was able to move their song "Talk to Me" into the mainstream national arena, including a performance on *American Bandstand*. When the group failed to produce another hit song, however, Meaux convinced Ozuna to turn to the Mexican ethnic market instead, despite the fact that Ozuna "hate[d] Spanish music."[49] As discussed further in Chapter 3, Ozuna and others like him resisted being confined to the Mexican American market until the Chicano movement of the late 1960s, when Mexican-origin music was validated as an expression of ethnic pride and self-determination, even among assimilated youths.

In 1967, the small Dallas-based Zarape Records coined the term "*Onda Chicana*" to link Little Joe and the Latinnaires' rock 'n' roll–inflected music to the Chicano movement, providing their hybrid musical style with a symbolically appealing moniker.[50] Ambivalence toward Mexican American rock 'n' roll remained, however, and Mexican American producers came to the conclusion that they would do better commercially with music more strongly grounded in long-popular local styles, such as polka-ranchera. Even Sunny Ozuna and Little Joe eventually embraced performance styles foregrounding more audibly Mexican aesthetics, and they established their own labels, Buena Suerte and Key-Loc, respectively, to produce it.[51] Performers of vernacular Mexican American music, whose music did not threaten to disrupt perceived ethnic boundaries, benefited from the continuing vitality of pioneering Texas-based labels such as Ideal and Falcon that had been established in the 1940s, as well as dozens of newer ones that sprouted up in the 1960s and 1970s. Some of these labels were started by musicians who could not get a record deal with an established label; Freddie Martinez, for example, founded the later hugely successful Discos Freddie in 1969 for just this reason.[52]

As for the East Coast music industry in the 1960s and beyond, if rock 'n' roll displaced New York Latin music as the dance music of choice for trend-conscious urban cosmopolitans—and disrupted the Latin music industry that had once catered to them—Spanish Caribbean music remained vital within New York's Puerto Rican community. The music did, however, move toward a more explicitly roots-oriented style that came to be known as salsa. As discussed further in Chapters 3 and 4, salsa was a grassroots phenomenon arising out of the urban decay and official neglect experienced by Latino New Yorkers in the 1970s, and it was nourished by the ideology of self-determination promoted by the Puerto Rican civil rights movement. Yet if salsa itself was a spontaneous grassroots musical phenomenon, its hegemonic image as the quintessential

sound of Latin music (and *latinidad* itself) acquired in the 1970s was the product of the savvy business practices of salsa's premier record label, Fania.

Founded in 1964 by the Dominican-born Johnny Pacheco and Jerry
Masucci, Fania was originally intended to replicate Alegre Records' earlier success in promoting Pacheco's pachangas.[53] Pacheco's first recordings with the
fledgling Fania label were literally peddled out of the trunk of a car, but, given
Pacheco's name recognition in Latino New York, the releases did reasonably
well based on word of mouth. What really stimulated Fania's success, however, was the confluence of several unfolding developments: the marginalization of music from Cuba as a result of the postrevolutionary U.S. embargo of
Cuba; the desires of New York's most well-known Latin musicians to leave the
ailing Tico, Alegre, and Seeco labels; and the dramatic expansion of the Puerto
Rican community in New York in the wake of labor surpluses created on the
island by the industrialization programs collectively referred to as Operation
Bootstrap.[54] New York Puerto Rican and Cuban musicians calculated that a
new label co-owned by Pacheco promised a better future, especially in the
context of the city's rapidly growing Puerto Rican community; within a few
years, Fania had signed virtually every significant Latin musician in New York,
from such well-established artists as Celia Cruz and Ray Barretto to newer up-
and-coming artists such as Ruben Blades and Willie Colón. Even Tito Puente,
discouraged from a disappointing experience with RCA, signed on with Fania.
Indeed, Fania's roster of Latin music stars was so extensive, and it produced
so many hit salsa records, it has been called "the Latin Motown."

Unlike Tico and Seeco, Fania did not (initially) attempt to appeal to
non-Latino mainstream audiences; nor, like Seeco, did Fania sign talent from
Mexico or other Latin American countries whose musics had long enjoyed
small but consistent audiences in the United States. Instead, to use a contemporary political term, it sought to appeal to its musicians' base, New
York's Puerto Rican and other Latino communities. By the early 1970s, having transformed salsa into the quintessential sound of Latin music in New
York, Fania began making skillful use of Spanish-language media to market
the Fania "brand" of New York–based Afro-Cuban and Puerto Rican dance
music to Latinos and Latin Americans beyond New York. Fania's 1972 film
Our Latin Thing, documenting a seminal collective performance by its biggest stars at the Cheetah nightclub, proved to be extraordinarily effective in
spreading dynamic images of Fania's Latino musicians of diverse national
backgrounds (and their enthusiastically dancing fans) to urban Latinos/as
in other parts of the United States as well as throughout Latin America,
bolstering salsa's image as a counterweight to the power of U.S. rock.
Throughout the 1970s, Fania was the undisputed powerhouse producer of
hip, sophisticated Spanish Caribbean Latin dance music that was virtually

synonymous with the concept of Latin music itself. In 1975, Fania extended its dominance of New York Latin music even further by purchasing Tico and Alegre from Levy as well as Goldner's Cotique label, giving Fania access to the rich back catalogue of music produced by the stars it had under contract. It has been said that Fania deliberately "scuttled the label [Tico] to eliminate competition with . . . Fania";[55] whether or not this is true, the significant fact is that Fania faced little competition from either Latino-owned or non-Latin labels during its formative decades.

By the end of the 1970s, Fania was becoming a victim of its own successes among urban U.S. Latinos and Latin Americans. As salsa became more profitable, Fania's stars were lured away by contracts with major record companies such as Elektra, A&M, and Columbia. Others left for smaller labels, because they believed they were not receiving royalty payments commensurate with Fania's international sales. In 1979, Fania ceased producing records, although it continued to release music from its back catalogue.[56] Contributing to Fania's decline, the hegemony of salsa itself as the quintessential Latin dance music came under challenge in the 1980s with the rise in popularity of Dominican merengue—even among salsa's core Puerto Rican constituency (see Chapter 5). By the early 1990s, Latino-owned record companies were sprouting up in New York to market Spanish Caribbean musics other than salsa, such as the Dominican-owned J&N, which specialized in merengue and bachata.[57]

Fania's centrality to New York's Latin music industry was further sidelined by the rise of Ralph Mercado, a concert promoter and artists' manager whose Latin music empire would dwarf Fania within a decade. Mercado, born of Dominican and Puerto Rican parents, began his career in the 1960s as a concert promoter, organizing dances in New York's Puerto Rican community. (He also promoted non-Latino artists, including James Brown.) In 1972, he established the RMM Management Company and began signing local artists, mostly salsa musicians, some of whom, such as Tito Puente, were Fania's top stars. As Puente noted, "Everyone took advantage of Latin musicians back then. . . . As a promoter Raffi [Mercado] was different. He respected us . . . and he's a man with ethics. Everyone who was anybody went with Raffi."[58] Since he was not directly competing with Fania in record production and distribution at the time, Mercado and Masucci collaborated frequently and effectively in promoting the New York salsa sound to their mutual benefit. Mercado, for example, was responsible for booking the Fania All-Stars into the Cheetah nightclub in 1971 and arranging for the filming of what became *Our Latin Thing*. Mercado also promoted major salsa concerts in New York, including the annual Madison Square Garden concert featuring the artists who recorded with Fania. Mercado's role in promoting Latin music in the post-Fania period is discussed in Chapter 7; for now, it is important to credit his groundbreaking work in promoting Fania's musicians in the early days of salsa, when New York's Latin music business, after years of dominance by non-Latinos, was reverting into Latino hands.

The mainstream music industry's disinterest in the vibrant sounds of cultural empowerment and resistance produced by New York Latino musicians in the 1960s and 1970s may have provided opportunities for Latino entrepreneurs, but their location within (primarily) New York Spanish Caribbean communities also prevented these musicians and styles from achieving the place they deserve in the history of U.S. popular music, despite their profound influence on a generation of U.S. Latinos and Latin Americans. As a *New York Times* columnist observed in 2006, when Emusica, the company that purchased Fania's catalogue in 2005, began reissuing high-quality recordings, "Today Motown looms gigantic in American cultural memory, a cornerstone of the 60's nostalgia industry, the subject of innumerable books and documentaries, its hits still ubiquitous on the airwaves decades after they made the charts. Fania, on the other hand, is recalled mostly by collectors and Latinos of a certain age. And where Motown's records have been endlessly reissued and anthologized, Fania's catalog languished for years, its master tapes moldering in a warehouse in Hudson, N.Y."[59]

In subsequent decades, the segmented, layered nature of the Latin music business would once again change shape in the wake of major waves of immigrants from all over Latin America, who began transforming the cultural demographics of the major U.S. Latino record-producing centers—New York, Los Angeles, and Texas—and contributing to the emergence of a new center: Miami. The mainstream music industry, which had largely ignored the musics being produced within U.S. Latino communities since the 1950s, reconsidered their position in the late 1980s when the economic potential of so many Spanish-speaking newcomers became impossible to ignore. As the majors re-entered the Latin music business, smaller independent, Latino-owned labels that once had the field to themselves found themselves competing with the powerful, deep-pocketed majors—although this time, music industry personnel, even in the majors, were far more likely to include Latinos than in the past. The growing U.S. Spanish-speaking, Latin American–oriented market segment, however, created new dilemmas for a music industry gearing up to market ethnically marked "Latin" music across ethnic and geographic lines, within the United States as well as to Latin America. While growing numbers of foreign-born Latinos reinforced the Latin American image of Latin music, most Latinos continued to be U.S.-born, bicultural, bilingual, and culturally distinct from the newcomers.[60] How the music industry responded to this dilemma is the subject of Chapter 7.

3

To Rock or Not to Rock

Cultural Nationalism and Latino Engagement with Rock 'n' Roll

When Tito Puente wrote his now-anthemic song "Oye Como Va!" in 1963, the United States was poised on the brink of profound social and cultural upheavals that, in the seven short years between Puente's original recording and Carlos Santana's 1970 rock version, would profoundly alter the context, nature, and meaning of Latino musical practices. In the early 1960s, thousands of economically displaced Puerto Ricans, including Puente's family, had arrived in New York in search of opportunity—just as the city was beginning to lose its manufacturing base, condemning many of the new arrivals and their mainland-born children to lives of chronic unemployment, poverty, and racial discrimination. Increasingly negative images of Puerto Ricans and their culture began appearing in the media, such as John Frankenheimer's 1961 film *The Young Savages* and the 1961 film *West Side Story* (based on the 1957 play). In this context, Puente's Cuban-inspired version of "Oye Como Va!" found receptive ears in New York's Puerto Rican community, but the rest of the nation was turning its back on the Spanish Caribbean mambos and cha-chas once synonymous with tropical festivity and cosmopolitan glamour, dancing instead to rock 'n' roll.[1] Elsewhere in the Americas, the economic restructuring that anticipated (and prepared the way for) an increasingly globalized economy was setting in motion massive human displacements that would bring millions of Mexicans searching for better lives into the United States, among them Santana's family.

In 1963, however, these processes had not yet made themselves fully felt. The Vietnam War had not yet mobilized the nation's youths to rebel against authority, and young second-wave feminists were only beginning to issue calls for the end of patriarchy. Psychedelic drugs and alternative visions of how society could be organized had not yet caught the imaginations of young people around the globe. The Beatles were on the eve of their dramatic arrival in the United States but had not yet become global countercultural icons. The country's racist structures were being challenged by the civil rights movement, although the intersecting impacts of race and ethnicity later foregrounded by the Chicano and Puerto Rican movements in the 1970s had not yet surfaced, nor had these activists issued their manifestos calling on Latinos to resist assimilation and to retain their cultural heritage and distinct identities.

By 1970, in contrast, when Santana's version of "Oye Como Va!" burst onto the *Billboard* charts, these groundbreaking, paradigm-shaking transformations had been set in motion. Increasingly frustrated with their persistent marginality and inspired by cultural nationalism, young Latinos heeded the call to maintain and to celebrate their traditional Latin American cultural heritages. But at the same time, many of them, especially bilingual and bicultural Latino youths, continued to embrace the mainstream styles that had provided the soundtracks to their daily lives. As I argue in this chapter (and develop further in Chapter 4), Latinos were not outsiders looking in or passive consumers of mainstream styles; they were active (if often unrecognized) participants in musical developments that incorporated, but went beyond, practices considered by cultural nationalists as appropriate for representing their ethnic identities.

There was nothing new, of course, about the layered quality of U.S. Latino musical practices, which have always been far more complex than surface-level correspondences—for example, between Puerto Ricans and salsa or Tejanos and conjunto—would suggest. U.S.-born Latinos, particularly in their youth, have routinely consumed their own communities' traditional musics as well as the same mainstream popular music and culture as their non-Latino contemporaries. Latino engagement with mainstream styles has encompassed jazz, swing, and Tin Pan Alley in the 1920s, 1930s, and 1940s; rock 'n' roll, pop, and various subgenres of rock in the 1950s, 1960s, and 1970s; and, since the 1980s, rap and hip-hop. Such engagements, however, were particularly fraught in the late 1960s and 1970s, when cultural nationalism stimulated by the African American, Chicano, and Puerto Rican civil rights movements rendered cultural hybridity, long vexing to a nation loathe to acknowledge it, increasingly problematic to Latinos themselves as well as to non-Latinos trying to interpret their cultural productions.

Significantly, Latino responses to developments in mainstream popular music in the rock era, which coincided with the rise of cultural nationalism, have taken quite different forms; these different responses are the subject of this chapter. Chicanos have engaged with rock 'n' roll directly, consistently, and (relatively) successfully. Santana's version of "Oye Como Va!"—in which he blended two styles, Afro-Cuban cha-cha and guitar-based rock, neither of which was considered an authentically Mexican style—exemplified Chicanos' familiarity and comfort with cultural and musical hybridity. Many of Santana's New York Puerto Rican contemporaries, in contrast, were deliberately distancing themselves from mainstream, English-language rock in favor of music unambiguously rooted in Spanish Caribbean sonorities that were closer in spirit and aesthetics to Puente's original version.[2]

Concepts and Comparisons: Historical Perspectives

In order to unravel the differences between West Coast Chicano and East Coast Puerto Rican engagement with rock 'n' roll, several variables must be considered: the groups' immigration histories; the characters of their most important receiving cities, Los Angeles and New York, including their residential patterns and demographic compositions; their relationships with local and national music industries; the position of each Latino community in the U.S. racial hierarchy, especially vis-à-vis African Americans; and, finally, their interactions with musical developments in the sending regions of Mexico and Puerto Rico.

At first glance, the positions of Chicanos and New York Puerto Ricans within U.S. society seem remarkably similar, even taking into consideration important differences, such as the fact that Chicanos trace their origins in what is now U.S. territory well back into the Spanish colonial period, centuries before California was seized from Mexico after the 1848 Mexican-American War; in contrast, Puerto Ricans did not begin migrating to New York in substantial numbers until after the 1898 Spanish-American War that brought the island under U.S. colonial rule. Both communities were relatively small at the turn of the century: Mexicans, for example, comprised only 5 percent of the population of Los Angeles in 1900,[3] while Puerto Ricans in 1920 numbered only twelve thousand in the entire U.S. territory.[4] Similarly, both communities became larger, better established, and more internally diverse after World War II thanks to the concurrent accelerations in processes of assimilation and immigration, making both of them the most culturally influential Latino group in each receiving city.[5]

Some crucial differences between the two communities, however, influenced their identities and their musical practices. Mexican Americans' and Puerto Ricans' racial identities had evolved quite differently within the United States as a result of their distinct colonial histories. As discussed in Chapter 1, Mexican Americans are predominantly mestizos of mixed European and

Amerindian heritage and have therefore fallen outside the long-standing U.S. racial binary.[6] (Indeed, because they lacked clear and obvious African antecedents, at various points in U.S. history, Mexican Americans were able to lay legal claim to whiteness.)[7] Puerto Ricans, in contrast, are the racial and cultural descendants of the Spanish colonizers, indigenous Taínos, and the enslaved Africans brought to island. Many Puerto Ricans disavow their African heritage; nonetheless, as Juan Flores and others have pointed out, Puerto Ricans have unmistakable historical and cultural commonalities with African Americans that Mexican Americans do not share.[8] Because of their mixed racial ancestries, both Mexican Americans and New York Puerto Ricans were subjected to racial discrimination, and they often resided in segregated neighborhoods in close proximity to African Americans. New York, however, has always been more spatially concentrated than Los Angeles, with its characteristic metropolitan sprawl; as a result, Puerto Ricans, particularly in Spanish Harlem and the South Bronx, lived and worked in closer physical proximity to African Americans than did Mexican Americans in Los Angeles, where Mexican American barrios have been comparatively more removed from African American neighborhoods (with some exceptions, such as Watts); for example, African Americans predominated in South Central Los Angeles, while Mexican Angelenos were concentrated in downtown and East Los Angeles.[9]

As for the relationships between Chicanos and New York Puerto Ricans and musical developments in their respective homelands, particularly in regard to rock, both Mexico and the island of Puerto Rico developed active rock 'n' roll scenes as early as the 1950s.[10] In both locations, rock 'n' roll was initially associated not with rebellious working-class youths but rather with lighter-skinned, upper-class young people, whose desire to participate in its associated modernity was perceived by nationalists as reflections of a colonized mentality. In Mexico, however, rock 'n' roll was indigenized when a working-class Mexican rock scene evolved in dialogue (albeit unequal and nearly one-sided) with developments in the United States (U.S. rockers took little interest in Mexican rock). In Puerto Rico, in contrast, rock 'n' roll—regardless of whether the musicians were African American or white—continued to be perceived as an intrusive and unwelcome product of U.S. imperialism, against which salsa became a symbolic bulwark.[11] Given Puerto Ricans' equation of salsa with authenticity and nationalism, and rock 'n' roll with U.S. cultural imperialism, it is not surprising that aesthetic moves in the direction of rock were not received more enthusiastically within the working-class and intensely nationalistic New York Puerto Rican community. Chicano nationalists, in contrast, could look upon Mexico's vibrant rock scene with pride; no less a figure than Santana, whose career as a rocker began in Tijuana, was a product of that scene.

West Coast Mexican Americans and Rock 'n' Roll

As an expanding body of scholarship has made clear, the most important influences on Mexican American rock 'n' roll musicians were their African American neighbors, with whom they shared the experience of racial and economic oppression and segregated, marginalized urban spaces.[12] African American groups routinely played in East Los Angeles venues, and they were familiar with Mexican American culture, which they incorporated into some of their music, much to the delight of their Mexican American fans. As far back as 1953, for example, Texas-born African American sax player Chuck Higgins wrote the song "Pachuko Hop" (referring to the zoot-suited Mexican American youths known as "pachucos"), which became enormously popular among Mexican American youths in Los Angeles.[13] In the 1960s, the Penguins recorded a song called "Hey Señorita," and one of their later songs was entitled "Memories of El Monte," the East Los Angeles stadium where a mixed crowd of Mexican American, African American, and white teens saw their favorite rock 'n' roll groups.[14] In the 1970s, the song "Lowrider" by the group War explicitly celebrated the customized cars so closely associated with Mexican Angelenos; indeed, the song has become an anthem to Mexican American lowriders.[15]

Despite their affinities with African Americans, Mexican American forays into the rock 'n' roll arena were by no means limited to African American styles: Trini Lopez worked in the folk rock style, Chris Montez recorded soft pop ballads, and Bobby Espinosa started his career playing surf music with a group called Mickey and the Invaders before going on to become a founder of the 1970s group El Chicano.[16] Rubén Guevara collaborated with avant-garde rocker Frank Zappa on Zappa's album *Cruising with Ruben and the Jets,* and Guevara later formed an actual neo-doo-wop group—as opposed to the fictitious one mocked on Zappa's album—called Ruben and the Jets. Even acid rock, so closely associated with white middle-class hippies, had important Mexican American participants, most notably Santana but also his brother Jorge's group Malo, and other groups, such as Sapo and Azteca.

Some scholars have suggested that Mexican American rockers developed a characteristic sound, attributed to their extensive use of the Farfisa organ sometimes used in conjunto ensembles[17]—an intriguing suggestion, to be sure, although it does not account for the full range of styles played by Mexican Angelenos in which the Farfisa organ was not employed.[18] Indeed, even when aesthetics from Mexican or other Latin/o American music were incorporated, the effects tended to be quite subtle, rendering scholars' efforts to describe the distinctiveness of Mexican American rock 'n' roll rather imprecise. Guevara, for example, explains the Mexican influences in the music of the self-identified 1950s Mexican American rocker L'il Julian Herrera (a Hungarian American Jew raised by a Mexican American family) as follows: "It was very much in the black style, but something about it—the accent, the voice, the *attitude*—made it different."[19] Matt Garcia is similarly vague in identifying a Mexican American sound in a more "intense" rhythmic pattern and the presence of a brass section, especially the saxophone.[20] The point here is not that these characterizations of Mexican American rock 'n' roll are incorrect but that most casual listeners would not likely have been able to identify the music as distinctively Mexican American.

Rock 'n' roll produced by Mexican Americans in the 1950s and 1960s was as remarkably successful as it was stylistically varied. Those who attained national hits included Cannibal and the Headhunters, whose "Land of a Thousand Dances" (1965) earned them the spot as openers for the Beatles on their second U.S. tour; Chris Montez with "Let's Dance" (1962), "Call Me" (1966), "The More I See You" (1966), and "There Will Never Be Another You" (1966); Trini Lopez (Texas-born but performing in Los Angeles when he was discovered) with his folk-rock version of "If I Had a Hammer" (1963), "Kansas City" (1963), "Lemon Tree" (1965), and "I'm Comin' Home Cindy" (1966); and the Premiers with "Farmer John" (1964). Dozens of other East Los Angeles bands, such as Rene and Ray, the Blendells, Thee Midniters, and the Romancers, charted locally or on the Top 100 chart nationally. These bands, whose song titles and lyrics often celebrated local cultural practices and geographies (the most famous example being Thee Midniters' 1965 song "Whittier Boulevard," named after Chicanos' favorite strip for cruising), enjoyed the support of a large and enthusiastic community of East Los Angeles teenage fans, who flocked to performances held in the city's largest venues, such as the Paramount Ballroom and the El Monte American Legion Stadium.[21] Indeed, in Los Angeles, so much Mexican American rock was produced between the 1950s and 1970s that a term was coined to refer to it collectively—the so-called "East Side Sound."

Groups composed entirely or partially of Mexican Americans from other parts of the country also made the national charts during this period, demonstrating the vitality and range of Mexican American rock 'n' roll in the 1950s and 1960s. Texan Mexicans were particularly successful: Sunny and the Sunglows with "Talk to Me" (1963); Sam the Sham and the Pharaohs with "Woolly Bully" (1964), "Ju Ju Hand" (1965), "Ring Dang Doo," (1965), "Lil' Red Riding Hood" (1966), and "The Hair on My Chinny Chin Chin" (1966);[22] the Sir Douglas Quintet with "She's About a Mover" (1965), "The Rains Came" (1966), and "Mendocino" (1969);[23] and Rene and Rene with "Lo Mucho Que Te Quiero" (1968). Tejano musician Freddy Fender's English and Spanish versions of his rock 'n' roll songs "Mean Woman"/"Que Mala" and "Holy One"/"Hay Amor" became local hits in the 1950s,[24] and he later scored four number-one hits on the national country charts, which then crossed over to the pop charts—although, with the exception of "Before the Next Teardrop Falls" (1975), to somewhat lower positions. The Detroit-based ? (Question Mark) and the Mysterians also made the national charts in 1966 with "96 Tears," followed the next year with "I Need Somebody."[25]

While collectively Mexican Americans' successes are noteworthy, the fact that their songs were largely sung in English and were aesthetically very similar to—if not indistinguishable from—mainstream rock 'n' roll enabled Mexican Americans to step into the mainstream popular music arena in the 1950s and 1960s.[26] To be sure, included in the substantial body of Mexican American rock 'n' roll produced between the 1950s and 1970s were some remakes of Spanish-language songs; examples include Ritchie Valens's version of "La Bamba," based on a traditional Veracruzan folk song, and various versions of the classic Mexican bolero "Sabor a Mí." Nonetheless, as discussed in Chapter 2, in the 1960s, the mainstream music industry and the English-speaking public had lost their appetites for Latin American music.

The cultural nationalism inspired by the Chicano movement in the late 1960s and early 1970s, in contrast, stimulated Chicano rockers to ethnically mark their music by employing a variety of performance strategies—although they did not abandon the rock 'n' roll idiom in favor of more "authentically Mexican" styles. The group originally called the VIPs, for example, which played music ranging from the Beatles' "Lady Madonna" to Eddie Floyd's "Knock on Wood," changed their name to El Chicano in 1969 but continued to play the same repertoire.[27] Instrumentation was also employed to convey ethnicity, such as the prominent mariachi horns in Yaqui's bilingual song "Time for a Change (Es Tiempo Para un Cambio)" (1973). Other musicians released songs with Spanish titles, such as El Chicano's 1970 hit song "Viva Tirado," named after a Mexican bullfighter—despite the fact that the tune, written by Los Angeles jazzman Gerald Wilson, was an instrumental and had nothing to do with bullfighting.[28] Album cover art also made explicit musicians' links to the ideology of the Chicano movement, a noteworthy example being the iconic image of an indigenous warrior and princess featured on the cover of Malo's 1972 eponymous recording, which invoked Chicanos' southwest homeland, the mythical Aztlán (see Figure 3.1).[29]

In response to the Chicano movement's emphasis on cultural roots, traditional Mexican music was imbued with additional value, particularly within the farm workers' struggle, where cultural activists such as Luis Valdéz employed Mexican *corridos* and conjunto music in their drive to unionize workers.[30] Nonetheless, the sources many Chicano rockers drew on, even in this highly politicized period, were not Mexican but Spanish Caribbean,

Figure 3.1. Artwork on a 1972 Malo recording reflects the Chicano movement's focus on the indigenous ancestral Chicano homeland, Aztlán. *(Courtesy of Rhino/ Warner Brothers.)*

thereby invoking a more generalized pan-Latino identity. Santana's "Oye Como Va!" and "Evil Ways" are certainly the most famous examples of such Spanish Caribbean–infused Chicano rock, but other groups, such as Malo, Sapo, and Azteca, similarly blended rock with Spanish Caribbean aesthetics, particularly in the domain of percussion. Spanish Caribbean Latin music had always been popular in Los Angeles,[31] but it should be noted that those most responsible for developing the Afro-Latin rock style were Chicanos/Latinos from San Francisco. Significantly, Santana's first group, the Santana Blues Band, began, as its name clearly indicates, not as a rock band but as a blues band, specializing in Chicago-style blues; Latin percussion and stylings were introduced when conga player Mike Carabello joined the band and were later enhanced with the addition of José "Chepito" Areas and Pete and Coke Escovedo.[32] Los Angeles Chicanos, in contrast, generally favored a more African American–oriented R & B/funk sound, although some gravitated to the new punk style that emerged in the 1970s.[33]

By the end of the 1970s, the Chicano movement, like other social movements originally stimulated by cultural nationalism and identity politics in the 1970s, was being modified by more nuanced views of ethnic identity generated by Latinos, especially feminists and gays, who contested essentialist, monolithic (and masculinist) constructions of what it meant to be Chicano. Ethnic identity and pride remained important, but the range of opportunities for articulating them through music expanded. Chicano punk rockers such as the Plugz and The Brat, for example, reflected the political tenor of the times by harshly critiquing the establishment. Other punk groups, such as Los Illegals, insisted on incorporating Spanish into their lyrics, but they rejected the heroic nationalism adopted by their predecessors in terms of their performance styles and the iconographies invoked in their cover art. The changing political environment can be observed in the trajectory of the rock group Los Lobos: They had begun playing rock 'n' roll in their youth, but when they formed the band in the early 1970s as the Chicano movement was in ascent, they turned to traditional Mexican music; they returned to English and the rock 'n' roll idiom in the 1980s; and since then, they have maintained a successful career based on their ability to play both traditional Mexican music *and* straight-up guitar rock as well as zydeco, blues, and country and western.[34] Achieving national acclaim with their 1984 bilingual recording *How Will the Wolf Survive?* followed by their role in Luis Valdéz's successful 1987 biopic *La Bamba* (based on the life of Ritchie Valens), Los Lobos' command of the full range of U.S. and Mexican popular music styles—sometimes blending them, sometimes not—allowed them to sustain a fan base of both ethnic Mexican and mainstream audiences.

The career of Chicano Elvis impersonator El Vez (Robert Lopez), who began his musical career in the Los Angeles–based punk rock group the Zeros, similarly articulates Mexican Americans' increasingly creative and strategic use of their hybridity. El Vez's music is designed primarily for listeners who are bilingual, bimusical, and bicultural, all of which are necessary traits for understanding his unique brand of ironic humor and social commentary. Take, for example, his song "Nunca He Ido a España," from his CD *Fun in Español.*[35] The song is a parody of Three Dog Night's 1972 hit "I've Never Been to Spain," in which El Vez subverts the original song's idea of Spain as an exotic travel destination: In his (Spanish) lyrics, he explains that since he has never been to Spain, he should not be called Hispanic, but since he *has* been to Mexico, he should be called Chicano. But his humor also functions at a musical level: After a few verses closely following the Three Dog Night original, the tune switches to a parody of George Harrison's 1973 song "Wah Wah." Here, El Vez substitutes the chorus of "wah wah" with the word "agua," the Spanish word for water, and lyrically switches his narrative to the consequences of Columbus's voyage across the ocean. The full richness of El Vez's commentary on Mexican and Mexican American identities depends on listeners who not only understand English and Spanish but also are thoroughly familiar with the rock 'n' roll canon. Monolingual and monocultural listeners might enjoy the music, but they will not get the jokes.[36]

In summary, Mexican Americans, especially those from Los Angeles, have a long, continuous, multifaceted engagement with rock 'n' roll and, by extension, with U.S. mainstream popular music. Although some of their musical productions have been bilingual and even fewer have been entirely in Spanish, the majority have been in English. Mexican American rockers certainly encountered barriers created by the disinterest (if not the racism) of the mainstream music industry, and artistic recognition and economic success eluded most of them, but enough of them achieved mainstream success that Mexican Americans must be considered coparticipants in the development of U.S. rock 'n' roll. Most germane to this discussion, however, is the idea that Mexican American rockers, whether or not they made the national charts, received consistent support from within the Mexican American community, because rock 'n' roll was perceived as their birthright.

New York Puerto Ricans and Rock 'n' Roll

On the East Coast, young New York Puerto Rican teens in the 1950s were, like their West Coast counterparts, listening avidly to rock 'n' roll as well as to their parents' Spanish Caribbean musics. As the subsequent decades unfolded, however, New York Puerto Rican musicians and fans did not dedicate themselves to rock 'n' roll with the same enthusiasm and consistency as their Mexican American counterparts. With the exception of the short-lived boogaloo and two Puerto Rican musicians, José Feliciano and Tony Orlando, New York Puerto Rican musicians' engagement with rock 'n' roll and the English-language mainstream popular music arena in general has been more tenuous and ambivalent, and, when it has taken place, it has been primarily with those styles at the African American end of the rock 'n' roll continuum. Indeed, other than Feliciano and Orlando (who are discussed further below), only two New York Puerto Rican musicians made the national charts between the 1950s and the late 1990s, when Ricky Martin and Jennifer Lopez burst onto the pop charts: Ray Barretto with "El Watusi" (1963) and Joe Cuba's boogaloo "Bang Bang" (1966). Significantly, Barretto's and Cuba's tunes, both hybrids of R & B with Spanish Caribbean styles, were, with the exception of some Spanish phrases, primarily instrumental.

The first step in unpacking New York Puerto Ricans' relationship to rock 'n' roll is to emphasize the fact that, well before the 1950s, Puerto Rican musicians in New York had always engaged with U.S. popular music, albeit more often with African American styles than with the mainstream-oriented Tin Pan Alley music.[37] Like their Mexican American counterparts, New York

Puerto Ricans were victims of racial discrimination and shared with African Americans not only the same segregated neighborhoods but also often the same tenement buildings—and, as one New York Puerto Rican acerbically noted, the same cockroaches.[38] Unlike Mexican Americans, however, many New York Puerto Ricans were of African ancestry, which, coupled with the spatial concentration of New York's minority neighborhoods—compared to Los Angeles's more ethnically specific neighborhoods and metropolitan sprawl—brought New York Puerto Ricans closer culturally and physically to their African American neighbors. Indeed, Flores has argued that the constant social and cultural interactions between these two groups in New York City encouraged New York Puerto Ricans to engage laterally with African American culture rather than assimilating into the dominant white mainstream culture.[39] Nevertheless, New York Puerto Ricans' relationships with African Americans, if close, have not been unproblematic, as writer Piri Thomas and many others have observed: New York Puerto Ricans have resisted the effacement of their cultural distinctiveness when misidentified as African Americans, a confusion that was not experienced by Mexican Americans, who were more likely to be mestizos.[40]

New York, the country's premier immigrant city and historically the center of the nation's recording industry (see Chapter 2), had long been a magnet for talented musicians from the Caribbean and Latin America as well as African Americans and whites from throughout the United States, rendering it fertile ground for musical exchanges and creative experimentation. When rock 'n' roll emerged in the 1950s, New York–based Puerto Rican musicians were enjoying the benefits of being embedded within a dynamic music scene solidly grounded in Spanish Caribbean styles as well as being in close proximity to the international music industry—both of which offered clear professional advantages to those musicians interested in working in Spanish Caribbean idioms. Given the dynamism of the local Latin music scene at the time, New York Puerto Rican musicians had less motivation to look beyond the boundaries of Spanish Caribbean repertoires, even when English-language R & B and doo-wop groups began routinely including Latin-tinged songs in their repertoires in the 1950s.[41]

In addition to witnessing the florescence of mambo and cha-cha on the national stage, New York Puerto Rican teens in the 1950s were experiencing another quite distinct but extraordinarily vibrant musical moment: the eruption of rock 'n' roll, which was being performed live in venues across the city, including the Apollo theater in Harlem, as well as on locally produced (but nationally broadcast) television variety shows, such as Ed Sullivan's. Young New York Puerto Ricans, most of whom had arrived as children during the surge of migration from Puerto Rico in the 1940s, were among those who avidly embraced rock 'n' roll, especially doo-wop. Doo-wop, being primarily vocal, was an easily accessible musical style that required no instruments and could be performed by anyone, anywhere. Doo-wop's sentimental lyrics were particularly appealing to young New York Puerto Ricans raised in a culture that had long valued romantic music, the quintessential example being the bolero.[42] Three Puerto Rican musicians achieved nationwide success in doo-wop, although in both cases they were assumed by most listeners to be black: Herman Santiago and Joe Negroni of Frankie Lymon and the Teenagers, and Harold Torres, who sang with the Crests (of "16 Candles" fame).[43] Other New York Puerto Rican vocalists began their careers singing doo-wop in the 1950s. Jimmy Sabater, for example, sang with a doo-wop group called the Viceroys before later scoring a hit with Willie Torres's Latin soul ballad "To Be with You";[44] and Joe Loco (a pianist who had performed with the legendary Afro-Cuban bandleader Machito) released a version of "Gee," which had been a major hit for the African American doo-wop group the Crows. (Loco's Latinized doo-wop song is considered to be the first Latinized R & B vocal, but it did not make headway in the market.)[45]

Throughout the 1950s, Latin stylings continued to show up in rock 'n' roll music produced by both white (e.g., Bobby Darin) and African American artists (e.g., Betty Everett), but, by the end of the decade, the attraction of Latin music for mainstream audiences was on the wane. In part, this was due to the saturation of schlocky mambos and cha-chas that had flooded the marketplace, but more importantly, Latin music was displaced by the exploding popularity of the newer sounds of R & B and rock 'n' roll, followed by Beatlemania and the so-called British Invasion in the early 1960s. Another blow to the Latin music scene in New York was the U.S. blockade of revolutionary Cuba, which abruptly cut off musical interactions with the island that for decades had served as an incubator of new rhythms and sounds.[46] To older and well-established Puerto Rican and Cuban bandleaders accustomed to sophisticated and vibrant Latin musics rooted in their own communities, rock 'n' roll was of little interest, but they were unable to compete with its appeal to young people; instead, they continued to churn out mambos and cha-chas that did not comparably reflect the tumultuous new decade.

In the 1960s, some of New York's well-established Latino musicians attempted to revitalize Spanish Caribbean music by infusing it with new rhythms and energy, resulting in scores of flute- and violin-based *pachanga* and *charanga* recordings. Some of these cha-cha-inspired charangas and pachangas (such as Tito Puente's "Oye Como Va!") were solidly grounded in Spanish Caribbean aesthetics, although others (such as Johnny Pacheco's "Acuyuyé") had a subtle R & B rhythmic feel. It was precisely this combination of Latin and R & B sonorities that sent Ray Barretto's instrumental "El Watusi" to the top twenty on the national pop charts in 1963.[47] That same year, Cuban-born percussionist Mongo Santamaría also made the charts with his R & B–inflected "Watermelon Man." These mainstream hits, however, did not reflect the sensibilities and preferences of that generation; indeed, Barretto is said to have been uncomfortable with the pressure to replicate the success of "El Watusi" and, instead, returned to more patently Spanish Caribbean aesthetics in his 1964 recording *Guajira y Guanguancó* (which anticipated the more roots-oriented style he would develop with Fania a few years later).[48]

However, a younger generation of New York–born or New York–bred Puerto Rican musicians, such as Johnny Colon, made more dramatic and sustained attempts to renovate what they perceived as their parents' old-fashioned "hick music" by mixing it with R & B, creating a new musical hybrid called "boogaloo," or *bugalú*[49] (much of which was released on Goldner's Tico label; see Chapter 2). The boogaloo was based not on the complex 3-2 (or 2-3) Cuban clave rhythm that had underpinned most Spanish Caribbean Latin music but rather on rock 'n' roll's steadier 4/4 rhythms. The trap drums added to Spanish Caribbean percussion further expressed the musicians' layered experiences as Puerto Ricans and as urban U.S. teenagers who liked rock 'n' roll. Significantly, boogaloo was most heavily influenced by soul and funk—that is, the African American end of the rock 'n' roll spectrum—which is not surprising given the physical and cultural commonalities between the two communities, referred to above. Indeed, Flores sees the creation of the boogaloo as a deliberate attempt to get "Black Americans involved and onto the dance floor."[50] The fact that most boogaloos were either in English or bilingual facilitated such crossovers, and in 1966 Joe Cuba's "Bang Bang" hit the mainstream charts at number 63. Other boogaloos, such as Pete Rodríguez's "I Like It Like That" (1966) and Colon's "Boogaloo Blues" (1966), did not chart nationally but became instant hits within New York.

Boogaloo's Latin percussion- and horn-based textures were noticeably closer to Spanish Caribbean dance music than to the electric guitar–based rock 'n' roll being produced at the same time in East Los Angeles by groups such as Cannibal and the Headhunters. However, a noteworthy point of convergence between East and West Coast Latino rock 'n' roll in the 1960s reflected how the spirit of the times was being articulated by young Latinos. Many of the recordings produced contemporaneously by Los Angeles Chicanos and New York Puerto Ricans featured raucous party sounds and celebratory shouts in the background that expressed the uninhibited informality of the 1960s and their refusal to conform to the constraints required of a well-defined "song." Indeed, Flores's description of the boogaloo sound as "a bawdy happening at the peak of its emotional and sexual energy, with instrumentals and vocals playing in full and wild association with the crowd" could just as well describe the Premiers' "Farmer John" (1964) or the Blendells' "La La La La" (1964).[51] In this regard, the boogaloo and its West Coast counterparts expressed the liberatory spirit of the 1960s, in which conventions and boundaries were gleefully transgressed. Whether boogaloo could or should be categorized as a variant of rock 'n' roll is certainly open to debate, although it should be noted that Santana's Spanish Caribbean and rock hybrids—which are sung in Spanish—*are* considered to be rock. The boogaloo, however, preceded Santana's successful combinations of rock 'n' roll with Afro-Cuban music by several years.

Despite boogaloo's promising success in New York, New York Puerto Rican musicians in the 1960s were unable to achieve levels of national visibility in the mainstream arena comparable to those of Chicano rockers in that decade. One issue was that the boogaloo did not receive adequate support from New York's Latin music industry. On the contrary, despite Goldner's efforts to promote boogaloo on his Latin music–oriented Tico label, the genre faced active hostility from established bandleaders (including Tito Puente) who considered it musically primitive but were clearly threatened by the competition.[52] More crucial to the fate of boogaloo, however, was the rise of Puerto Rican cultural nationalism and the contemporaneous emergence of salsa, a music that, unlike boogaloo, was deeply rooted in Spanish Caribbean musical traditions.

Salsa's intense symbolic importance to New York Puerto Ricans in the 1970s was directly related to the appalling social conditions and urban decay imposed on Latino and black neighborhoods as the first rumblings of economic globalization began to make themselves felt in New York. The city's manufacturing base was eroding as factories relocated to other locations with cheaper and more tractable labor, while changes in immigration policies in 1965 were opening up the doors to hundreds of thousands of new immigrants from Latin America (and other parts of the globe). The flight of white middle-class residents to the suburbs drained city coffers just as the need for public services was rising, contributing to the decay of New York's once vital Puerto Rican neighborhoods. Inspired by the black and Chicano civil rights movements, militant Puerto Rican cultural nationalists, particularly the South Bronx–based Young Lords, sought to defend their communities not only by challenging the city's neglect but also by fostering community empowerment, urging their ethnic cohorts to rely on their own cultural resources as a source of strength and pride.

Salsa drew upon multiple contemporary musical sources, including R & B, jazz, and other Latin American and Caribbean genres, but at its core

nvigorated and celebrated the Spanish Caribbean musical aesthetics
..... nad flourished in New York in the 1940s and 1950s. The music of young
salseros such as Willie Colón could be differentiated from that of its Spanish Caribbean predecessors by its aggressive, busy energy and stinging lyrics
that reflected the salseros' struggles growing up in New York's besieged barrios. However, notwithstanding its distinct New York flavor, salsa's aesthetic
emphasis was solidly Spanish Caribbean—so much so that some of the older
musicians performing it, such as Tito Puente, insisted they were simply playing existing Latin dance musics such as mambo and cha-cha under a new
name.[53] Musical mixings and innovations did take place in the 1970s, as salseros incorporated jazz and African American R & B stylings, but they drew
little from the domain of guitar-based rock, at the time virtually synonymous
with U.S. cultural imperialism.

To activists such as Felipe Luciano, a member of the Young Lords, salsa
was the musical symbol of the Puerto Rican and Latino communities' political
and cultural resistance. Performed by a dizzying number of talented musicians
(many, but not all, of whom were Puerto Rican), salsa dominated the Latin
dance scene throughout the 1970s, not only in New York but also in other U.S.
cities, such as Los Angeles, with large Latino populations as well as throughout
urban, working-class Latin America.[54] Yet despite the polarizing rhetoric of the
times, New York Puerto Rican musicians, including some of the older and well-
established ones, made overtures in the direction of non-Latin mainstream
styles and English-language vocals. Roberto Roena's 1969 recording *Apollo
Sound,* for example, incorporates sounds reminiscent of the groups Blood,
Sweat, and Tears and Chicago, although it is noteworthy that these groups
were horn-based rather than electric guitar–based.[55] Even Latin music stalwart
Eddie Palmieri experimented by combining Spanish Caribbean sonorities with
R & B in the 1970s.[56] In 1973, Fania—salsa's premier record label—organized a
Madison Square Garden concert featuring its biggest stars entitled *Salsa, Soul,
Rock,* in which Jorge Santana, Carlos's brother and leader of the Chicano rock
group Malo, played straight guitar-based rock in a duo with prominent Puerto
Rican salsa singer Cheo Feliciano (although each in their own musical idiom).
Nevertheless, these gestures were the exceptions rather than the rule; overall,
salsa succeeded in pulling Spanish Caribbean music back to more traditional
Spanish Caribbean aesthetics, insisting on a rhythmic grounding in the clave
and rejecting the English lyrics and R & B rhythms used in boogaloo in favor
of Spanish lyrics, Latin percussion (congas, bongos, and timbales), and the big
brass sound of trumpets and trombones. As John Storm Roberts observed, "the
prevailing rhetoric was of roots, purity, and a concept (related to the growth of
Latino political awareness) of 'community music.'"[57]

If salsa and cultural nationalism dominated the soundscape and imaginations of most New York Puerto Rican dancers and activists in the 1970s, a small handful of New York–based Latin rock bands did appear in the late 1960s, most of whose musicians were New York Puerto Rican: Harvey Averne's Barrio Band; Toro; Seguida; Benitez; and, from the town of Woodstock (an hour's drive north of New York), the group Chango. These groups recorded very little and did not achieve much commercial success; indeed, they would most likely be forgotten but for their inclusion in a 1988 compilation CD entitled *Chicano Power! Latin Rock in the USA 1968–1976*. As the liner notes explain in reference to the New York–based bands, "The problem was ironically a product of the fact that in New York there was already a strong latin [sic] music industry spearheaded by the Fania record company. Whilst Fania brilliantly manipulated New York latin music into a worldwide marketable commodity, giving it the term Salsa, latin rock was unfortunately not really understood by the people who controlled the industry . . . [and] . . . few salsa purists accepted latin rock."[58] Interestingly, these New York Puerto Rican rock groups maintained aesthetic and personal connections with Chicano rockers as well as with their local Latin music counterparts. Harvey Averne's Barrio Band, for example, "featured the cream of New York's salsa musicians" (e.g., Andy González on bass and Hector Lavoe and Ismael Miranda on vocals), and one of their songs, "Cayuco," was covered by the West Coast bands El Chicano and Macondo.[59]

Before concluding, it is necessary to address two New York Puerto Rican musicians who did achieve mainstream success in the 1960s but were not grounded in the New York Puerto Rican community in the same way that their counterparts performing salsa were. In the 1960s and 1970s, Tony Orlando (born in New York of a Puerto Rican mother and a Greek father) had a string of pop chart hits (either solo or with his backup vocal group, Dawn), the most famous of which were his 1961 version of "Halfway to Paradise," his 1970 hit songs "Candida" and "Knock Three Times," 1973's "Tie a Yellow Ribbon 'Round the Ole Oak Tree," and his 1975 version of "He Don't Love You (Like I Love You)." Between 1974 and 1976, he even had his own television variety show, *Tony Orlando and Dawn*. José Feliciano, born in Puerto Rico but raised in New York from the age of five, attended P.S. 57, a public high school famous for the number of successful salsa musicians trained in its music program. Feliciano took up the accordion and the guitar, and at the age of nine performed at South Bronx's Teatro Puerto Rico, but while he was in high school, his musical performances were in Greenwich Village coffee shops rather than salsa clubs. His first U.S. mainstream hit, which reached number 4 on the pop charts, was an acoustic version of the Doors' "Light My Fire" that he recorded on the suggestion of his Los Angeles–based producer. The album it was on, *Feliciano,* won two Grammys in 1968, one for Best New

Artist and the other for Best Male Contemporary Pop Vocal Performance; it was also nominated for Album of the Year. That same year, Feliciano had another hit with his acoustic version of "High Heel Sneakers."[60] Feliciano did not have any additional Top-40 hit singles, but throughout the 1970s he headlined several sold-out performing tours and sessioned with major artists, such as John Lennon and Joni Mitchell.

How do these two extraordinarily successful New York Puerto Rican artists fit into the musical practices and preferences of the New York Puerto Rican community in the 1960s and 1970s? Feliciano was primarily a singer-songwriter-guitarist whose stylings were more indebted to jazz and folk than to rock, but his music, in content as well as in context, was unequivocally located within the mainstream rock 'n' roll arena. As for Orlando, thanks to such schmaltzy songs as "Tie a Yellow Ribbon 'Round the Ole Oak Tree," his particular strain of pop rock "had little street credibility,"[61] but seventeen of his songs charted in the Top 40, and numerous others made the Top-100 list—a feat that no Puerto Rican or Chicano musician has even come close to matching. In short, the achievements of these two musicians are noteworthy indeed, although they have often been overlooked by the journalists who gushed over Ricky Martin in the 1990s as if he were the first Puerto Rican artist to achieve mainstream success. Yet, in spite of Feliciano's and Orlando's undeniable importance in commercial terms, their music was not rooted in a local, community-based music scene, nor did they contribute to the development of an influential and recognizable style comparable to the East Side sound created and supported by West Coast Chicano musicians and their fans.[62]

Concluding Thoughts

If both East and West Coast Latinos were inspired by cultural nationalism and identity politics in the 1970s, their musical responses and trajectories diverged dramatically. West Coast Chicanos continued to perform guitar-based R & B and rock, although they devised a range of strategies to convey their ethnic consciousness within these idioms. Chicanos, like Puerto Ricans, demonstrated preferences for the horn- and percussion-heavy styles associated with African Americans, but they also routinely played the electric guitar–centered rock styles commonly associated with white groups. To be sure, the issues of assimilation and cultural nationalism raised by the Chicano movement in the late 1960s and early 1970s created a dilemma for young Chicano musicians sympathetic to their communities' efforts to celebrate their ancestral Mexican cultural traditions,[63] but they did not thereby categorically reject rock 'n' roll and English because they were the idioms of their oppressors; rather, they sought to use these idioms to express their grievances, their resistance, and their ethnic pride. As George Lipsitz notes of the musical choices of Chicanos, "Mexican-American musicians could stick to Chicano musical forms like ranchera and cumbia musics and find recognition and reward within their own community. Or they could master Anglo styles and be assimilated into the mainstream without anyone being aware of their Chicano identity. But Los Angeles Chicano rock-and-roll artists have selected another path. They have tried to straddle the line between the two cultures, creating a fusion music that resonates with the chaos and costs of cultural collision."[64] In short, Chicanos cannot be described as being more "assimilated" or less conscious of their ethnic identity, but, in terms of popular music in the United States, it is undeniable that, on the whole, they have been more willing to engage with rock than their New York Puerto Rican counterparts.

New York Puerto Ricans also engaged with a variety of non-Latin musical idioms, but their participation in the English-language mainstream popular music scene in the 1960s and 1970s was less consistent and less visible overall than that of their Chicano counterparts. Moreover, to the extent that they experimented with non-Latin styles, they tended to favor the African American end of the rock 'n' roll continuum. Significantly, in spite of a deep tradition of acoustic guitar music in Puerto Rico and elsewhere in the Spanish Caribbean, New York Puerto Rican musicians generally avoided the electric guitar that was so closely associated with rock 'n' roll. In contrast, cutting-edge Cuban dance bands in the 1970s such as Los Van Van routinely added the electric guitar and trap set as well as rock stylings to their ensembles, much to the delight of their young fans eager to hear updated versions of Cuban dance music.[65] This is not to suggest that New York Puerto Ricans did not influence developments in mainstream popular music during this period—indeed, their contributions in this regard (discussed further in Chapter 4) were significant; but their presence was more audible in terms of aesthetics rather than as visible center-stage participants. Chicanos, in contrast, were far less influential on developments in the domain of commercial Latin music, domestically and internationally.

While this chapter has focused on comparing West Coast Mexican Americans' and East Coast New York Puerto Ricans' relationships with rock 'n' roll, it is important to note that the musical practices of Mexican Americans in Texas and other parts of the United States generally were comparable to those of their Los Angeles–based counterparts. Miami's Cuban Americans, in contrast, were too recently arrived in the 1960s and 1970s, and too obsessed with the possibility of returning to Cuba, to become involved in the civil rights movements marking that tumultuous era; moreover, they did not perceive themselves as members of racially or socioeconomically subordinated groups. Thus, even though second-generation Cuban Americans gravitated toward rock 'n' roll in the same period, the cultural implications of their choices were quite dissimilar.

In comparing Chicano and New York Puerto Rican musical practices in the 1960s and 1970s, it is important to emphasize that this is not an attempt to valorize one community's choices and to devalue the other's but rather to acknowledge and learn from the local specificities of each. New York, for example, has always been the site of extraordinary cultural creativity, and historically it has been more ethnically diverse than Los Angeles; nevertheless, as a city that values traditions and continuity, it has retained many of its long-standing physical and cultural contours. Los Angeles, in contrast, celebrates—indeed, prides itself—on its newness, its progressive modernity, its ability to reinvent itself, and its inhabitants' willingness to do likewise.[66] In the most general contextual terms, then, New York has offered advantages to those musicians and fans seeking to maintain traditional repertoires, while Los Angeles has offered plenty of space for those seeking to reshape them.

But, ultimately, it is at the intersection of the historical, social, and cultural forces shaping each community's urban experience that we can most productively seek explanations for these differences. Los Angeles Mexican American mestizos defy the United States' black or white binary, giving them some flexibility in forming their racial identities; New York Puerto Ricans, in contrast, were more likely to be confused with African Americans. Moreover, while Mexican Americans' national origins in sovereign Mexico have always been a source of pride, the post-Chicano movement generation insisted on a U.S.-based ethnic identity and accepted the distinctions between here and there. Rubén Guevara, for example, explained why he celebrates Los Angeles as his "home" in his song "Con Safos," which contains an extensive narrative about Chicano history and identity: "The inspiration . . . came from a jarring culture shock I experienced in 1974 on my first trip to Mexico in search of my indigenous roots and identity. . . . I came to the painful realization that my social culture was not Mexican. My ancestral cultural roots were, but not my social culture—it was and is Chicano."[67] Regardless of whether one interprets Aztlán as myth or historical fact, its location in the Southwest provides Chicanos with a powerful symbolic basis for claims to national belonging and the rights of cultural citizenship.

New York Puerto Ricans' homeland, in contrast, was (and is) a colony, and even their U.S. citizenship, like their residence in New York, was perceived by many as the imposed and unwanted consequence of their colonial tragedy. New York Puerto Ricans commonly express the sentiment that no matter where they were born, no matter where they live, and no matter what language they might choose to speak, they are first, foremost, and always Puerto Rican. Nostalgic, loving images of Puerto Rico in New York Puerto Rican expressive arts are ubiquitous, while New York has often been rendered as cold, hostile, and unforgiving, or, at best, just a place to earn a living rather than a home.[68] Despite their ambivalence toward New York, many New York Puerto Ricans have never lived on the island and no longer speak Spanish—or, at best, speak a New York–inflected Spanish/Spanglish that is scorned on the island—and they are fully established within the New York communities in which they live. Numerous mainland-based Puerto Rican observers, from novelist Piri Thomas to filmmaker Frances Negrón-Muntaner, have commented on New York Puerto Ricans' contradictory experiences of not fully belonging either to the United States or to the island homeland—yet, at the same time, being attached to both.[69] This sense of in-betweenness seems to have produced more reluctance to lay similarly historical and celebratory claims to the geographical and cultural spaces of the United States among Puerto Ricans than among West Coast Chicanos.

The New York Puerto Rican community has relied more heavily on Spanish Caribbean–based cultural traditions as a steadying and unifying force, which is *not* to imply that they are backward-looking; indeed, their contributions to developments in Latin and mainstream styles, discussed in this and the following chapters, have been profound and significant. Nevertheless, many Puerto Ricans, particularly an older generation, still believe that their musical "essence" has been best expressed in salsa, whose most prominent and defining aesthetics are unequivocally Spanish Caribbean. For example, Ángel Quintero Rivera, referring to both Puerto Ricans on the island and on the mainland, sees the uninterrupted production of salsa for over thirty years as a victory over the threat of rock and the cultural impositions it is perceived to embody. He goes on to conclude that "the battle of 'resistance' seems to have been won" and notes that since rock is no longer a threat to salsa (and, by implication, to Puerto Rican identity), Puerto Ricans can now comfortably accept it.[70] Such sentiments did not, I might note, spare Ricky Martin in the 1990s from accusations that he sold out his Puerto Rican culture by performing electric guitar–based music in English for the U.S. pop marketplace.

Although a strong adherence to tradition may have discouraged a more radical reshaping and reinvention of Spanish Caribbean musical styles and may have deterred New York Puerto Rican musicians from venturing into the more lucrative rock arena in the 1960s and 1970s, it undeniably helped the community maintain its cultural coherence and integrity in years when it was under intense social and economic pressures. It is important to acknowledge and understand that maintaining a strong sense of ethnic identity is not necessarily dependent on any particular mode of engagement with mainstream U.S. musical practices: Communities and individuals must decide for themselves when and where it is appropriate to participate and when and where it makes more sense to withdraw and resist.

4

Turning the Tables

Musical Mixings, Border Crossings, and New Sonic Circuitries

The 1940s and 1950s are often considered the glory years of Latin/o popular music, thanks to the aesthetic developments and commercial success achieved in the national and international arena by the mostly Afro-Cuban–inspired dance musics emanating from New York City that virtually came to define "Latin music" in the U.S. imagination, particularly in the wake of the mambo craze. This characterization is particularly salient if compared to the 1970s and 1980s, when the national visibility of Latino musical practices was low and, in many ways, virtually off the national radar screen until the late 1990s, at which point Ricky Martin burst on the scene with his (English-language) rock/pop song "Livin' La Vida Loca" and ushered in the so-called "Latin boom." Yet in many ways, the decades between these two "booms" were even more interesting and significant eras in the evolution of Latino musical practices, as an extraordinary range of musical practices were percolating, often concurrently, within Latino communities nationwide. This was particularly true in the 1970s, when, even at the height of a highly politicized era defined by cultural nationalism and identity politics, young Latinos/as were contributing actively to emerging new styles not specifically associated with Latino cultures: In the 1970s, these included disco and rap; in the 1980s, house and freestyle; and in the 1990s, increasingly eclectic mixes, such as meren-rap, banda-rap, and *reggaeton*. Most of these involved turntable-based performances intended for dance floors, in which producers manipulating electronic technology, sampling and mixing a wide range of sounds and rhythms, became the artistic creators. Turntable-based performances represented a major departure from rock and salsa, both of which relied on musicians using conventional instruments to perform repertoires typically drawn from a (relatively) limited range of musical sources associated with each of these styles.

If the disco and rap being spun and mixed on dual turntable rigs in the 1970s drew mostly on records and sounds being produced in the United States (and, in disco's case, Europe), in the 1980s and 1990s, the range of recordings available for sampling and mixing expanded to include a greater diversity of sounds, particularly those from Latin America and Africa. Economic globalization and faster telecommunications facilitated the circulation of the records and sounds employed by DJs and producers, but the millions of new immigrants from Latin America, all carrying musical preferences brought from their homelands, further enriched the musical ingredients that could be combined to produce dance musics. Reggaeton and banda rap, both of which emerged in the late 1990s, are the most recent and noteworthy examples of such genre-jumping practices, but even Latino rock and Latin American *rock en español,* whose aesthetic sources had formerly been more limited by conventional notions of rock, began mixing genres more freely and frequently. This chapter analyzes these new musical mixings and their sociosonic circuitries,[1] paying particular attention to how they were simultaneously encouraged and obstructed by their hybridity—the racial and cultural hybridity of the musicians and fans themselves as well as the aesthetic hybridity of the dance musics they were producing and consuming.

Mixing It Up: Rap, Disco, and Freestyle

In terms of its cultural importance as well as the sheer numbers of its Latino producers and consumers, the 1970s were, without question, salsa's golden decade. Many young bicultural and bilingual New York Puerto Ricans in that seminal decade, however, resisted the essentialist, ethnically specific imagined community promoted by cultural nationalists, perceiving that their complex, multilayered identities could not be encompassed or articulated by salsa. Indeed, the very fact that salsa was so strongly linked to tradition made it appear antiquated to young people whose imaginations were being captured by two new rhythm-based musics just starting to circulate in New York's poor and working-class neighborhoods: hip-hop and disco. Young New York Puerto Ricans' enthusiasm for hip-hop in particular articulated their understanding of race relations in the United States: Unlike rock, hip-hop's connection to urban communities of color was unequivocal, and its defiant stance against racial subordination was assertive and compelling.

In considering the range of Latino musical practices in New York in the 1970s, it is important to keep in mind the appalling social conditions and urban decay imposed on African American and Latino neighborhoods by a combination of public and private disinvestment in working-class communities during that decade. City officials' inability (or unwillingness) to cope with an increasingly impoverished population compounded New York's economic and social troubles. New York's poorest welfare-dependent residents were corralled in formerly vibrant working-class neighborhoods such as the South Bronx, where landlords received above-market rents to accept them, but basic city services, such as garbage collection, were reduced or eliminated. Growing numbers of African American and Latino youths joined gangs and claimed city blocks as their own, terrorizing residents as they defended their territory from perceived intruders; the flow of highly addictive drugs completed the recipe for a perfect storm. The city did nothing to restore order; worse, absentee landlords with little motivation to maintain their deteriorating properties realized they could recoup their investments with insurance payments if their buildings burned down. As Peter Shapiro has noted, by the mid-1970s, the South Bronx was literally burning, suffering an average of twelve thousand fires a year; it became so bad that the *New York Times* began printing a daily listing of all the fires the day before, which came to be known by its readers as the "ruins section." In the early 1980s, when insurance companies finally stopped paying for the damage caused by fires, the arson stopped, but by then the South Bronx had lost 40 percent of its housing stock, and most of what was left was decrepit.[2] Indeed, the city's abandonment of the South Bronx was so deliberate and the effects on its residents so appalling that Marshall Berman refers to it as "urbicide."[3] Hollywood sensationalized the South Bronx's appalling physical landscape and social disintegration in the (highly controversial) film *Fort Apache, The Bronx* (1981), in which the South Bronx's lawlessness was compared to the Wild West.

While the South Bronx burned and gangs balkanized the neighborhood by attacking anyone "out of place," African American and Puerto Rican youths began employing various forms of artistic expression to "piece together," as Shapiro notes, "bits from this urban scrap heap,"[4] reassembling them through graffiti, DJing, emceeing, break dancing, and fashion—the cultural elements comprising hip-hop.[5] The history of Puerto Ricans' contributions to the development of hip-hop has been extensively documented and interpreted by Juan Flores and Raquel Z. Rivera, who note that when rap began to be commercially recorded in the late 1970s, record labels began marketing the new style as an exclusively African American form of cultural production, marginalizing Puerto Ricans.[6] The influence of Spanish Caribbean rhythms in the funk music that had propelled early hip-hop did not mitigate the obstacles encountered by Puerto Ricans as rap became increasingly African American–centric in the 1980s. Moreover, despite the fact that Puerto Ricans had been among hip-hop's most active break-dancers, when hip-hop began attracting wider public attention, the easily observable differences between break dancing's individualized and competitive moves and salsa's highly choreographed couples' dancing underscored the aesthetic distance between the two styles and, by extension, the perceived cultural dissimilarities between the two communities.

Under these circumstances, Puerto Ricans interested in pursuing careers as DJs were inclined to obscure (although not to disavow) their bicultural identities. DJ Charlie Chase from the Cold Crush Brothers, for example, recalled that since most DJs were African Americans at the time he began DJing, he created an English-sounding stage name in order to distance himself from the perceptions (of both African Americans and Puerto Ricans) that he could not excel as a DJ because of his Puerto Rican origins: "I liked playing this music, but I'm Spanish. I'm not going to be accepted if I go out there as DJ Carlos Mandes, just the name alone is going to make you not want to come in the door."[7] His participation in hip-hop was similarly perceived as "out of place" by his family, who encouraged him to turn his attention to Latino New York's then-burgeoning salsa scene: "In my house, my moms was, like, 'why aren't you playing some salsa like the other DJs? Look at Freddie down the block, he's coming home with a hundred dollars a night.' And I'm like, I don't wanna do that Mom, *this* is what I want to do."[8]

As rap in the 1980s and 1990s became the most culturally significant musical development since the emergence of rock 'n' roll in the 1950s, hip-hop's original connections to New York's Puerto Rican community disappeared from view. It is ironic, then, that until New York Puerto Rican rappers Big Pun and Fat Joe achieved mainstream success in the 1990s, the first nationally known self-identified Latino rappers were based not in New York but rather on the West Coast. (The first was the Cuban-born Mellow Man Ace, whose bilingual song "Mentirosa" was released in 1989, followed by the Chicano rapper Kid Frost, who saluted his Chicano musical forebears by sampling a loop from El Chicano's 1974 song "Viva Tirado" on his 1990 hit single "La Raza.")[9]

Disco was another DJ-based musical practice in which New York Puerto Ricans participated actively in the 1970s, although the outcomes for Latinos who chose to engage in it—in terms of interethnic relations as well as public recognition and economic success—were quite different from those affecting their counterparts who gravitated to hip-hop. Like rap, disco was also the product of the deteriorating social and economic conditions in New York, as the style developed in dances held in empty warehouses, churches, and other abandoned spaces that became available in the wake of the city's economic and social collapse. The audiences who attended disco dances were more diverse than those at early hip-hop events: mostly African American and Latino but also white and Asian; mostly gay but also straight; mostly working-class but also affluent. What disco dancers shared in common was a desire for escape and pleasure, achieved in long nights of highly rhythmic (mostly couples') dancing that, enhanced by drugs, produced physical states of ecstatic euphoria and powerful feelings of community among the dancers. Initially, many of these parties were invitation-only events, but clubs open to the public also became part of a network of discos that collectively nurtured the development of the musical style, first in New York and then nationally; I discuss this in more detail later.

Given disco's primary function—to stimulate dancers to dance—rhythm was at the center of the disco aesthetic. The primary sources for disco rhythms were recordings of African American funk and soul music (later driven by a constant 4/4 rhythm created by drum machines), but disco's genealogical roots also extended deeply into Spanish Caribbean music and culture. As John Storm Roberts has pointed out, when Latin boogaloo disappeared from view in the late 1960s (see Chapter 3), its innovative combination of Latin and R & B rhythms left an imprint on the African American R & B groups that subsequently laid the foundations for disco.[10] More directly, Latin rhythms underpinned some of disco's most seminal records, the most noteworthy of which was Joe Bataan's cover of Gil Scott Heron's 1974 song "The Bottle." In "La Botella," Bataan's "dirty sax and razor-sharp horn section overlaying a grinding salsa beat" turned it into one of the first disco hits.[11]

While not Latino himself, the African American and Filipino Bataan (born Peter Nitollano) served as a crucial link between salsa and disco via his recordings produced on the SalSoul record label. The early history of SalSoul is worth summarizing here, not only because it has received little attention in scholarship about Latino musical practices but also because it illuminates the multiethnic, interconnected, and overlapping character of New York's music scenes in the 1970s. The founders of the SalSoul label were three Jewish Syrian American brothers—Ken, Joe, and Stanley Cayre—who started in the lingerie business in Miami but, in the 1960s, on the advice of a cousin working in Mexico, formed a company called Caytronics to begin importing Mexican music. With the popularity of Latin music among mainstream audiences at a nadir in the 1960s, this upstart company was able to obtain the licensing or distribution rights to the extensive Latin catalogues of RCA and CBS, and it subsequently became a well-known name in the Latin music business.[12] The Cayre brothers relocated from Miami to New York in 1972, where they found a Latino community ardently engaged with locally produced salsa, with little interest in the Mexican and other Latin American music they were selling; they also learned that Fania already had the best salsa musicians under contract. Attempting to compete, they started a new record label called Mericana and signed a few minor local musicians. When Bataan, already well established as a performer of boogaloo and salsa, approached Caytronics to produce a record he wanted to perform in the new disco style starting to percolate in New York, the Cayre brothers jumped at the opportunity to work with a musician associated with Fania. In 1973, Mericana released Bataan's full-length album *SalSoul,* containing the song "Latin Strut," which became a hit on disco dance floors after the influential African American disco DJ Frankie Crocker gave it extensive play on his R & B radio program on WBLS.[13]

Columbia Records, sensing the possibility of crossing the song over to mainstream audiences, paid Mericana $100,000 for the rights to "Latin Strut." The song failed to make the national pop charts, but Columbia's payment provided the Cayre brothers with enough capital to start a new label that would focus on disco. They called the label SalSoul, because their idea, nurtured by Ken Cayre's close friendship with Bataan, was to create a new sound for the burgeoning disco dance scene that, combining elements of both salsa and soul, would be rhythmic but also instrumental and lush, "an R&B rhythm and Latin percussion with a pretty melody on top."[14] Regarding the origin of the name "SalSoul," Ken Cayre recalls, "It was used to describe a Spanish person but also from America that liked, in addition to the Salsa music, the dance music and that's the Soul part."[15]

The musicians whose work they admired most were from Philadelphia; most were African Americans, although jazz vibe player Vince Montana, long an admirer and performer of Latin music, was Italian American. Asked to hire the Latin musicians for the label's new band—named the SalSoul Orchestra—Montana brought in some of New York's finest Latin percussionists: Andy González,[16] Manny Oquendo, Roy Armando, and Peter Quintero. Disco DJ Frankie Crocker promoted SalSoul Orchestra's first recording on his radio show and brought its Latin-influenced sound to the attention of the disco world. The single "Salsoul Hustle" became a major hit on dance floors and a defining moment in the development of disco's so-called Philadelphia sound.[17]

The personal and professional identities of the musicians performing on the original SalSoul Orchestra's recordings highlight the interlocking relationships between salsa, disco, and rap in the 1970s. González and Oquendo, founding members of the influential ensembles Grupo Folklorico y Experimental Nuevayorkino and El Conjunto Libre, were key figures in the development of salsa in New York in the 1970s. Their emphasis on Spanish Caribbean traditions embodied the cultural nationalism of New York's Puerto Rican communities that inspired the younger generation of salsa musicians, but nonetheless they agreed to participate in the SalSoul experiments.[18] Bataan is noteworthy not only for his personal hybridity but also for his active and successful engagement with African American and Latino styles as well as his successful combinations of the two: He began his career in the 1950s singing doo-wop, made his name in Latin music with boogaloo and salsa, crossed back into R & B with Latin soul and disco, and in 1979 released and charted the song "Rap-o Clap-o," a fusion of disco and rap aesthetics considered one of the earliest rap records.[19]

The majority of the work produced by the SalSoul label in subsequent years was more R & B–oriented than Latin, and most of its musicians were African American, but Latin rhythms produced by Latino musicians remained one of its essential ingredients. In an online interview, Ken Cayre reflected on the nature and impact of the SalSoul sound: "Well, the first vision I had was for the SalSoul Orchestra . . . to make it the first Latin and Soul Dance Orchestra ever. You know, when we played in Madison Square Garden and Radio Music City Hall we had 42 pieces orchestra on stage [sic], we had the whole place jumping and dancing. I mean, it was a magnificent sound, it was very overwhelming and nobody ever done that before with the Congas on stage and the deep groove beat of the drums and the bass, and then the strings and horns. It was quite an overwhelming sight and sound."[20]

In addition to providing some of disco's foundational rhythms, New York Puerto Ricans and other Latinos from the South Bronx were also directly responsible for one of disco's most important dance styles, the hustle. The hustle, which was observed as early as 1972, was originally a couples' dance like salsa, but faster, with more flourishes and more acrobatics that one Bronx-born Puerto Rican dancer described as "aerials."[21] Shapiro describes the hustle as "a vision of romance floating gracefully out of the squalor and decay of Fort Apache. It was men and women dressed to the nines, spending whatever they could afford in order to attain that one minute of ecstasy that dancing on the rubble could provide."[22] Interestingly, the development of the hustle in the South Bronx was connected, in an inverse way, to the simultaneous emergence of hip-hop: In the 2006 documentary *From Mambo to Hip Hop*,[23] an African American DJ noted that when break dancing was developing in the early days of hip-hop, it was male-dominated and performed individually or in groups in a highly competitive manner. Consequently, girls often preferred going to the discos, where they could participate more actively (and equally) in couples' dancing.[24]

As the 1970s progressed, the hustle spread from Latino barrios into discos throughout Manhattan, where it inspired African American R & B singer Van McCoy's 1975 song "The Hustle," a fusion of R & B and Latin rhythms that topped the charts and earned him a Grammy.[25] Over time, a number of substyles to the hustle developed, rendering the original Latin hustle only one of many localized versions. (Other hustle styles included the line dance that accompanied McCoy's hit song, the Bay Area hustle, the West Coast hustle, the tango hustle, the American hustle, the rope hustle, and others.)[26] In 1977, national and international audiences saw the hustle in action (both the couples' and line-dance versions), as the New York Puerto Rican couple in the hit movie *Saturday Night Fever* out-danced the characters played by John Travolta and Karen Lynn Gorney. The film, it should be noted, acknowledged the pervasive anti–Puerto Rican sentiments prevailing in New York at the time: Travolta's character becomes distressed when the Puerto Rican couple is subjected to snide remarks by his friends and is then relegated to second place in the competition despite their spectacular performance.[27]

Disco's large orchestral ensembles, richly textured arrangements, Latin-inspired rhythms, relationship to complex couples' dancing, and its dancers' insistence on dressing up rather than down all located disco aesthetically much closer to salsa than to rap; nonetheless, important connections existed between the disco and rap simultaneously being developed in the South Bronx and other working-class Latino neighborhoods in the 1970s. Given that both the disco and rap scenes were record- and turntable-based, it is not surprising that rap and disco DJs were well aware of developments in each other's musical domains, attending each other's parties, sampling the same music, and sometimes working in both worlds simultaneously.[28] As Shapiro notes, "Through their use of much the same techniques, disco and hip-hop were in many ways the flip side of the same coin: one keeping the *groove* going in order to foster a communitarian, celebratory spirit, the other splitting and chopping the *beat* to highlight the virtuosic abilities of its participants. Both were after a sense of empowerment: one by the force of numbers, the other by individual heroics. It is little wonder, then, that at the very beginnings of hip-hop, it and disco were hard to separate."[29]

Nevertheless, profound differences existed between the ethos and outlooks of the audiences in each scene. Most notably, disco was predominantly gay or gay-friendly, while rap emphasized an exaggerated (and often homophobic) masculinity. The disco scene was also attractive to straight Latinos and Latinas who had grown up enjoying a social context in which intricate couples' dancing and dressing up were the norm. While some disco clubs were exclusive to one group or another (e.g., gay only or African American only), the disco scene was characteristically multiracial; hip-hop, in contrast, grew more Afro-centric as it developed, excluding even Puerto Ricans.[30] Michael Corral, a Bronx-born Puerto Rican who established a local reputation as a dancer in hustle competitions, recalled his discomfort with the ethno-racial boundaries of the hip-hop scene: "The only hip-hop parties I would go to was the [pioneering Jamaican hip-hop DJ] Kool Herc parties. . . . When I went to Herc parties, they was cool, but I wasn't wanted there because I was a light-skinned child and everybody was black in there. It was like a racial thing going on, so I felt intimidated."[31]

As disco fever spread, the range of rhythms employed by DJs moved beyond African American funk and R & B to include those found on recordings of African, Caribbean, and Latin music (e.g., Manu Dibango's "Soul Makossa," Babatunde Olatunji's "Drums of Passion," Carlos Santana's Latin rock, and songs by the Caribbean African group Osibisa), bringing a diversity of rhythms and stylings onto the dance floor that had not been possible in traditional band-based performances.[32] Even Fania, salsa's premier record label, was among the record companies contributing products to the record pools from which disco DJs drew their dance tracks. But as commercially oriented disco recordings became more formulaic, disco was increasingly disparaged for what were perceived to be its excesses, and by the end of the 1970s, disco's star was on the wane. As Tim Lawrence observes, "The fact that disco was foregrounding rhythm to such an extent that it was sidelining the key symbols of rock's authority—the lead vocalist and the lead guitarist—constituted a significant challenge, and the ideological nature of this conflict was reflected in the contrasting identities of the two constituencies. Whereas white heterosexual men dominated rock, disco was teeming with African Americans, gays and women."[33] Lawrence notably and inexplicably neglects to mention Latinos and Latinas, without whom disco's rhythms, sound textures, dances, and audiences would have been profoundly different.

A few Latino DJs emerged from the disco scene and later became well known among dance culture enthusiasts, including David Rodríguez, David Morales, and John "Jellybean" Benitez. It is curious, however, that despite the influence of Latinos and their aesthetics on disco music and dance, few New York Puerto Rican musicians benefited from this Latin percussion-influenced musical craze, and not one New York Puerto Rican disco recording star emerged on the national stage alongside the numerous African American and white disco artists who hit the charts in the 1970s. This may, perhaps, explain why Lawrence, Shapiro, and other authors of recent histories of disco have given only passing attention to Latinos, even in the domain of dance. For example, Shapiro traces the 4/4 rhythms underpinning disco dancing back to the marriage of Spanish Caribbean and jazz rhythms in mambo and cha-cha, and he extensively cites an interview with Michael Corral, one of the Puerto Rican hustle dancers whose frequent appearances in disco clubs throughout the city as well as on nationally televised dance competitions were responsible for disseminating the hustle.[34] But he does not elaborate on the cultural implications of the obvious connections between disco and the couples-based salsa dancing (including the importance of sartorial elegance) permeating the Puerto Rican community in the 1970s, particularly when contrasted with the aesthetics and sensibilities of the concurrently emerging hip-hop scene. To be sure, salsa and disco are rhythmically very different—salsa rhythms are based on a 3-2 (or 2-3) *clave* beat, while disco's signature rhythm is an incessant 4/4 bass drum—but to what degree is disco dancing simply a rhythmically simplified, "squared" version of salsa dancing that non-Latinos could easily dance to? Latino participation in disco, in fact, has yet to receive the same sort of attention given to salsa, which admittedly was more central to New York Puerto Rican musical practices at the time but was not the only form of music being consumed and produced by Puerto Ricans. Nor has disco stimulated the same sort of recovery work done by Flores and Rivera, who (re-)situated New York Puerto Ricans within the history of hip-hop.

The demise of disco in the early 1980s did not mean the end of dance music created by DJs and studio producers. In Chicago, house music, a new form of electronic music inspired by disco but faster, was even more eclectic, drawing on everything from European disco, R & B, salsa, and disco to new wave, reggae, and hip-hop. House music moved dance music in new aesthetic and geographic directions, including, as I discuss below, to the West Coast, where it joined rap and rock as one of the musics popular among young Mexican Americans. In New York, house attracted Latino fans as well, but there, young Puerto Ricans created a uniquely Latino form of electronic dance music that combined hip-hop beats and the faster speed and synthetic sound effects of the substyle known as electro with romantic, often melodramatic lyrics that were always sung in English.[35] The music was called freestyle or, in a nod to its ethnic roots, Latin freestyle or Latin hip-hop.

Freestyle, which, like rap and disco, circulated mostly on singles rather than on full-length albums, began as a local New York phenomenon, becoming popular in neighborhood clubs catering to young Spanish Caribbean Latino audiences and on local radio stations, although its popularity later spread to other cities with large Latino populations, especially Miami and metropolitan Los Angeles. The DJ credited with popularizing the style was Jellybean Benitez, the DJ at the now-legendary Funhouse in New York's warehouse district, who had a well-established reputation in New York's dance scene, first in disco and subsequently in house. He and his successor at the Funhouse, Lil' Louie Vega, drew in flocks of teenagers of every ethnicity, but particularly Latinos. Shapiro's description of freestyle reflects the style's multiple sources and porous borders: "In this mechanical matrix, New York Latinos heard ancestral echoes of salsa piano lines and *montuno* rhythms. In the hands of producers like the Latin Rascals, Paul Robb, Omar Santana, and Andy 'Panda' Tripoli, the Pac-Man bleeps, synth stabs, and Roland TR-808 claves became a robotic jam session called freestyle."[36]

The musical and cultural interactions between African Americans and

Latinos have been credited both for the birth and the decline of freestyle. Rivera argues that the very origins of freestyle were located in the exclusions experienced by Latinos as the then-burgeoning rap business was identifying hip-hop as an exclusively African American style.[37] Bronx-born Puerto Rican freestyler George Lamond, who began his career in hip-hop as a B-boy and graffiti writer, recalls the increasing segregation of a scene once shared by Latinos and African Americans: "It was ours . . . and yet at one point, suddenly it wasn't ours anymore."[38] Comments by freestyle musician K7 of the group TKA further illustrate the ethno-racial exclusions experienced by Puerto Rican freestylers in the 1980s. K7 notes that TKA's song "One Way Love" was being regularly requested on one of New York's major black music radio stations, but it was summarily removed from KISS FM's playlist once the singers' identities as Latinos became known: "They loved us . . . until we showed up in person, at the station. When they saw that we were Hispanic, that was that."[39]

New York Puerto Ricans' response to their marginalization from hip-hop was to reemphasize melodic vocals and romantic lyrics, aesthetic domains they could claim ownership of while at the same time maintaining their independence from the more narrowly defined realm of Latin music. The Puerto Rican musicians who provided the vocals for freestyle recordings were fully bilingual and bicultural, but, given their precarious location at the intersection of the Latino and hip-hop communities, they often concealed their ethnicity. One of freestyle's first stars, Lisa Velez, went by the name Lisa Lisa, and her group was called Cult Jam; George Lamond, whose 1990 song "Bad of the Heart" reached number 25 on *Billboard*'s Hot 100, was born George García.[40] For a while, it looked as though freestyle might break out nationally, particularly when Madonna copied the style as her career began to take off, but instead freestyle slipped into obscurity in the early 1990s.

Several explanations have been offered for the decline of freestyle in New York. Some date it to the moment when Hot 103, the only radio station in New York willing to play freestyle—Spanish-language radio refused—went to an exclusively hip-hop format in 1992 (renamed Hot 97). Others observe that New York Puerto Rican freestyle artists did not receive adequate promotion from their record companies. Moreover, their record companies, hoping to capitalize on what looked like a breaking trend, began signing dozens of attractive young women with little musical talent and using the same production style for all of them, weakening rather than strengthening the style.[41] d. u. proserpio points to freestyle's marginalization from hip-hop at a time when hip-hop's popularity was in ascent as an additional factor: "The terming of freestyle as 'Latin' in the form of 'Latin freestyle' or 'Latin hip-hop' terminally underscores the isolation that aided in creating the style of freestyle and downplays the genre as not having an impact beyond the parameters of hip-hop."[42]

Freestyle never completely disappeared, but, lacking opportunities to advance their careers, the most successful freestyle producers went to other genres, and its most talented musicians, including La India (Linda Viera Caballero) and Marc Anthony, eventually turned to salsa, where they were welcomed as sheep returning to the fold and encouraged to sing in Spanish.[43] In a 1998 interview posted on the Internet, India recalled the suggestions she received from *salsero* Hector Lavoe, the uncle of her husband, Louie Vega: "He felt I should forget about the dance music I was doing at the time and start looking to do salsa. . . . He would say, 'you're wasting your talent in the American Market. What you should be doing is focusing on being here with us.'"[44] La India's and Marc Anthony's move to salsa was highly successful, and they have been credited with revitalizing salsa and repopularizing it with younger Latinos by infusing it with hip-hop and house music stylings and incorporating some English lyrics. While their professional success as salsa stars certainly represents a happy ending, the early careers of these young New York Puerto Rican musicians clearly suffered from their unstable racial and cultural location between African American and Latino musical practices.

Mixing It Up, West Coast Style

When disco fever swept the nation in the 1970s, it also became popular in Los Angeles, where Mexican Americans enthusiastically danced to it at private parties and in Los Angeles's numerous disco clubs.[45] Nonetheless, the nature and degree of Chicanos' engagement with disco remains even more shrouded than the disco dancing of their East Coast counterparts.[46] In part, the dearth of information on Chicanos and disco can be attributed to Chicanos' far more significant engagements with rock during these years; as I discuss in Chapter 3, a vibrant Mexican American rock scene remained strong throughout the era of cultural nationalism inspired by the Chicano movement. As disco rose to mainstream prominence in the late 1970s, however, rock fans' disparagement of everything about disco—the music, the dance, the dancers' fashion statements—became widespread and produced the infamous "Disco Sucks" crusades led by FM rock stations and rock critics. Nonetheless, Chicano musician Rubén Guevara recalls that Chicanos' overall preference for rock did not prevent them from enjoying disco dancing in clubs and private house parties, nor did they participate in antidisco campaigns.[47]

If disco itself disappeared from view in the 1980s, Los Angeles's disco DJs left behind an important legacy: Their power to excite and to control a crowd of dancers with skillful mixing of rhythms inspired an extraordinary East Los Angeles subculture that at its peak involved hundreds of thousands of Mexican American young people. Since dance clubs were relatively expensive for many working-class youths to attend and were off limits to those underage, "promoter crews" (or "party crews") of young Mexican Americans, many of them still in high school, began organizing DJ dance parties in family backyards, charging a few dollars for admission.

Gerard Meraz, who has analyzed the history and development of the DJ culture of East Los Angeles,[48] explains that promoter/party crews ranged in size from a handful of youths to larger organizations with officers and members with specific responsibilities, including raising money, identifying a family willing to loan or rent its backyard for the party, publicizing the event through fliers or cards (and word of mouth), hiring a DJ and a sound system, arranging for security, and so on, demonstrating these youngsters' considerable organizational skills. Initially, these were neighborhood events, but, as word got out, these parties began attracting youths from other Mexican American neighborhoods throughout greater Los Angeles, sometimes from considerable distances. The Mexican American young people who "cruised" these events, for example—sometimes several parties in a single evening— were often members of local social groups organized around shared interests in a particular style of music, a particular fashion statement, or a favorite type of car or motorcycle, and each group had its own name, such as the Rebels, Wildstyle, Mods, GQs, and the Cha Chas.

DJs were at the center of these backyard parties, and their success depended on their skills in mixing rhythms, phrases, and other sounds they selected from records.[49] As Meraz notes, each DJ developed his or her own particular sound and identity: Some specialized in a particular style of music, such as house, hip-hop, new wave, or techno; others specialized in mixing rhythms and other sonic elements from a range of styles. None of it was Mexican or "Latin" music per se, although Latin rhythms could be included in DJs' mixes. Nonetheless, the backyard parties and the promoter crews who organized them were deeply grounded in Mexican American cultural practices.

At the height of their popularity in the 1980s, East Los Angeles backyard parties involved thousands of DJs, thousands more people in the crews supporting them, and hundreds of thousands of young people who attended them regularly (see Figures 4.1 and 4.2). As Meraz notes, these DJs "brought the night club environment to the back yards of the East Side [of Los Angeles] with lights and great sound systems 'imitating' the clubs. They gave the street and backyard parties their own identity outside of the club, not trying to mimic them. They gave the scene a fashion, a sound, and a new perspective of partying with the DJs in the streets. To the youth of the East Side the scene provided a space where they could be glamorous, meet lots of cute girls or boys, be important, make some money, be responsible for massive sound systems, and listen and dance to music in the streets."[50] As these parties became larger

Figure 4.1. Flyer for a promoter-crew-organized birthday party in 1986. *(Courtesy of Gerard Meraz.)*

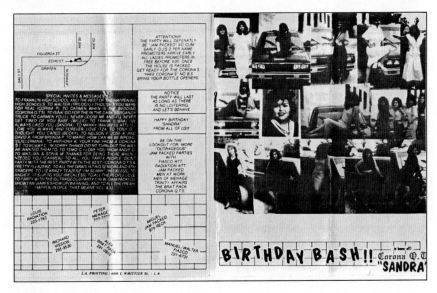

Figure 4.2. Reverse of the flyer. *(Courtesy of Gerard Meraz.)*

and more profitable—a successful party could generate $500 to $1,000—the scene also became more competitive, attracting both gangs and police, which contributed to the decline of backyard DJ parties in the early 1990s. The DJs and the dance music they mixed did not disappear, however, but moved into clubs, where an underground scene continued to evolve and to thrive.

Although semiprivate parties with music provided by DJs and MCs had also been common in New York during the 1970s and were crucial to the development of hip-hop in its early stages, Los Angeles backyard DJ parties in the 1980s were strikingly different. In terms of social context, New York parties typically took place in abandoned buildings and public parks in the South Bronx, in contrast to the backyards of modest single-family houses characteristic of Los Angeles housing tracts. In terms of musical aesthetics, the musical styles incorporated into DJ performances at Los Angeles backyard parties were considerably more diverse than on the East Coast, reflecting Mexican American fans' familiarity and comfort with a wide range of musical styles. Rock, especially classic rock, was often part of Los Angeles DJs' mixes, because they knew their fans were familiar and comfortable with it. Indeed, as Meraz notes, some DJs got their start playing between sets at Chicano rock concerts.[51] Connections between the East and West Coast turntable- and DJ-based music scenes were more noticeable in the domain of house music, particularly in clubs, where the more successful DJs plied their trade. Because their music was based on mixing beats and sounds rather than on any particular ethnically defined sound, East and West Coast DJs often knew about each other and attended each other's events when they toured: East Coast DJs Lil' Louie Vega and David Morales, for example, played in Los Angeles, while Los Angeles DJ Irene (Gutierrez) played in New York.[52] Notwithstanding such similarities and overlaps between East and West Coast turntable-based practices in the 1980s, however, nothing developed on the East Coast analogous to the sheer geographical extent and number of people involved in the backyard party phenomenon or to the high degree of organization characteristic of East Los Angeles's party crews.

By the 1990s, Los Angeles club DJs were routinely weaving a range of sources into an evening's performance—from classic rock, reggae, and house to salsa, Andean music, flamenco, and beyond. The San Francisco–based Latino youth–oriented magazine *Frontera* called this sort of blending "esoteric, post modern, or just straight up fresh,"[53] but the trend was also referred to as "genre jumping" and as "traveling music" (the latter by a fan unfamiliar with James Clifford's concept of "traveling cultures").[54] Despite the popularity of such sounds among youths, however, these developments threatened the integrity of formerly distinct categories of Latin music, angering some Latinos. One DJ, for example, commenting on the resistance he encountered from the Latino community because of his genre mixing, noted that "the salsero won't open his hands to me because I do salsa y [and] house."[55] Despite or perhaps because of such anxieties, Mexican American DJs deliberately continued to employ mixing "as a way of making political change in the musical community, where divisions run deep."[56]

Instrumental groups performing in Los Angeles's underground music scene were similarly wide ranging in their sources, the most well-known example being the thoroughly eclectic and multiethnic group Ozomatli, founded in 1995. As Yvette C. Doss observes of these musical mixings and border crossings, the underground Chicano music scene was "the product of a generation of fans and artists whose cultural and musical sensibilities haven't been expressed by either the Latin America–oriented *rock en español* or traditional 'Anglo' rock scenes, nor by the popular Mexican sounds of banda or mariachi. The artists produce music that is an urban blend of traditional and modern, retro and futuristic: turntable scratching and conga beats, *jarochos* alternating with rock and soul, and manic punk-tinged ska and blues accompanied by tales of frustration and heartbreak in a city some call 'Los(t) Angeles.' It is a music that is a direct reflection of the participants' hybrid identity in Los Angeles society."[57]

Given Mexican Angelenos' proclivity for musical hybridity, it is not entirely surprising that even strongly rural-oriented genres collectively referred to as regional Mexican became subject to fusions, mostly with rap; the language of their lyrics also expanded to include English and Spanglish. The most successful of such fusions was produced by the banda-rap group Akwid, whose CD *Proyecto Akwid,* a blend of hip-hop beats and the brass-band sounds of banda, sold over a quarter of a million copies in 2003. Akwid's success clearly reflected the bilingual, bicultural realities of Mexican Los Angeles at the turn of the millennium. The group was composed of the Gómez brothers, Francisco and Sergio, who were born in Michoacán, Mexico, but raised in South Central Los Angeles. They became obsessed with the mixing art of the DJs who played at backyard parties, and as teens in the 1990s they purchased a sound system and began producing mixes and rapping in English under the name Juvenile Style. Modeled after African American acts, such as NWA and Snoop Dogg, they gained a following in the local hip-hop DJ scene, but, as they honed their production and lyrical skills, they acquired the desire and confidence to incorporate some of the Mexican sounds they had grown up listening to at home, in part because of charges that they were simply imitating African Americans and not using Spanish.

Anticipating criticisms about their language choices when they released *Proyecto Akwid,* they included a spoken prelude (only slightly over a minute) entitled "Se Habla Español." The cut begins in English, with the following phrases: "Yeah check this out, I got something I wanna get off my chest. You know I been shoppin' my demo around, showin' it around to people, and they be saying like, yeah that shit's tight, but y'all are Mexican, y'all be Mexican, how come you never bust in Spanish? And I say yo, that's not my thing. You know I flip my style the way I do and that's just me. You know, why you sweatin' me? But anyway check this out."[58] The lyrics that follow, however, now rapped in Spanish, establish their street credibility by referring to their tough upbringing and other tropes of hypermasculine rap. The next cut, in contrast, opens with the distinctive sound of a tuba, banda's signature instrument, but a novelty, if not distinctly out of place, in the arena of mainstream rap. As Sergio Gómez notes of this deliberate layering of languages and styles, "When you're young and growing up in an environment that is totally different than your culture, you find yourself being forced to adapt and assimilate, only to later evolve and reunite with your own roots."[59] To the Gómez brothers, reuniting with their Michoacán roots meant finding a way to fuse hip-hop and banda but "without losing the essence of each one and without compromising either style, that's the idea and the basic foundation of our sound."[60]

In the wake of Akwid's success, other Los Angeles groups, such as Mexiclan, Azteca, ATM, and Jae P, as well as the Texas-based group Lil' J, began adding hip-hop beats to the signature sounds of regional Mexican *norteño* music, such as accordions and *cumbia* rhythms. Making these unlikely fusions work required Mexican American musicians to risk alienating their hip-hop audiences as well as fans of traditional Mexican music. Indeed, despite stated intentions not to "compromise" traditional sounds in their fusions, the requirements of blending such disparate styles entailed disrupting the aesthetic boundaries of both. As Francisco Gómez notes, "We've implemented more instruments into the entire product to break the notion that banda music does not have a guitar or that norteño does not have a piano; this is truly blending instruments according to what makes sense to us and what sounds good together."[61] Not surprisingly, not everyone understood or liked the new sounds. Mexiclan's Sem "Leon" Vargas, for example, comments, "The norteño groups are telling us that we're not respecting the music, so we really try to show them that we really respect norteño and Mexican music with songs like 'Me siento bien' and 'Mi Papa Lloraba'"[62]—the latter a fusion of rap with the romantic (often melodramatic) bolero, whose lyrics are about a son telling his father, nostalgic for Mexican ways, that he has to live his own life in his own way.

The mixture of genres with such profoundly dissimilar aesthetics also confounded the music industry's efforts to categorize and to market such musics according to once (presumably) bounded criteria. Akwid's 2003 single "No Hay Manera," for example, improbably charted on *Billboard*'s Latin, Regional Mexican, and Tropical/Salsa charts, while their album was nominated for Best Spanish Rock/Alternative Album and won the awards for Latin Rap/Hip-Hop Album of the Year *and* the Regional Mexican Album of the Year, New Artist. The result was a new industry term coined to describe banda-rap and similar fusions: "urban regional," an unlikely linguistic combination of contrasting cultural referents. By 2005, urban regional appeared to be on the upswing on the West Coast, inspiring bombastic press releases by record labels, particularly Universal, which had invested heavily in promoting the new sound: "Akwid, the most important and talked-about musical and cultural phenomenon in recent Latin music history" and "Akwid is the new voice of the twenty-first century and without a doubt, the new sound of America." Unfortunately, such bold predictions about the future of urban regional were premature, as a new musical hybrid was arriving from the East Coast that better articulated the layered identities of Latino youths of all national origins: reggaeton.

New Social and Musical Circuitries in the New Millennium: Reggaeton

If the musical sources drawn upon by West Coast DJs and musicians demonstrated a notable openness to incorporating styles coded as non-Latino (e.g., rock, house, and electro), their counterparts on the East Coast more typically focused their efforts on mixing hip-hop with the Spanish Caribbean styles they had grown up listening to at home. In the 1990s, New York Puerto Rican and Dominican groups such as Proyecto Uno and DLG (Dark Latin Groove) began playfully mixing languages and bending genre boundaries, producing hybrid styles that combined salsa and merengue with hip-hop and house but also incorporated Jamaican reggae and dancehall.[63] Some of these hybrids were in Spanish, some were in English, and some were completely bilingual. (These fusions, it should be noted, were similar in spirit to the subsequent banda-rap of such groups as Akwid, but aesthetically the distance between hip-hop and merengue or salsa was much smaller—and thus less difficult to bridge—than the gap between hip-hop and banda's brass-band sonorities). DLG and Proyecto Uno, who achieved modest commercial success with their musical hybrids, clearly expressed the bilingual and bi- or multicultural identities of a young generation of New York Spanish Caribbean Latinos, which by the 1980s included many of Dominican origins. Notwithstanding the common Afro-diasporic origins of styles incorporated into these blends, many Latin music purists as well as hip-hop fans denigrated meren-rap and salsa-rap as commercially motivated deviations lacking authenticity and value. Meren-rap and salsa-rap did not coalesce into distinct and sustained styles, but their musical mixings did anticipate their successor, reggaeton, a style with similarly diverse Caribbean sources that developed in Puerto Rico in the late 1990s and then crossed back to New York in the new millennium.

Like the other musics discussed in this chapter, reggaeton originated in DJ and dance club cultures, but, in this case, club cultures in four dispersed locations—Jamaica, Panama, Puerto Rico, and New York. Reggaeton was consolidated as a genre and received its name in Puerto Rico in the late

1990s, but, as Wayne Marshall has documented extensively, the sociocultural matrix that nourished reggaeton aesthetics was the product of decades of people and musical styles moving through a spatially and temporally criss-crossing network of transnational fields linking the Caribbean and the United States.[64] Reggaeton's primary root genres are Jamaican dancehall, mediated via Panamanian *reggae en español* and U.S. hip-hop. All of reggaeton's ante-cedent genres, however, are themselves historically interconnected: Jamaican and Puerto Rican immigrants in New York City, for example, were copartici-pants in the early development of hip-hop in New York in the 1970s, while in the 1980s, Jamaican dancehall, influenced by U.S. gangsta rap, moved away from the mellower "roots" reggae of earlier artists such as Bob Marley and Peter Tosh. (Dancehall's debt to gangsta rap can be heard in its reliance on drum machines rather than on live bands, as well as in its lyrics celebrating masculine physical prowess.)

By the late 1980s, the sounds of dancehall reggae were being heard beyond Jamaica, not only in New York City but also throughout the Carib-bean, among poor working-class urban youths of African descent.[65] In Panama, vernacular Spanish lyrics were superimposed on Jamaican dancehall beats by local youths, among them the descendants of Jamaicans who had migrated to work on the construction of the Panama Canal in the early twentieth century, some of whom spoke English and maintained an active interest in Jamaican culture. Referred to as *reggae en español,* the earliest Panamanian songs pro-duced in the mid-1980s were lifted directly from, or were close replicas of, the original dancehall tracks, although it did not take long before local artists, such as Renato y las 4 Estrellas and El General (Edgardo Franco), were pro-ducing original songs[66] (although even original compositions often employed currently popular Jamaican dancehall backing tracks known as *riddims*). The most influential of these riddims was referred to as the *dembow,* after the 1991 song of that name popularized by Shabba Ranks; it was incorporated into so many *reggae en español* tracks that fans began referring to the style itself as dembow.[67] By the turn of the decade, *reggae en español* hits from Panama joined the flow of black dance musics circulating throughout the Caribbean and the U.S. eastern seaboard—particularly Puerto Rico, where conditions were ripe for another round of fusion.[68]

Hip-hop, which by the 1980s had become a major component of the musical flows crisscrossing the Caribbean,[69] was well-established in Puerto Rico early thanks to New York Puerto Ricans' involvement in its development since the 1970s, coupled with the constant circular flows of people and goods between the island and the mainland. On the island, urban youths—especially those who were poor and black—embraced hip-hop despite its U.S. origins and English lyrics, because its clearly audible cosmopolitanism and defiant attitude resonated with their own experiences of and resistance to racial and economic marginality.[70] Initially, the hip-hop heard in Puerto Rico consisted of the same English-language productions by African American artists popular on the mainland, but by the early 1990s, rapping in Spanish, inspired by seminal (New York–born) Puerto Rican rapper Vico C, could be heard on street corners, private parties, and especially in DJ clubs, such as the seminal San Juan club The Noise. The style was referred to as "underground," because its blatantly sexual and uncompromisingly aggressive lyrics expressing the realities of San Juan's urban poor were banned from the airwaves and subjected to public campaigns against "indecency."[71] (As a result, it circulated primarily via mix tapes made by club DJs and passed along hand-to-hand.) The equally sexually explicit *reggae en español* arrived in Puerto Rico from Panama in the early 1990s with El General's hit songs "Pu Tun Tun" (aka "Tu Pum Pum" and "Tu Pun Pun") and "Muévelo;" henceforth, Puerto Rican underground DJs began incorporating dancehall riddims to their mixes, although these arrived from Panama or from New York rather than directly from Jamaica.

In Puerto Rico, significant overlaps between hip-hop and the new dembow-based style blurred the boundaries between these genres, especially when Puerto Rican artists originally known as rappers and MCs began moving into reggaeton as it became more commercially profitable than hip-hop. Moreover, as Marshall has pointed out, Puerto Rican DJs developed a characteristic style that employed musical collages of sampled hip-hop sources that were already familiar to Puerto Rican ears, thus audibly linking the newer style not only to Panamanian and Jamaican reggae but also to U.S. mainland hip-hop.[72] Nevertheless, as the dembow riddim became increasingly dominant in the mid-1990s, the term "reggaeton," which distinguished the Puerto Rican style from its other antecedents, foregrounded its links to Jamaican dancehall reggae rather than to U.S. hip-hop.

Complicating this polymusical matrix, Jamaican "roots" reggae had also been transplanted on the island. Puerto Rican reggae fans were primarily white middle-class rock-oriented youths attracted more to reggae's countercultural trappings, such as dreadlocks and ganja, than to its antiracist, anti-imperialist militancy. Nonetheless, reggae was audibly connected to dancehall and *reggae en español*. In short, despite significant class, racial, lifestyle, and identity differences characterizing various segments of the Puerto Rican public, the distinctions between rap, underground, reggae, and reggaeton became so blurred that the terms were often used interchangeably.[73] Notwithstanding its multiple sources, as reggaeton coalesced into a distinct and recognizable style, it was coded on the island as quintessentially Puerto Rican; as its popularity exploded internationally in the mid-2000s, it became a powerful symbol of national pride to island youths (although not to their parents).

Despite its audible hybridity and links to hip-hop, reggaeton was not immediately accepted on the U.S. mainland, where young U.S.-based Latinos, including New York Puerto Ricans, felt more engaged with and represented by the domestic hip-hop they had grown up listening to. When reggaeton did hit, however, it surprised everyone, Latinos and non-Latinos alike, with the speed and intensity with which it exploded—first on Spanish-language radio on the East Coast around 2003, then in Latino communities throughout the nation, and, by 2005, into the English-language hip-hop and mainstream arenas. When Daddy Yankee's groundbreaking 2004 single "Gasolina" made *Billboard*'s Hot 100 and his CD *Barrio Fino* hit number 26 on *Billboard*'s Top 200 Albums, it was the first time a Spanish-language song that was not a "novelty" had charted in decades, generating hyperbolic media stories heralding reggaeton as "the next big thing" in popular music, whose trajectory from ghetto authenticity to commercial success and media lime-light was compared to hip-hop's.

Reggaeton's success in the United States (discussed in more detail in Chapter 7) has been attributed to many factors, including crucial race-based strategic collaborations with African American hip-hop stars, the most promi-nent example being the African American and Puerto Rican rapper N.O.R.E., whose video for "Oye Mi Canto," a collaborative effort with up-and-coming Puerto Rican and Dominican reggaeton artists, was credited with introducing reggaeton to MTV and BET audiences. Others point to its catchy, sexually charged lyrics and videos and danceable rhythms invoking Caribbean festiv-ity, coupled with the grittier and more assertive hip-hop aesthetics that all young people in the United States, regardless of ethnicity, had grown up with. But reggaeton's success must also be attributed to the dramatic increases in the sheer numbers of young, urban Latinos born and raised in the United States. These youths embraced reggaeton, because it offered a more cosmo-politan version of *latinidad* that blended the modernity of hip-hop's urban aesthetics with a more identifiably "Latin" sound that powerfully articulated the layered identities of the new Latino generation. As one young Dominican American student expresses it, "Reggaeton is the first type of music that second-generation Latinos can say is their music because merengue, salsa, bachata, you sort of pick up on it because of your parents—the way you grow up, it's part of your culture. And then hip-hop and R & B is mainly considered part of black culture, African American culture. So for the first time, you have a type of music that you can say is your music, and that it's a very unique genre, and that's why it's picked up so much in popularity."[74]

Reggaeton's inclusiveness was facilitated by its structural flexibility, which encouraged artists to mix international and local sonorities to construct not only new combinations of sounds but also images and lyrics that Latinos of all national backgrounds could relate to. *Village Voice* reporter Raquel Cepeda, for example, was struck by the number of different flags carried by fans at the sold-out Madison Square Garden reggaeton concert in March 2005, commenting, "It looks like closing night at the summer Olympics."[75] Some might argue that reggaeton's appeal to different nationalities in such songs as "Oye Mi Canto" and Don Omar's anthemic "Reggaeton Latino" was simply a crass commercial ploy to expand reggaeton's fan base beyond Puerto Ricans, but clearly it resonated with fans seeking ways to express and to perform their increasingly layered and blended identities. Like their antecedents in previous decades, they resisted narrowly defined concepts of national or ethnic identity and gravitated toward musical idioms capable of expressing the increasingly globalized experiences and transnational identities characteristic of postmillennial urban youths—although, as the prominence of national flags in videos and concerts demonstrates, the *idea* of being connected to a specific Latin American homeland retained its symbolic potency, however removed that homeland might be from the actual day-to-day lives of Latino fans.

As reggaeton became entrenched among U.S.-born bicultural youths, particularly those in musically cosmopolitan cities, such as Los Angeles, Chicago, and Miami, the multilateral musical circuits that produced reggaeton in the first place continued to multiply, to cross over, and to double back, producing an ever-expanding number of new combinations. In Miami, for example, reggaeton was mixed with Caribbean, regional, and local musical styles (including Latin freestyle) in uniquely local ways. Jose Davila's description of the *crunkiao* movement in Miami—characterized by rhyming in Spanglish, Spanish, or English over hip-hop rather than dembow beats— captures the complexities of these musical circuitries: "Much in the same way that reggaetón artists once created their own movement by freely incorporating aspects from Jamaican dancehall and American hip-hop, crunkiao musicians are mixing Latin elements with the sounds of southern hip-hop (especially Atlanta-based crunk), Miami bass/'booty music' (a local predecessor to crunk), and freestyle, an 80s pop style that drew heavily on electro funk as well as Latin elements—all of which mingle in the Miami soundscape."[76]

Concluding Thoughts on Musical Mixings and Border Crossings

Even as the intensity of identity politics subsided in the 1980s, essentialist notions of what Latino musical practices should or could be continued to strain and to constrain bicultural musicians and fans engaging in cultural and aesthetic border crossings. Nonetheless, the musical vocabularies generated by Latinos in the latter decades of the twentieth century deliberately and self-consciously destabilized traditionally defined borders in order to carve out new artistic and cultural spaces capable of incorporating multiple sources and articulating layered identities. The turntable- and mixer-based dance cultures that nurtured rap and disco in the 1970s, freestyle and Los Angeles's eclectic DJ parties in the 1980s (and beyond), banda-rap and meren-rap in the 1990s, and reggaeton in the 2000s have all, in their own way, crossed racially and ethnically defined boundaries and, in many cases, linguistic boundaries as well. The engagement of Latinos with such a diverse range of styles over so many decades demonstrates clearly that such musical hybridity is not anomalous but rather a fundamental feature of U.S. Latino cultural practices, as much so as engagement in more "traditional" styles, such as salsa and banda. Far from being signs of assimilation or imitation, these musics make audible the experiences of Latino musicians and fans whose cultural roots are not located unambiguously in Latin America or in the United States but instead at the crossroads of the Latin American, Latino, black diasporic, and Anglo-American worlds.

The development of musical styles such as rap, disco, freestyle, and reggaeton within the United States is also significant because of the ways they have encouraged vigorous, if not always unproblematic, intercultural musical negotiations among Latinos, African Americans, and Euro-Americans, as well as with and among Latinos of different national backgrounds and cultural traditions. The fates of such musics as boogaloo in the 1960s and freestyle in the 1980s, for example, speak to both the creativity and the dangers of being at the crossroads. Indeed, the tangled, interconnected histories of these musical styles remind us of George Lipsitz's cautionary words: "Inter-cultural dialogue does not automatically lead to inter-cultural cooperation, especially when participants in the dialogue speak from positions of highly unequal access to power, opportunity, and life chances."[77] New York Puerto Ricans' exclusion from the hip-hop arena as it became increasingly identified as an African American cultural form in the 1980s is one case in point. Reggaeton, discussed further in Chapter 5, was similarly coded by many island-based Puerto Ricans as a Puerto Rican–only creation despite its multiple sources— although, as I discuss in Chapter 7, it has since moved on to become a symbol of pan-Latin/o identity.

5

New Immigrants, New Layerings

Tradition and Transnationalism in
U.S. Dominican Popular Music

In 1997, Fulanito, a group of young Dominicans raised in Upper Manhattan's Washington Heights neighborhood, released a recording called *El Hombre Mas Famoso de la Tierra* (*The Most Famous Man on Earth*).[1] The images on the front cover, inside flap, and disc show the five members of the band posing dramatically in chic, tropical gangster-style white suits and fedoras (see Figure 5.1). The image on the back cover, in contrast, features five stick figures fashioned of multicolored neon tubes, whose tourist-shop, doll-like heads are topped by the easily recognizable straw hats associated with the Dominican peasantry (see Figure 5.2). These figures are singing and playing instruments used in more traditional merengue ensembles—accordion, *tambora* drum, and saxophone; the instrument carried by one of the figures is not visible, but presumably it is the metal *güira* scraper.[2] The fifth figure is holding, somewhat improbably, a *palo* long drum whose red, white, and blue coloring instantly signals its Dominican-ness. Palo drums, however, are not commonly associated with merengue but rather with Afro-Dominican religious practices that for decades have been shunned by most urban Dominicans. Who is Fulanito appealing to in these images: tradition-steeped, island-based Dominicans or their U.S.-based, urban Dominican counterparts?

The music on the recording offers similarly mixed messages. The lead song, "Guallando,"[3] contains the hallmark elements of the *típico* style of Dominican merengue invoked by the folkloric sounds of the accordion, güira, and tambora, emphasized with the virtuoso performance of an older, well-known típico accordion player, Arsenio de la Rosa. Fulanito's lyrics,

Figure 5.1. Front cover of Fulanito's 1997 *El Hombre Mas Famoso de la Tierra. (Courtesy of Cutting Records, Inc. Photography: Natalie Quinn. Graphic design: Amy Bennick. Executive producers: WinDose and Amado and Aldo Marin.)*

Figure 5.2. Back cover of Fulanito's 1997 *El Hombre Mas Famoso de la Tierra. (Courtesy of Cutting Records, Inc. Photography: Natalie Quinn. Graphic design: Amy Bennick. Executive producers: WinDose and Amado and Aldo Marin.)*

however, are audibly influenced by the cadences and sonorities of hip-hop, and their references to iconic features of Dominican life, such as the island's mountainous landscape and Barceló rum, are interspersed with English phrases, such as "move your body" and "reach out!" De la Rosa's accordion clearly marks the song as "roots" merengue, but its distinct urban edge made the song a major hit among urban U.S.-born or U.S.-raised Dominican youth brought up on a steady diet of hip-hop, who otherwise were unlikely to embrace sounds so closely associated with the island's rural past. It also became a hit in the Dominican Republic, a nation being transformed by the intertwined forces of globalization and transnational migration: With over a million Dominicans living in the United States (over 10 percent of the total Dominican population),[4] many of them in constant contact with their non-migrant kin and friends, Fulanito's combination of Dominican traditions and New York sonorities was understood by Dominicans in both places.

How do we make sense of music such as Fulanito's, that derives its unique energy and appeal from its young bicultural, bilingual Dominican performers located in the cosmopolitan city of New York but at the same time is able to retain its power to invoke feelings and images of cultural authenticity and imperviousness to change? In this chapter, I address this question by examining the musical practices of U.S.-based Dominicans in the context of the dense social and cultural networks, facilitated by advances in communication (especially the Internet and digital technology), that connect the lives of Dominican migrants and nonmigrants alike. These so-called transnational fields have provided a matrix in which all sorts of musical genres and their symbolic associations have been circulating freely between home and host societies, allowing U.S.-based immigrants, their U.S.-born children, and their island-based counterparts to simultaneously experience and participate in musical developments in both locations. Paradoxically, however, the same transnational fields that allow immigrants in the United States to remain connected to their homeland traditions also accelerate changes in these same practices in the sending area.

The complexities and nuances of second-generation Latino musical practices are particularly important to understand, because the majority of new immigrants from Latin America over the past few decades have been of child-rearing age and have contributed to the rapid growth of a domestically born second generation. Robert Suro and Jeffrey Passel, for example, have noted that "although the Latino immigrant population can be expected to continue increasing, the growth rate for the second generation has already gained sufficient momentum that it will remain higher than the first generation's even if immigration flows accelerate. Second-generation births are a demographic echo of immigration and the high fertility among immigrants. So, larger numbers of Latino immigrants will simply produce larger numbers of second-generation Latinos."[5] As I discuss below, second-generation Dominican youths have been exerting an increasingly audible influence on the sounds and circulation of Dominican popular music. Linked to their homeland through their parents' transnational fields but at the same time fully engaged in cultural developments in the United States, these young people are the primary subjects of this chapter.

Transnational Theory in Historical Context

Despite a history of racist immigration policies and outbreaks of anti-immigrant sentiments, the oft-invoked identity of the United States as an immigrant nation is well grounded: Over the past two centuries, a steady stream of Latin Americans (and others) have been arriving in the United States and have established families and communities—albeit with varying degrees of hardship and success. Immigration from Latin America has always been diverse in terms of origins—colonial California received immigrants from Chile and Peru during the gold rush, while New York at the turn of the twentieth century was home to immigrants from throughout the globe. Nevertheless, until the 1970s, large-scale immigration from Latin America originated primarily from three countries—Mexico, Puerto Rico, and Cuba—all with long histories of entanglement with the United States. These patterns began to change in the wake of the Immigration and Nationality Act of 1965, which privileged family reunification, making it easier for applicants with family members in the United States to receive residence visas. As newcomers from other Latin American countries experiencing internal political or economic turmoil began arriving in the United States, they took advantage of these changes to sponsor family members, setting in motion "chain migrations" that, intensified by millions of undocumented immigrants and their families, significantly altered the historic profile of the U.S. Latino population. Between 1970 and 2000, the Latino population in the United States grew by 25.7 million to 35.3 million, and almost half the increase was due to the arrival of first-generation newcomers.[6]

Immigrants from Latin America, especially those marked by darker skin, have seldom found it easy to incorporate themselves into the fabric of life in the United States. Nonetheless, successive cohorts of immigrant parents have discovered to their dismay that their children and grandchildren all too easily lost their ability to speak Spanish and that their attraction to U.S. mainstream culture and music resulted in either a loss of interest in homeland traditions or a desire to reconfigure them. This is emphatically *not* to say that the "melting pot" theory of inevitable assimilation has been successfully at work: The continuing marginalization of long-established Mexican American and mainland Puerto Rican communities over many generations amply demonstrates that it does not. But as the musical practices of these foundational Latino communities discussed in earlier chapters have demonstrated, second-generation youths in particular have engaged with their cultural surroundings more effortlessly than their parents, although the nature and outcomes of these interactions have varied considerably over time and space in response to local conditions. For example, Puerto Rican youths have tended to assimilate laterally into African American culture,[7] while Cuban American youths have more readily assimilated into the more Eurocentric mainstream culture of the United States.[8]

The adaptive strategies employed by more recent immigrants and their U.S.-born children have, in general, been more complex than those employed by their predecessors, because advances in telecommunications and transportation have allowed them more opportunities to stay better connected to cultural developments in their homelands. Furthermore, significant aspects of "home" have actually been relocated to the United States, as extended networks of families and friends, often from a single region or village, have resettled close to one another, concentrating cultural practices from the sending region in relatively bounded geographical spaces. A large percentage of residents from the Dominican town of Baní, for example, have settled in Boston's Jamaica Plain neighborhood. As Peggy Levitt has demonstrated, the interactions between *Banileños* in both locations are so extensive, they are effectively able to participate simultaneously in many aspects of daily life in both locations—for example, watching the same television shows, listening to the same music, and routinely sharing information about new developments by phone.[9] Within ethnically concentrated neighborhoods such as New York's Washington Heights or Boston's Jamaica Plain, Dominican immigrants no longer need to interact as regularly with members of the host society, and the possibility of holding dual citizenship avoids having to relinquish their political and emotional affiliations to the Dominican Republic.

Since migrants and nonmigrants become senders as well as receivers of goods and information, the cultural flows facilitated by transnationalism are circular rather than unidirectional. In an effort to interpret these changes, the influential theory of transnationalism emerged in the 1990s, arguing that new immigrants' social, cultural, and economic networks were so effectively straddling home and host countries, the distinctions between "here" and "there" were significantly eroded.[10] Transnational theory did not argue that assimilation was no longer taking place; rather, it proposed that the relationships between immigrants and their host and home countries were qualitatively different than in the past, and, therefore, the very nature of immigrant identity formation has been altered.

Transnational theory has generated many critiques, among them that it is a fancy new name for behaviors that have always characterized immigrants, especially the first generation.[11] Another charge is that the term "transnationalism" has been so broadly defined and overused that it is analytically meaningless. Others note that it does not adequately account for the impact of racial, class, and cultural differences among new immigrants (not to mention local differences within host communities). Still others observe that the transnational model accounts best for the behavior of first-generation immigrants but less well for their children and grandchildren, whose connections to the host country quickly become as strong as or stronger than to the home country, often within a generation. Alejandro Portes, for example, noted in 2002 that "there is no evidence at present that economic and political transnationalism is transmitted inter-generationally. Indeed, existing studies of the immigrant second generation in the United States point to a very rapid process of acculturation including the loss of parental languages."[12] Other theorists, such as Levitt and Mary C. Waters, have insisted that transnationalism and assimilation are not mutually exclusive but rather simultaneous; moreover, engagements between host and home countries may be periodic and situational rather than constant and inevitable. The negotiations between the second generation's "newland" and homeland cultural practices in particular are "an interactive, bumpy journey along nonlinear pathways."[13]

U.S.-based Dominicans and their musics offer a valuable case study of such negotiations and how they have increased the complexity of U.S. Latinos' already hybrid and layered identities. Dominican migration is relatively new compared to that of Mexicans and Puerto Ricans, but nonetheless it is substantial enough to have nurtured the dense web of social and cultural connections that is transnationalism's signature feature. Moreover, the transnational fields in which Dominican immigrants' and their children's experiences are embedded are segmented and stratified rather than homogenous, shaped by each individual's race, class, and regional backgrounds. These vectors of social difference are further overlain (and complicated) by differences produced by the chronological time of migration and the sociocultural particularities of the settlement location.

New York's Dominican community began growing in the mid-1960s and expanded dramatically with a later, steady flow of immigrants whose numbers peaked in the 1980s and 1990s. Concurrently, a large cohort of second-generation U.S.-born Dominicans was emerging, whose identities were being forged in New York's multiracial and multicultural cauldron. Other Dominicans relocated to Puerto Rico instead of New York, but they became enmeshed in existing networks there that had long connected Puerto Ricans in New York to their home island counterparts. Each of these cohorts was (and is) crosscut by significant differences in social class, region of origin, gender, race, degree of urbanization, and aesthetic outlooks, particularly its preferences for musics that index tradition or modernity, regionalism, nationalism, or pan-nationalism.

Thanks to the vibrant transnational fields linking Dominicans in the United States and on the island, U.S.-based Dominicans within these distinct but often overlapping social categories have been able to select from a range of musics from home to express and to perform their Dominican identity. These range from the big-band merengue that has long served as the quintessential symbol of Dominican national identity to genres associated with more regionally, socioeconomically or racially specific sectors of Dominican society, such as merengue típico, bachata, and the syncretic palo music deeply rooted in rural Afro-Dominican culture. More recently, reggaeton, which coalesced as a style in Puerto Rico in the late 1990s, has also been embraced by U.S. mainland–based Dominican youths, especially as it has been "Dominicanized" with merengue and bachata sonorities. Each of these musics arrived in the mainland United States at different times and in very different contexts, but all of them have been profoundly transformed by virtue of being part of the webs of transnational connections linking island-based Dominicans and diasporic Dominicans embedded in the United States' multicultural soundscape. The symbolically and aesthetically layered musical practices of second-generation Dominican groups, such as Fulanito, clearly demonstrate the power of transnational fields, but, by moving beyond the more traditional sonorities of merengue and bachata retained by their first-generation parents, it is clear that these youths are also seeking newer, more nuanced, and layered ways of "being Dominican." Inevitably, without even physically leaving the United States, they have also been transforming the popular music landscape of their homelands.

Dominican Music, Migration, and Identity: Merengue and Bachata

Merengue, long considered the most powerful musical symbol of Dominican national identity, was the first Dominican music to arrive in the United States; therefore, it is the most obvious place to begin looking at the relationships between music, transnational migration, and Dominican identity in historical context. Merengue, a creolized variant of the European contredanse, emerged in the Dominican Republic in the eighteenth century as an urban elite salon music.[14] Considered scandalous because of the couples' dance that accompanied it, merengue eventually fell out of favor in urban ballrooms but spread to the countryside, where rural folk adapted it for small *conjuntos* (groups) whose instruments were easily obtainable: stringed instruments such as guitar or *quatro,* the tambora drum, and the gourd güiro scraper (later replaced by the metallic güira). As elsewhere in Latin America, the accordion arrived in the Dominican Republic from Europe in the 1870s, and, thanks to its brighter and louder sound, it largely displaced the stringed instruments rural conjuntos had long used to perform music for dancing. By the 1930s, the accordion had become merengue's signature instrument, especially in the northwestern Cibao region.

In the aftermath of the 1924 U.S. occupation of the Dominican Republic, nationalist sentiments rendered musical styles associated with the United States (such as the then-popular fox-trot) unpalatable to the Dominican elites. In this context, the merengue was revalidated as an authentic form of vernacular Dominican culture, and it was reintroduced into elite urban contexts—but only after it was adapted to a more socially acceptable jazz-band format. By the end of the 1930s, these jazz bands had evolved into larger *orquestas* modeled after the international Latin dance bands popular at the time. The accordion-based style associated with rural popular culture, on the other hand, remained excluded from elite venues. To this day, a distinction exists between the big-band *orquesta* merengue popular in urban contexts and the accordion-based merengue típico popular among country folk. This distinction has made its way into the United States, although, as the music of Fulanito demonstrates, not without undergoing changes in its symbolic valence.

Commercially oriented merengue was introduced to the United States in a similar fashion as other Spanish Caribbean musics: In the 1920s, Columbia Records brought a trio of Puerto Rican and Dominican musicians to New York City to record a variety of guitar-based styles popular at the time, and merengue was among them.[15] During the three-decade dictatorship of Rafael Trujillo (1930–61), however, most Dominican musicians were unable to travel to New York (or elsewhere), because Trujillo closed the border and denied exit visas to all but his most (presumably) loyal followers who could be trusted to return. Further limiting communication between Dominicans on the island and the tiny number of exiles residing in New York[16] was Trujillo's personal interest in merengue. Trujillo supported the country's finest big-band *orquesta,* grandiosely named the Orquesta Generalissimo Trujillo after Trujillo himself, but he actively discouraged the development of a Dominican recording industry that would have allowed Dominican popular music to circulate abroad alongside other then-fashionable Latin musics. The little recording that did take place during the dictatorship was done under the close scrutiny of Trujillo and his similarly merengue-loving (and equally unsavory) brother Petán, to whom musicians had to demonstrate their loyalty by employing lyrics slavishly celebrating the regime.[17] Thus, unlike Puerto Rican and Cuban musicians in New York at the time, whose musical practices evolved in the context of constant interactions with musical developments in their respective islands (and vice versa), Dominican musicians in New York and their counterparts in the Dominican Republic had very little contact with each other. This is particularly significant given that the decades between

1930 and 1960 were crucially important in the development of Latin music in New York.

A handful of Dominican musicians did manage to leave the Dominican Republic and go into exile; some of them ended up in New York, where they either performed in smaller accordion-based conjuntos or played in one of the city's many Cuban- or Puerto Rican–led bands.[18] The most successful of New York's Dominican-identified bands was the Conjunto Típico Quisqueyano, led by piano-accordionist Angel Viloria and featuring vocalist Dioris Valladares. Despite the accordion's working-class associations, Viloria's merengues were sophisticated and urban-sounding, and his band dressed in fashionable suits, distinguishing their music from the button accordion used in merengue típico played by ordinary folk in the Dominican countryside. Viloria later became part of another accordion-based group called Conjunto Típico Cibaeño, whose name invoked the Cibao region where accordion-based merengue was most widespread (although the band was founded by a Puerto Rican, Rafael Pérez).[19] The presence of these conjuntos demonstrates that some of New York's Dominicans appreciated hearing accordion-based music from home, but others were not interested in identifying with conjunto-style merengue because of its lower-class associations.[20] The exiled Dominican intellectual Nicolas Silfa, for example, witnessed a parade organized by the Dominican consulate and reacted with scorn to the tamboras and güiras played by the "crazed gang circulat[ing] through the most aristocratic city of the United States, seeming to have emerged from the most remote and uncivilized regions of the world."[21] Granted, the exiled observer may have been reacting to the performance of merengues with lyrics glorifying the hated dictator Trujillo, but Silfa's palpable contempt for the aesthetics of accordion-based music was not atypical of those of his class.

Although Viloria and others like him found gigs in New York, the clubs they played at were often smaller neighborhood venues, and their more folkloric-sounding and clearly "ethnic" music was of little interest to radio programmers at a time when more sophisticated Latin styles such as mambo were in vogue. Al Santiago, for example, owner of Alegre Records, recalled that the Caborrojeño club where Valladares often played "was not really for our type of music."[22] As for big band–style merengue, it lacked a significant presence in the commercial market but was, nonetheless, a minor part of New York's Latin music scene.[23] Paul Austerlitz notes, for example, that in New York, two Dominican musicians—Josecíto Román and Napoleón Zayas—organized a big band–style merengue group.[24] Max Salazar reports that in 1947, Román's band, Orquesta Quisqueya, was among the six bands that played on the opening night of the Palladium, New York's soon-to-be-legendary Latin music ballroom.[25] Merengue arrangements were also occasionally incorporated into the repertoires of New York Latin music bands as a novelty and a change of pace from the Cuban and Puerto Rican styles dominating the Latin music scene at the time.[26]

In the 1950s, the New Jersey–based Latin music label Ansonia began recording Viloria and other New York–based Dominican típico musicians, initiating the export of accordion-based merengue produced in New York to Latin America. These recordings did not, however, circulate in the Dominican Republic, where Viloria's music remained largely unknown. In short, if merengue occupied a special niche in New York's burgeoning Latin music scene, it did not develop in dialogue with developments in the Dominican Republic itself, nor did it enjoy equal footing with the far more numerous and popular Cuban and Puerto Rican bands whose sonorities virtually defined Latin music for decades to come.

With the assassination of Trujillo in 1960, Dominicans and their musics could finally move beyond the island, ending decades of isolation. Hungry to catch up with contemporary social and cultural developments, Dominicans affluent enough to do so likely would have traveled to New York anyway, but the turmoil into which the country fell as competing sectors of society struggled for power set in motion the first significant and sustained migration of Dominicans to the United States. In 1963, democratically elected President Juan Bosch was deposed by a right-wing coup, after which his supporters staged a counterrevolution to return him to power. In 1965, the United States, fearing that the reforms sought by Bosch would turn the island into "another Cuba," sent in the Marines to prevent this from happening. In order to relieve the heightening political pressures created by the occupation, the U.S. embassy facilitated visas for Dominicans wishing to leave. While the exodus included Dominicans of varied socioeconomic backgrounds, many of them were educated and middle-class critics of the postcoup regime of Joaquín Balaguer, Trujullo's former vice president, whose authoritarian government was being supported by the United States as a bulwark against communism. Most Dominican émigrés went to New York City because of the advantages offered by its well-established Spanish Caribbean community, although Puerto Rico also became a destination for those attracted to the similarities to home in that island's language, climate, and culture.

Balaguer's modernization policies failed to benefit the country's working classes, and, as economic conditions worsened throughout the 1970s, many came to the conclusion that the only solution was to migrate to the United States. Those lucky enough to have relatives who had left earlier obtained family unification visas, but thousands of others lacking such connections entered with tourist visas and simply overstayed. Those without bank accounts and who could not afford the round-trip airline tickets required for tourist visas began piling into rickety boats called *yolas* and crossing the treacherous Mona Straights to Puerto Rico; from there, some of them subsequently made their way to the U.S. mainland. As the exodus intensified in the 1980s, those entering the immigrant stream were, in general, progressively poorer (and darker-skinned) working-class and rural folk, who had more trouble than their antecedents incorporating themselves into the city's shrinking unskilled labor force.[27]

Dominicans who arrived in New York in the 1970s found a Latin music scene dominated by salsa and the Puerto Ricans who were producing it. At the time, salsa was at the apogee of its popularity in New York as well as among the urban working classes in many Latin American countries, including the Dominican Republic. Many Dominican immigrants, then, were not only familiar with salsa; they were also enthusiastic fans. Moreover, Dominicans' own big-band merengue style shared some aesthetic commonalities with salsa, particularly its overall sonic textures created by the layering of brass instruments and polyrhythmic Afro-Caribbean percussion. However, some important differences between them did exist. In salsa, trumpets and trombones were prominent, and its rhythms, solidly grounded in the 3-2 clave characteristic of the Cuban *son*, were extensively syncopated. *Orquesta* merengue's signature instruments, in contrast, were the saxophone, the tambora, and the güira, and its steady two-step rhythm was easier to dance to.

In the 1980s, the number of Dominicans residing in New York more than doubled, to over 125,000, making them the second-largest Latino population in New York after Puerto Ricans.[28] The desires of this rapidly growing cohort of Dominican newcomers for dance music from their own homeland provided merengue musicians with new opportunities; in the mid-1980s, merengue was being regularly performed in New York by touring island-based bands as well as by highly accomplished New York–based Dominican *orquestas,* such as Milly Jocelyn y Los Vecinos, La Gran Manzana (The Big Apple), and the New York Band. Accordion-based merengue, which had been present in New York for decades, continued to be performed in local neighborhood settings but did not move into significant commercial circulation as the *orquestas* did in the 1980s.

In New York, Dominicans were at the core of *orquesta* merengue's most devoted fans, but, as the popularity of the highly danceable merengue began to spread, it also benefited from changes occurring beyond the Dominican community itself. In the 1980s, salsa was being aesthetically transformed (and, to some critics, weakened) by the homogenizing impulses of the recording industry.[29] Fania, salsa's premier label, had refocused its efforts on promoting the unthreatening, balladlike *salsa romántica* to middle-class consumers throughout Latin/o America, disrupting salsa's original connections to the sensibilities of New York's working-class Puerto Rican and Latino communities. Merengue, in contrast, was bright, cheerful, and brassy, and its lyrics about the vicissitudes of urban life employed skillful wordplay and humorous double entendres about women and sex. This was party music, pure and simple, but homogenized and bland it was not. Merengue was also easier to dance to than the choreographically intricate salsa and thus was more accessible to New York's increasingly heterogeneous Latinos from Central and South America, who were less attached to Puerto Rican and Cuban clave-based rhythms. As merengue moved into center stage beside salsa in New York's Latin music scene in the 1980s, salsa lost its hegemony as the city's representative Latin music—even among Puerto Ricans.[30] Thus, just as Latino New York was no longer synonymous with Puerto Ricans, Latin music in New York was no longer synonymous with salsa: It was salsa *and* merengue.

Similar developments took place in Puerto Rico, where the demand for merengue was so strong in the 1980s that some of the Dominican Republic's most successful merengue musicians, such as Toño Rosario and Jossie Esteban, moved to Puerto Rico to take advantage of that island's better-paying gigs. Record companies took note of merengue's ascent among former salsa fans and began devoting more resources to aggressively promoting merengue abroad, especially to Latin American countries, such as Colombia, where *música tropical,* with salsa at its core, was already well established.[31] Jumping on the merengue bandwagon, salsa musicians throughout the hemisphere began to incorporate merengue into their repertoires, in some cases turning exclusively to merengue. Indeed, some of the most successful *merengueros* in the 1990s, such as Elvis Crespo and Olga Tañon, were Puerto Rican.[32]

Dominicans were proud of merengue's success in the international marketplace, but its diffusion also meant that this music, the quintessential symbol of Dominican national identity, was no longer rooted primarily in the Dominican Republic itself. Moreover, as merengue (like salsa before it) became commercialized internationally, it similarly began losing its grounding in uniquely Dominican traditions and sensibilities: Its lyrics relied less on the narrative jaunts in Dominican vernacular that had always characterized merengue and more on catchy but repetitive phrases (often explicitly sexual) that were easily digestible by non-Dominicans; as *New York Times* reporter Ben Ratliff notes of Crespo's merengues, "His hits slow down merengue's galloping tempos and leach it of coded slang: they're for worldwide consumption, songs about the idealized eyes and smiles of women."[33] At the same time, the faster *maco* rhythm popularized in the 1980s by Dominican bands such as Jossie Esteban y La Patrulla 15 and Pochi y Su Coco Band (whose two beat pulses were, as Austerlitz notes, "evocative of disco" and other North American dance rhythms) became more prevalent in merengue performances in the 1990s.[34] This move away from the 4/4 percussion patterns characterizing merengue from the Cibao was controversial, and some Dominicans believed that the style was not even merengue.[35]

The changes to *orquesta* merengue's aesthetics, production, and circulation did not mean that the Dominican Republic had become irrelevant to *orquesta* merengue, but its Dominican performers and fans were becoming increasingly dispersed among several distinct national and cultural settings beyond the Dominican Republic—Puerto Rico, New York, and other northeastern U.S. cities, such as Boston, Salem, and Lawrence in Massachusetts; and Providence, Rhode Island. Diasporic Dominicans remained attached to merengue, but the disconnect between *orquesta* merengue's historical associations with their homeland and its newer, internationally oriented aesthetics, coupled with the new geocultural and economic realities of merengue's production and consumption, opened up space for other genres of Dominican music to fulfill Dominican desires for a sonic connection to and symbol of their homeland. One of the most important of these has been a relative newcomer to the Dominican popular music scene: bachata.

Bachata's roots are located in a variety of Spanish Caribbean, guitar-based musical traditions historically popular among the Dominican peasantry, particularly the Cuban bolero and Puerto Rican *jíbaro* music; to a lesser extent, bachata is also indebted to the working-class male-oriented sensibilities of Mexican *rancheras*. Bachata's roots, in other words, are not unambiguously Dominican. In the 1950s and 1960s, before bachata coalesced as a style, it was referred to as bolero *campesino* (country-style bolero) or simply as *música popular*.[36] When thousands of campesinos (farmers, country folk) migrated to Santo Domingo in search of work after the fall of Trujillo and ended up in the city's worst shantytowns, the style began to lose its original rural character. The instrumentation remained the same—two guitars, maracas, and bongos—but the romantic lyrics that once characterized guitar-based music were replaced by cruder sentiments about sexual desire, often accusing women of treachery or promiscuity or, in more humorous moments, referring to their sexuality and sexual organs with thinly veiled double entendres. Yet, in contrast to the lyrics' macho bravado, the voices of the men singing them were more often than not plaintive and overwrought, expressing emotional pain as well as anger. As I have argued elsewhere,[37] such lyrics reflected the performers' and fans' economic vulnerability as well as the social dislocations set in motion when migrant women entering the workforce displaced men from their traditional roles as family breadwinners. Other sectors of Dominican society, however, perceived this new style of guitar-based music as crude, vulgar, and lacking any redeeming social or cultural value, and they began referring to it as bachata. The word "bachata" originally referred to a spontaneous social gathering enlivened by food, music, and dance, but in this case it was deliberately resignified to disparage the music by invoking plebeian artlessness. To its fans, however, bachata's down-to-earth lyrics and grassroots aesthetics resonated with their own lives far better than the glamorous and fashionable merengue (and salsa) being performed by the big-band *orquestas* dominating the airwaves.

Despised by all but the country's poorest and most marginalized citizens, and lacking clear genealogical origins in traditional Dominican culture, bachata was an unlikely candidate to challenge merengue's hegemony in the United States, either commercially or as a symbol of Dominican identity among U.S.-based Dominicans. In the earlier years of the Dominican diaspora, such an unpolished music had no place in New York's cosmopolitan Latin music arena, especially during the 1980s, when *orquesta* merengue was on the upswing.[38] The increasing numbers of working-class Dominicans arriving in New York in the 1980s, however, expanded the pool of immigrants comfortable with bachata. If bachata's low-class associations had formerly rendered it anathema to anyone with middle-class aspirations, in New York, where immigrants of diverse social backgrounds were sharing similar experiences of economic hardship and social dislocation, such social pressures began to lose ground to immigrants' powerful desires for more "authentic" sounds of home.

Another turning point in bachata's trajectory came in 1990, when Juan Luis Guerra, a successful, conservatory-trained musician from Santo Domingo whose musical roots were originally in jazz and rock, released a recording entitled *Bachata Rosa*.[39] The music on this album was mostly big band–style merengue and salsa, but several songs were bachatas, which, like their grassroots models, were guitar-based, and Guerra's singing style imitated the plaintive quality of grassroots bachata singers. Nevertheless, their sophisticated lyrics and arrangements reflected Guerra's middle-class background and formal musical training, rendering his bachatas acceptable to middle-class tastes. *Bachata Rosa* became a major international success, and when it won a Grammy in 1992, Dominicans everywhere began seeing bachata in a different light. As a result, grassroots *bachateros,* once unwelcome on the Dominican national media, gained access to the mainstream commercial arena.

Henceforth, a younger generation of musicians of humble rural origins—such as Luis Vargas, Joe Veras, and Raulín Rodríguez—now playing electroacoustic guitars and dressing in trendy urban clothing modeled after those worn by *Dominicanyorks,* were able to promote their recordings on television and on the top radio stations and then, via transnational networks, to New York–based Dominicans eager to express their Dominican-ness in a more unequivocally Dominican register. Vargas continued in the tradition of writing raunchy and humorous sexual double-entendre lyrics, but others, including Rodríguez and Veras, cultivated cleaner images, singing only of love, loss, and longing. An even more romantic style of bachata performed by male-female duos, such as Monchy y Alexandra, further established bachata as a "nice" music that could be listened to in the home by women and children. Another successful strategy employed by this new cohort of working-class bachateros was to incorporate merengues into their repertoires. The fresh and lively sound of merengues played by small guitar-based ensembles, sonically so distinct from that produced by the large *orquestas* and the traditional accordion- or sax-based *típico* ensembles Dominicans had long been familiar with, allowed dancers to perform their national identity in an entirely new way.

In the wake of these changes, bachata reached unprecedented levels of popularity among Dominicans, particularly those in the diaspora. Women, who constituted over half the Dominican immigrant stream,[40] embraced this cleaned-up, romantic bachata, whose emotional lyrics expressing longing for departed or lost loved ones resonated with their own experiences of separation and displacement. Some of the old prejudices remained, and not all Dominicans liked bachata, especially older, first-generation immigrants from urban backgrounds who still perceived it as a marker of low-class status. But contrary to the usual pattern of second-generation immigrant children rejecting the "backward" music of their parents' generation in favor of whatever is more "modern" at the time, post-1990s bachata was enthusiastically accepted by young Dominicans born or raised in the United States. To these young Dominicans, bachata effectively articulated their emotional and symbolic connections to their national homeland—even if they had not lived there themselves—and they were unperturbed by the genre's low-class associations. Indeed, bachata's aesthetic simplicity, once responsible for its rejection by those with aspirations to cosmopolitan modernity, was precisely the quality perceived as more suitable for reconnecting diasporic Dominicans to the cultural essence of their homeland.

Throughout the 1980s, merengue and bachata were recorded primarily in the Dominican Republic by Dominican labels, which then exported the recordings for consumption by Dominican expatriates in the United States and in Puerto Rico. Beginning in the 1990s, however, the direction of flow became more circular as the economic center of gravity of the Dominican music business shifted from Santo Domingo to New York. Despite the low socioeconomic status of most New York Dominicans relative to other immigrant groups, they nonetheless had more disposable income than their working-class counterparts on the island, giving their musical preferences a disproportionate influence on the Dominican music business. Indeed, according to an executive of the New York–based record label J&N (one of the biggest labels promoting bachata that was established by two Dominican immigrants in 1990), by the turn of the millennium, sales in the United States accounted for over three-quarters of the company's income.[41] The United States also offered more lucrative performance venues than the island; as a result, some of the top Dominican bachata musicians began spending months of every year touring in the United States, and some even established residence in New York, although the latter continued to tour regularly and extensively in the Dominican Republic in order to maintain a fan base there. The transnational networks in which bachata was produced and consumed thus remained vibrant, but the Dominican Republic, beset by extensive and chronic poverty (and rampant piracy), accounted for a smaller portion of the earnings derived from bachata performances and sales. As one New York–based Dominican record executive noted, "Every CD that sells here has an impact there, not the other way around."[42]

In the 1980s and 1990s, bachata hits were expected to break first in the Dominican Republic before being exported to the United States, because the genre's authenticity was considered to be quite literally grounded in the homeland. By the end of the 1990s, however, the cultural center of gravity for bachata production also shifted, enabling developments in New York to achieve more parity with those on the island. The music of Aventura, a bachata group formed in New York by four young Dominican Americans, is emblematic of these changes and sonically articulates the cultural dialogues between island-based Dominicans and U.S.-based Dominicans. Aventura maintained bachata's signature guitar-based sound, but their guitars and bass were electric, slung low over their hips like rock musicians—a distinct contrast to the way the older generation of acoustic guitar players held their instruments high, over their chests. They also introduced nontraditional instruments, such as synthesizers, and R & B stylings. Their highly romantic lyrics were mostly in Spanish, although they also moved, as in the song "Cuando Volverás," quite fluidly between Spanish and colloquial English.[43] Moreover, all of their recordings have had English titles, from *Generation Next* (1999), to *We Broke the Rules* (2002), to *K.O.B. Live* (2006).[44] The visual images on their recordings and videos are also decidedly U.S.-based: In addition to the group in hip urban clothing, they feature New York streetscapes rather than iconic symbols of the island homeland such as palm trees and beaches.

Such changes have generated anxieties among bachata musicians and fans favoring sonorities and images unambiguously grounded in island-based

Dominican culture. Bachata producer David Wayne, for example, describes the response of more grassroots bachateros to Aventura's music and style:

> The group has remained almost a footnote among bachata's traditional listeners and artists. With the exception of "Obsesión," the plethora of local cover bands in New York has made almost no attempt to learn and perform the group's songs. Additionally, the members of the group have had acrimonious on-stage conflicts with such traditional icons as Luis Vargas and Frank Reyes. While bachata's other "breakthrough" group, Monchy y Alexandra, is in good standing with bachata musicians, Aventura, despite having recorded songs with stalwarts like Antony Santos and Leonardo Paniagua, seem to belong to another world. This can be due in part to the band's fashion statement; from the beginning, they have cultivated a cosmopolitan image, intentionally distancing themselves from the rural, humble, and nationalistic image of the traditional music. While their own young audience has identified strongly with this, many longtime bachata listeners criticize the band's style as extravagant, denying furthermore that its music is really bachata. . . . As such, Aventura has not become, as they originally imagined themselves, the precursors of a new style of bachata; rather, they have thus far been an idiosyncratic, if enormously successful, exception to the "Rules" that they claim to have broken.[45]

For Dominicans comfortable with their layered identities, however, Aventura's music effectively and explicitly articulates the simultaneity of the quality of being "here and there." Aventura has become enormously popular among young U.S.-based Dominicans as well as among nonmigrant youths whose lives or imaginations are in sync with the experiences of their diasporic peers. As Anjelina Tallaj has noted, Aventura's deliberate biculturalism would not have been accepted in the Dominican Republic a decade ago, but "nowadays . . . part of the local appeal of Aventura is that they are seen as *Dominicanyorks* who have proudly embraced their Dominican roots and achieved money and success."[46]

Bachata was not the only working-class music to become embedded in and transformed by the transnational fields linking Dominicans in New York and on the island. As Sydney Hutchinson's work on merengue típico demonstrates, this style, historically associated primarily with rural folk from the Cibao region and working-class residents of the Cibao's capital city of Santiago, has also enjoyed a renaissance in New York thanks to the arrival of working-class immigrants from the Cibao.[47] The similarities and contrasts between developments in bachata and merengue típico illuminate the internal segmentation of Dominicans' transnational fields, across the axes of region, class, gender, and generation.

If bachata benefited from the changes stimulated by Dominicans' transnational networks, the impact of these connections on the production and consumption of merengue típico has been considerably more complex as well as more controversial. As Hutchinson has argued, despite the timelessness implied by its name, merengue típico has evolved significantly since its emergence as a style in the late nineteenth century. The signature instruments of merengue conjuntos still include the accordion, tambora drum, and güira (and sometimes the large *marimbula* thumb bass). However, other instruments, such as saxophones, conga drums, and electric bass guitars, were added as early as the 1960s by such pioneering musicians as Tatico Henríquez and subsequently by such musicians as El Cieguito de Nagua and female accordionist Fefita la Grande; Hutchinson refers to these expanded ensembles as "neo-traditional."[48] Until the Dominican diaspora exploded in the 1980s, merengue típico, whether performed by the more folkloric accordion-based trios or the larger neotraditional ensembles, did not circulate widely in the Dominican Republic beyond the northwestern Cibao region, where it has always flourished as a vital element of the region's live and recorded music scene. (A limited market for this music has existed at upscale tourist hotels elsewhere in the Dominican Republic, where foreign guests lounging at the swimming pool are entertained with "authentic" Dominican music.) Despite its low national profile, however, merengue típico has remained a potent symbol of the Dominican Republic's rural past and its associated traditional values, explaining why conjuntos típicos are often on hand at the international airport at holiday times to welcome back returning migrants.

In the diaspora, merengue típico had always indexed "authentic" Dominican-ness in settings such as cultural heritage–oriented events, but, as Hutchinson notes, after migration from the Cibao increased in the 1990s, an active live típico music scene also developed in newer Dominican enclaves in Brooklyn and Queens, where many recently established Cibaeños had settled. In contrast, their Dominicanyork counterparts hailing from the capital city of Santo Domingo, where *orquesta* merengue reigned supreme (at least until the ascent of bachata), were more likely to live in Manhattan's older Dominican neighborhoods, Washington Heights and Inwood.[49] By the dawn of the new millennium, the cultural (and economic) revalorizations of bachata and merengue típico in New York were challenging *orquesta* merengue's long-standing status as the quintessential Dominican style. Anjelina Tallaj, born in the Dominican Republic to an upper-middle-class family, recalls her perceptions of these changes when she relocated to New York to attend college: "I realized that *merengue de orquesta* was not the music that represented Dominican-ness to all Dominicans, and in New York, *Dominicanyorks* listened more to *bachata* and *merengue típico* than to *merengue de orquesta*. Listening to this music was, for me, the beginning of a new awareness of my own culture."[50] Such diasporic-driven cultural revalorizations have deepened anxieties in the Dominican Republic, where Dominicanyorks have been perceived with a mixture of scorn and envy when they return to the island, conspicuously displaying their stateside fashions and attitudes.[51]

Notwithstanding the desires of some Dominican immigrants for consistently predictable sounds from home, merengue típico, like bachata, has been transformed in the United States, creating new fissures and layers within merengue típico's region-centered fan base. In addition to Fulanito, other groups composed of young Dominicans born or raised in the United States have sought to resignify traditional aesthetics by combining them with the diverse non-Dominican musical aesthetics comprising their sonic landscape: Krisspy, for example, infused the vocal sonorities and instrumentation of big-band salsa and merengue (e.g., keyboards, congas, and timbals) into a típico sound, while the group Aguakate combined típico with reggaeton rhythms. Moreover, these groups presented themselves on their CDs and in concerts with decidedly U.S.-based urban clothing and attitudes rather than deploying images and iconography traditionally invoking rural Dominican culture. Many young U.S.-based Dominicans, regardless of their regions of origin or class identities, embraced these stylistic and performative innovations, and, as occurred with bachata's fans in the late 1980s, their spending power has created a significant market in the diaspora and on the island for such hybridized styles.

By deliberately combining the aesthetics and iconography associated with both homeland and host cultures, these groups transcend and transgress the very authenticity that confers their more "modern" styles with their emotional and symbolic power in the first place. Despite such contradictions, bachata and merengue típico, including their modernized variants, serve to index an authentic Dominican-ness for U.S.-based Dominicans—although the identities they articulate are quite differently inflected. Típico remains associated with rural traditional culture from the Cibao. Bachata, in contrast, is associated with a more mixed rural and urban working-class culture and its economic, social, and physical displacements; moreover, as a more recently emerged music with multiple pan-Caribbean antecedents, it is less cloaked with expectations of cultural continuity. The highly romantic lyrics characterizing postmillennium bachata that have endeared it to female fans also distinguishes bachata from the brasher, more assertive merengue típico, which (notwithstanding the noteworthy presence of women accordionists such as

Fefita la Grande and María Díaz) has never been imagined as a vehicle for expressing softer (feminized) emotions and vulnerability.

Another noticeable contrast between the trajectories of bachata and típico in the United States can be discerned in their reception by non-Dominican Latino groups sharing the United States' complex soundscape. Bachata's characteristic lyrics about longing for loved ones departed or left behind have resonated deeply with other working-class Latino immigrants living transnational lives and experiencing comparable feelings of displacement and emotional loss. No transnational connections link bachata to Mexico or South America, but immigrants from these regions do arrive with comparable traditions of guitar-based music with highly emotional lyrics; to them, bachata is more familiar than the more locally specific and cheerful merengue típico. As the aforementioned officer of J&N Records notes, "Bachata is guitar music, it's like the Dominican blues, and so grassroots, like the blues. Also, not only the instrumentation, but the subject matter is very popular, very street, everybody can relate to it. Mexicans love to drink, and that's the kind of music to get a bottle of rum for. . . . The character of the voices, like other folkloric musics, blues, son, bachata, there's so much in common in the quality of the voice, in the vibrato. It's rough, a little crying going on."[52] Whether bachata's power to index an "authentic" Dominican-ness will diminish as it spreads beyond the Dominican community, as *orquesta* merengue did in the 1980s, remains to be seen.

Reconceptualizing Race

Given the sociocultural segmentation of the transnational fields in which Dominican musics circulate, Dominican conceptions of race must also be brought to bear in understanding the trajectory of Dominican musics in the diaspora. Preferences for *orquesta* merengue, merengue típico, and bachata have always been filtered by individual listeners' class and regional origins, but—despite the fact that in the Dominican Republic class and race are strongly correlated—these genres have not generally been thought of in racial terms (i.e., none of them is associated with any particular racial group). This is not to say that they lack African-derived aesthetic influences but rather that they are typically perceived as simply Dominican—and historically, "Dominican" has specifically meant "not black" (thereby distinguishing themselves from their Haitian neighbors who *are* considered black).[53] Since musics perceived as "too black" have long been disparaged and rejected in the Dominican Republic,[54] merengue's clearly audible debt to African-derived aesthetics was erased by describing it as a creolized variant of European forms of music making, particularly the ballroom-oriented contradanse. No attempts were

made to celebrate merengue as a music whose mixture of African, indigenous, and European racial and cultural antecedents symbolized the nation's
own mixed heritage (as occurred with *cumbia* in Colombia; see Chapter 6).
Indeed, as late as the 1970s, when a Dominican folklorist pointed out that
merengue, the quintessential symbol of Dominican identity, had roots in African traditions, he was accused in the press of being unpatriotic.[55] In such a
context, genres associated with syncretic Afro-Dominican religion practiced
by rural folk, such as palo, *congos*, and the creolized *salves*, have historically
been subject to particularly derogatory judgments.[56] Considered the cultural
remnants of primitive and superstitious people who had failed to progress,
the urban Dominicans who controlled the commercial production of music
were not interested either in recording them, incorporating them into contemporary arrangements, or giving them visibility in any form. As a result,
while these genres flourished in rural areas, until recently they made little
impact on the Dominican Republic's commercial musical landscape.

Of the several forms of traditional Afro-Dominican musics, palo in particular offers a unique lens through which to view how conceptions of race
have influenced and have been influenced by Dominicans' transnational cultural fields. "Palo" refers to the long drums that, along with other small percussion instruments, provide music at religious ceremonies, such as wakes
and *promesas* (ceremonies thanking the deities for granting a request), that
traditionally have taken place in front of altars in people's homes or structures
set up specifically for such events, but the term is also used for the music
and dancing associated with the drums. Palo was traditionally performed
only on religious occasions by skilled but nonprofessional members of the
community, but since it was rejected by Dominicans with even modest social
aspirations because of its associations with the poorest and blackest sectors
of Dominican society, it appeared to be losing ground as young people left the
countryside in search of better jobs in urban areas, whether on the island or
abroad, prompting ethnomusicologist Martha Ellen Davis to report in 1994
that palos appeared to be on the decline.[57] When the migration flows to New
York began incorporating increasing numbers of poor and darker-skinned
(and often undocumented) Dominicans of rural origins, however, rather
than falling further into disuse, palo traveled with them, entering Dominican
transnational cultural fields. As Hannah Gill has noted in her pioneering
work on the impact of transnationalism on palo, promesa ceremonies accompanied by palo music began to be held more frequently to thank the deities
for successful border crossings and safe arrivals.[58] These ceremonies could
be held either in the sending or receiving country, so the demand for palo
musicians in both locations increased in tandem with the rate of poor, rural,
undocumented immigrants leaving for the United States.

In the United States, and to an increasing degree in the Dominican Republic, palo music, once strongly rooted in (and limited to) sacred rural practices, has moved into secular and urban contexts and has even entered the realm of commercial production and distribution. Gill notes, for example, that palo groups on the island and in the United States now play not only on religious occasions, as they once did, but at dance parties as well. She also observed thoroughly secular palo shows being performed as entertainment in U.S. nightclubs attended by Dominicans of multiple social and racial backgrounds. Indeed, palo musicians in the Dominican Republic as well as in the United States were enough in demand that they began organizing themselves into professional groups, recording CDs and composing original secular songs (some of which narrate aspects of the migration experience).[59] The CDs recorded by island- and U.S.-based palo groups are now exchanged and sold in both locations, although the circulation is more often informal, from individual to individual, than promoted by commercial record labels.[60]

In the late 1990s, palo made an entrance into the commercial arena when prominent *orquesta* merenguero Kinito Mendez recorded a merengue/palo fusion song called "Suero de Amor," which, as Gill notes, was presented to the public as merengue rather than as palo and went on to win an award for "Merengue of the Year."[61] In Mendez's subsequent 2001 recording entitled *A Palo Limpio,* palo figures even more prominently, not only in the CD's title and repertoire but also in the cover art, which features images that clearly invoke Afro-Dominican religious practices.[62] Mendez had been exposed to palo drumming as a child when his parents took him to Afro-Dominican ceremonies at which palos were played, so, even though he had made his name and fortune as a member of Coco Band (one of the *orquestas* responsible for introducing the maco rhythm to merengue in the 1980s), he was able to claim the authority to perform and to represent palo. Mendez earned a Grammy nomination for *A Palo Limpio*; although it did not win or have as dramatic an impact as Guerra's *Bachata Rosa* did on the status of bachata, the public affirmation of palo by such a well-established island-based *orquesta* merenguero served to bring palo into public view and in a highly favorable light.

As happened with típico and bachata, changes in palo's status and circulation have been simultaneously the cause and effect of a major shift in palo's symbolic valence among nonpractitioners, moving beyond the primitiveness and superstition it invoked on the island to being considered, in the United States, a more authentic and unmediated expression of folk Dominican-ness. But unlike the ascent of bachata, which was linked to the changing social-class status of its fans, the trajectory of palo in the United States is related to changing notions of racial identity, particularly among Dominican migrants. Despite Dominicans' long-standing disavowal of their African heritage, over

90 percent of them have some degree of African ancestry (deliberately masked by the term *indio,* applied to those with darker shades of skin).[63] Upon arriving in the United States, many Dominicans were discomfited to realize that, regardless of their shades of brown, in this country they were categorized as black. Over time, and inspired by the racial pride of African Americans and other Afro-Caribbean immigrants, many of them have learned to accept their African heritage and have embraced an Afro-Dominican identity. For U.S.-born or U.S.-raised Dominicans interested in recovering and revalidating this particular aspect of their cultural heritage, palo became an ideal vehicle for articulating it.

Such notions have been met with dismay in the Dominican Republic, where *afrophobia* runs deep, but they have nonetheless generated public dialogues about race and opened up new spaces for Afro-Dominican culture. Gill, for example, notes that the number of palo groups in Baní and the nearby town of Monte Cruz increased from four in 1994 to twelve in 2004, stimulating a somewhat astonished older man to tell her, "The kids are burning to play those drums, they all want to be *paleros* now."[64] By 2004, when Gill did her research, Boston had three palo groups,[65] while in New York even larger numbers of folk revival groups have emerged,[66] contributing to the dissemination (and legitimation) of palo and other Afro-Dominican music in the diaspora by performing at Dominican cultural festivals, schools, and cultural centers.[67] Young U.S.-born Dominicans undeterred by the racial prejudices of their parents, including some of my own students, are eagerly seeking out opportunities to learn about and to perform these once-denigrated musics.

Reggaeton and the Puerto Rican Connection

Of the well over a million Dominicans living in the United States in 2000 (over six hundred thousand of them in New York City), one in three had been born in the United States.[68] Their musical preferences will continue to influence the aesthetics, meaning, and circulation patterns of Dominican popular musics in both the United States and the Dominican Republic. Second-generation Dominicans clearly value their connections to their home culture but find it increasingly difficult to maintain a single unmixed, unhyphenated identity. As one young U.S.-born Dominican college student told me, "I've felt most Dominican at my family parties, where all they play is merengue, bachata, and maybe salsa—anything from the U.S., they don't play. I feel most Dominican, because the same party here can be definitely happening in the DR."[69] At the same time, she and others like her also recognize that their upbringing in the United States—speaking English and participating in U.S. hip-hop culture—has distinguished them from their island-based counterparts in fundamentally crucial ways. Another student, for example, noted that when she returned to the island, she was not considered to be fully Dominican either: "The fact that we live in the United States automatically makes us American from their point of view. But when you are up here, we are not considered American; we are the Other."[70]

These statements reflect the complexity of second-generation Dominican identity, in which their affiliation with the Dominican Republic serves as what Jose Itzigsohn and Carlos Dore-Cabral call an "anchoring identity," but their identities include multiple other layers as well.[71] They know, for example, that they are "American" by virtue of their U.S. citizenship and immersion in U.S. mainstream culture, but they do not readily identify as such because they perceive "American" to be a construct inextricably associated with a white Eurocentrism that excludes them. For these Dominicans, the panethnic term "Latino" (or "Hispano") provides an additional identity category that positions them within the United States in proximity to other young people of different national backgrounds who share similar experiences.[72] Moreover, the panethnic Latino identity sits quite comfortably next to a national identity, as they are not mutually exclusive. Reggaeton, whose multiple roots include U.S. hip-hop and Spanish Caribbean (including Dominican) musical aesthetics, effectively articulates this pan-Latino layer of identity.

Reggaeton's Puerto Rican origins and its popularity among young Dominicans also bring to light another significant but often overlooked dimension of Dominicans' transnational cultural practices.[73] Since the 1970s, a growing number of Dominican migrants have settled in Puerto Rico and have remained, like Dominican immigrants in New York, closely connected to cultural and musical developments taking place in the Dominican Republic. But because of their location in Puerto Rico, they have also become enmeshed within the long-established Puerto Rican cultural circuits linking Puerto Ricans on the island and those in New York. Puerto Rico–based Dominican musical practices, which have included reggaeton since its inception in the late 1990s, demonstrate that bipolar "here and there" models of transnational simultaneity must be expanded to incorporate additional nodes.

When the Dominican diaspora was set in motion in 1961 after the fall of the dictator Trujillo, some Dominicans chose Puerto Rico as their destination because of its geographical proximity and familiar language and culture. If the earlier arrivals were socioeconomically mixed, later arrivals were more typically the Dominican Republic's poorer and more uneducated citizens whose only options for migrating entailed the dangerous journey to Puerto Rico by yola. Coming from a nation where class correlates closely to race, they were also the Dominican Republic's darkest citizens. In metropolitan San Juan, where most Dominicans settled, they ended up in the city's poorest and most undesirable neighborhoods, living next to Puerto Ricans who were similarly poor, poorly educated, and often dark. The presence of so many dark-skinned Dominicans in Puerto Rico stimulated Puerto Ricans' racial anxieties, as Dominicans—numbering approximately one hundred thousand by the turn of the millennium—threatened to "blacken" a population that has historically considered itself to be whiter than Dominicans.[74] As Jorge Duany notes, anti-Dominican prejudices generated "strong resentments against foreign newcomers to the island, especially Dominicans. . . . An ever expanding repertoire of ethnic jokes and folk stories perpetuates the myth of the dumb, ignorant country bumpkin from the Cibao."[75] Sixty percent of the Dominican immigrants, however, were young, single women, and notwithstanding such prejudices, a high rate of intermarriage or sexual unions with Puerto Ricans ensued.[76] Their offspring, Puerto Rican–born mixed-race youths of Dominican ancestry, grew up attending public schools alongside Puerto Ricans and absorbing whatever music was being listened to by their counterparts. Throughout the 1990s, that music was primarily the increasingly popular (if publicly censured) underground rap.

As discussed in Chapter 4, hip-hop from New York had originally been transferred to the island via long-established cultural circuits linking Puerto Ricans on the mainland to their counterparts on the island; the style was indigenized in the mid- to late 1980s when island-based musician Vico C and his successors began rapping in Spanish. *Rap en español* became enormously popular among marginalized youths (including Dominicans), who shared the island's poorest and darkest neighborhoods. At about the same time, Dominican merengue, on the ascent in New York in the wake of Dominican migration there, was also making inroads in Puerto Rico, not only among Dominicans but among Puerto Ricans as well. As merengue began to vie with salsa as the island's most popular dance music, a handful of top Dominican merengue *orquestas* took up residence in Puerto Rico, because the economically better-off island offered more and better-paying performance opportunities. When the highly successful Dominican-based merenguero Toño Rosario separated from his group Los Hermanos Rosario in the late 1980s and moved to Puerto Rico, he became Puerto Rico's top merengue performer.

One Puerto Rican entrepreneur, Jorge Oquendo, co-owner of Prime Records, the record label that had signed Vico C and first commercialized *rap en español*, took advantage of these popular but nonintersecting musical trends and by doing so contributed to laying the foundations for what was later to become reggaeton. Oquendo conceived the idea of combining the two genres—rap and merengue—by encouraging collaborations between his most popular rap artists and his most popular merengue artists. Among the rap artists were Vico C; one of Vico C's dancers, Lisa M (born of a Dominican mother and Puerto Rican father); and Francheska; the merengueros included Rosario and Jossie Esteban.[77] The resulting fusion, called meren-rap, appealed to young people who liked the cheerful, danceable merengue but at the same time were attracted to the innovative sounds of rap that they knew were beginning to define urban youth culture in the United States and other parts of the Americas.

Around 1990, Oquendo was touring in New York with Rosario, whose popularity among Dominican and Puerto Rican New Yorkers was at its height. There, Oquendo met and signed a young Panamanian musician named El General, who was rapping Spanish lyrics over dancehall reggae beats. Again recognizing a promising new sound, Oquendo signed El General to Prime Records and released what turned out to be a wildly successful and influential recording, "Merenrap," containing the anthemic *reggae en español* songs "Pu Tun Tun" and "Muévelo," today recognized as antecedents to what would later become known as reggaeton.[78]

Meren-rap was a studio experiment rather than a grassroots musical development, and it was short lived:[79] as Puerto Rican rappers embraced *reggae en español*'s dancehall beats, meren-rap was all but eclipsed. It continued to develop in New York City, however, with groups such as Proyecto Uno and DLG—both composed of Dominican and Puerto Rican musicians. Fusions of merengue with rap and dancehall reggae would not be produced again on the island until after the turn of the millennium, after reggaeton had coalesced as a distinct style. The reappearance of Dominican aesthetics may have reflected the growing number of Dominican reggaeton fans on the island, but it also coincided with the arrival in Puerto Rico of the Dominican-born production team Luny Tunes, whose professional trajectories perfectly illustrate the transnational circuits moving Dominican people and aesthetics between the Dominican Republic, the United States, and Puerto Rico. Luny (Francisco Saldana) had moved to Puerto Rico from the Dominican Republic with his mother and sisters as a child, and he grew up in one of San Juan's working-class barrios listening to Puerto Rican underground rap. When he was a teen, his family moved again, this time to the Boston area, where he met and subsequently began producing music with Dominican-born Tunes (Victor Cabrera). In 2000, Luny received an opportunity to work in pioneering reggaeton producer DJ Nelson's studio in Puerto Rico, and Tunes accompanied him. There, they produced a string of successful releases for reggaeton artists from Ivy Queen to Daddy Yankee. Luny Tunes also collaborated with Tego Calderón on his influential 2003 recording *El Abayarde*,[80] whose song, "Pa' Que Retozen" featured the unmistakable guitar sounds of Dominican bachata—although, interestingly, Puerto Rican DJ Joe, not Luny Tunes, is credited with that particular production. Luny Tunes' own 2003 hit compilation, *Mas Flow,* also included a Calderón song, "Métale Sazón," which exhibits bachata's signature guitar arpeggios and merengue's characteristic piano riffs.[81] Subsequently, merengue and bachata aesthetics were widely incorporated into Puerto Rican reggaeton—examples include Ivy Queen's "La Mala," Don Omar's "Díle," and Daddy Yankee's "Brugal" (named after a well-known brand of Dominican rum).

In the wake of successful infusions of Dominican aesthetics into reggaeton, bachata-inflected collaborations between established Puerto Rican reggaeton and Dominican bachata stars also began to appear; one example was Dom Omar and Aventura's song "Ella y Yo," whose melodramatic lyrics about a love triangle narrate the destruction of a friendship between two men as a result of female infidelity. Expressions of emotional vulnerability had long been hallmarks of bachata lyrics, but their appearance in reggaeton, whose lyrics had characteristically articulated aggressive male braggadocio, represented a significant new development. In 2005, Puerto Rican producers went further, remixing existing reggaeton hits with bachata's characteristic guitar sounds and marketing them as *bachaton,* defining the style as "*bachata a lo boricua.*"[82]

If reggaeton's early development was incubated in Puerto Rico, the transnational fields created by Dominican immigrants quickly moved the genre beyond the island to the Dominican Republic and New York. Reggaeton's circulation and symbolic valences in these locations, however, were strikingly dissimilar. Reggaeton (and its antecedents rap, meren-rap, and *reggae en español*) had been circulating between Puerto Rico and the Dominican Republic since the 1990s, but Dominican artists in the Dominican Republic performing these styles lacked the advantages of access to the capital, technology, and media available to Puerto Rican musicians thanks to the commonwealth island's connections to the U.S. economy. As a result, despite the back-and-forth movement between the two islands, developments in the Dominican Republic were not correspondingly influential in Puerto Rico. Indeed, despite reggaeton's roots in U.S. hip-hop and Jamaican dancehall and its increasingly prominent Dominican aesthetics, it was widely perceived in Puerto Rico as a Puerto Rican–only creation.[83]

New York, in contrast, was another story. Reggaeton's popularity there did not explode until the new millennium, deterred, in large part, by the long-standing preference of young New York Latinos for U.S. hip-hop. When reggaeton did begin to make a mark in the early 2000s, however, it was perceived as a quintessentially hybrid Afro-diasporic or pan-Latin genre that could easily accommodate Dominicans and Puerto Ricans (as well as other Latino nationalities). The combined economic potential of New York's hip-hop and Latin music industries, coupled with the demographic realities of hundreds of thousands of Dominicans and other Latinos of all ethnicities, quickly transformed New York into an important center of reggaeton production and consumption. Collaborations between Puerto Rican and Dominican musicians, which were nothing new in New York (e.g., in the aforementioned meren-rap group Proyecto Uno), simply expanded to accommodate the growing interest in reggaeton. One example of such collaborations was the Queens-born Dominican producer Manuel Alejandro Ruiz, aka Boy Wonder, whose seminal compilation CD and DVD documentary on the history of reggaeton, *The Chosen Few,* sold over five hundred thousand copies and charted on *Billboard* for months, many of them in the top five.[84] Other highly visible examples include the aforementioned duet between Aventura and Don Omar; the performances of U.S. Dominican artists Gem Star, Big Mato, and LDA with Puerto Rican artists Daddy Yankee and the female duo Nina Sky in (the U.S.-based Puerto Rican and African American rapper) N.O.R.E.'s 2004 major international hit "Oye Mi Canto."

In short, reggaeton constitutes yet another layer of the musical practices embraced by urban Dominican youths wherever they are found, whether in the United States, Puerto Rico, or the Dominican Republic—although how it articulates Dominican identity differs in each location. In Puerto Rico, the prevailing negative stereotypes of Dominicans have dampened Puerto Rican and Dominican reggaeton musicians' inclinations to publicly foreground their Dominican identity: Several of reggaeton's biggest stars are of Dominican ancestry,[85] but they are seldom represented, or represent themselves, as anything other than Puerto Rican. This inclination to submerge their Dominican identity contrasts markedly with their counterparts in multiethnic New York, where Dominican musicians born or raised in the United States, performing in a variety of styles, have embraced every opportunity to display their national heritage.

Concluding Thoughts

As the dissimilar trajectories of merengue, bachata, palo, and reggaeton demonstrate, the ways Dominican identity has been imagined and performed within transnational fields have been neither uniform nor predictable but segmented and subject to crosscutting variables, such as class, race, gender, generation, migratory status, and regions of origin and resettlement. Dominican musical practices since the 1980s have been particularly sensitive to the sensibilities of second-generation youths, who have grown up embedded in U.S. hip-hop culture but share their first-generation parents' desires to remain visibly and audibly connected to their homeland. Yet despite U.S. Dominican youths' desires to embrace their homeland's "authentic" musical practices, such as típico merengue and palo, these have also been subject to the forces of relocation and resignification. In the Dominican Republic, some individuals, especially older nonmigrants, have interpreted the cultural revalorizations of bachata, típico, and palo as signaling the loss of traditional values and behaviors of which they are (presumably) the rightful stewards. These observations are, in fact, correct: The island's traditional hierarchies as well as its historical patriarchal authoritarianism *have* been disrupted by the circular flows of people, behaviors, and values between the island and its diaspora, creating new ways of imagining Dominican identity that are no longer necessarily defined within the Dominican Republic itself.

6

From Cumbia Colombiana
to Cumbia Cosmopolatina

Roots, Routes, Race, and Mestizaje

In a 2008 *Daily Telegraph* article by Gervase de Wilde entitled "Why the World Is Catching On to Cumbia: The Infectious Music of Colombia Is Spreading across the Globe," Colombian music producer and musician Ivan Benavides explains that cumbia is "the foundational Colombian rhythm" but, at the same time, "part of a wider movement which some refer to as 'cosmopolatino.'"[1] De Wilde parses the term "cosmopolatino" as "this global Latin culture of ideas [that] allows sounds and styles to travel and evolve locally in exciting new forms," and he gives as examples urban-based groups, such as the Colombian fusion rock group Bloque and the eclectic Los Angeles–based group Very Be Careful.[2] A Web search for "cosmopolatino" turns up similar definitions referencing "young, urban, and bilingual [individuals who] are fusing aspects of Latin America with other global trends to create a unique cultural space in New York and other cities."[3] Such definitions do not, however, make any references to race or to the racial locations of cumbia's musicians or fans.

Cumbia does fit the descriptions of being well-traveled and having evolved into numerous styles, although the sophisticated gloss provided by the term "cosmopolatino" obscures cumbia's much more humble roots and complicated routes through the Americas over the past century. Cumbia's aesthetic origins are in pre-twentieth-century coastal Colombian folk culture, where it articulated the hybrid sensibilities of that region's tri-ethnic population of mixed African, European, and native ancestries. In the 1940s and 1950s, commercialized variants of cumbia were popularized throughout Colombia and then spread to other parts of Spanish-speaking Latin America to the south (Ecuador, Peru, and Argentina) and to the north (Central

America and Mexico), where it became embedded and resignified in (primarily) working-class and mestizo communities—and then, via Mexican immigrants, to the United States as well. Cumbia remains deeply rooted in working-class Latin/o American communities, but its recent global variants have become unmoored from any particular social group or location.

Cumbia's extraordinary northward journeys from Colombia to Mexico to the United States and then to the global stage are the subject of this chapter. I also necessarily track its close cousin, the Colombian vallenato, whose international trajectory has been closely linked to that of cumbia. As I map the origins of these styles in Colombia and their subsequent arrivals in the United States, I foreground the complex relationships between the social and aesthetic transformations that occurred along the way. While most musics undergo significant changes in style and social context as they move from one location to another, cumbia's trajectory in particular stands out as unusual and often paradoxical. Unlike most Latin American musics, such as merengue, bachata, or banda, which have been brought to the United States by immigrants hailing from these genres' birthplaces, cumbia was originally brought into the United States by Mexicans, who arrived prior to, and therefore unconnected to, the influx of Colombian immigrants escaping the increasing levels of violence that exploded in Colombia in the 1990s. Indeed, when Colombian immigration to the United States began to surge, it was vallenato, not cumbia, that enjoyed the status as a quintessential symbol of Colombian identity.

Today, the largest proportion of cumbia fans in the United States are not Colombians but Mexican immigrants—although the cumbia they listen to little resembles the technologically sophisticated cumbia fusions produced by DJs in trendy dance clubs for pan-Latin cosmopolatinos, which are far more likely than their working-class counterparts to be celebrated by the mainstream media. While some of the cumbia listened to by Mexicans is still produced in Colombia, most of it is produced by Mexicans, in Mexico as well as in the United States, most successfully by the working class–oriented *norteño* bands that now account for well over half of Latin music sales in the United States (see Chapter 7). Indeed, by the turn of the millennium, Mexicans had reconfigured and resignified cumbia to such an extent that many Mexicans believe cumbia is of Mexican origin. Paradoxically, despite Mexicans' far greater numbers in the United States, since the new "cumbia/vallenato" category was added to the Latin Grammys in 2006 to reflect the growing interest in these styles, all but one of the nominees and winners have been vallenatos.[4]

The cultural significance of cumbia's and vallenato's complicated travels to the United States and beyond cannot be properly understood without referring to the nature and meaning of the cultural (and racial) mixing that originally produced these genres in Colombia. Moreover, these genres did not originate in the primarily mestizo interior areas that later sent most immigrants to the United States but, rather, on Colombia's tri-ethnic northern coast, whose people are the racially mixed descendants of Africans, natives, and Europeans. The aesthetic sensibilities of contemporary Colombia's Afrodescendants, whose "tropical" polyrhythmic aesthetics were credited for propelling cumbia into international circulation back in the 1950s, have since been largely overlaid or replaced by the cultural sensibilities of mostly working-class mestizo people, first in Colombia and then in Peru, Ecuador, Argentina, and Mexico. The more recent variants of global cumbias circulating in cosmopolitan cosmopolatino dance clubs, in contrast, seem to be re-Africanizing cumbia's rhythmic orientation, although, as I note below, in a problematically unreflective way.

The Roots and Routes of Cumbia (and Vallenato) in Historical Perspective

In order to properly understand the interlocking relationship between cumbia's roots and its pan-American (and then global) routes, Colombia's geocultural complexities must first be taken into account.[5] One of the most geographically diverse countries in Latin America, Colombia's geocultural regions include Amazonian lowlands and vast Orinocan grasslands that are home to indigenous groups and more recent mestizo colonists, as well as dense rainforests along the Pacific Coast coinhabited by the black descendants of escaped slaves and the region's remaining indigenous communities. The regions most pertinent to this discussion, however, are the primarily mestizo Andean mountains and valleys of the interior, and the tri-ethnic northern Caribbean coast of Colombia, colloquially known simply as *la costa*. Most of the coast's original indigenous groups were decimated during the Spanish invasion, but vibrant (if struggling) indigenous communities still inhabit various parts of Colombia's coastline.[6] In the colonial period, enslaved Africans were brought to the coast to construct the massive fortifications surrounding the economically crucial port city of Cartagena, from which the riches plundered from the interior of the continent were loaded aboard galleons headed for Spain. Enslaved Africans were also put to work as boatmen on the Magdalena River, which served as the primary transportation link to the interior where the capital city of Santa Fé de Bogotá was located. The descendants of these Africans, connected by maritime trade to the Afro-Caribbean island cultures to the north, have given the coast and its culture a distinctively Afro-Caribbean flavor. Today, the majority of the contemporary *costeño* population is a mix of blacks, mulattos, *zambos* (offspring of black and Indian parentage), mestizos, and whites. The more recent descendants of European (especially Italian) and Middle Eastern (especially Lebanese) immigrants who settled in Colombia in the first half of the twentieth century have further complicated the coast's diverse demographic and cultural profile. Phenotypically speaking, the population inhabiting the *sabanas* (lowland plains) surrounding Cartagena tends to be blacker, while those inhabiting the more easterly region surrounding the Sierra Nevada are more likely to be mestizo; whites tend to be concentrated in urban areas. Despite these variations, in terms of culture, costeños—regardless of color—are perceived (when compared to other regions) as relatively homogeneous.

In contrast, the people inhabiting the country's Andean mountain ranges stretching north-south through the interior sections of the country are predominantly mestizo; a notable exception is the population of the interior lowlands of the Cauca Valley and its primary city of Cali, which have a larger percentage of inhabitants of African descent. The mostly mestizo inhabitants of the cities of Bogotá and Medellín (known in the vernacular as *cachacos* and *paisas,* respectively), but especially their white or light-skinned ruling elites, have historically prided themselves on being more entrepreneurial, modern, and "civilized" than those in other regions with larger proportions of black or indigenous inhabitants. The racially mixed inhabitants of the northern coast in particular have been stereotyped as indolent, promiscuous, vulgar, and loud. This regional hierarchy is crosscut by a highly stratified class structure that correlates strongly with race, with white and light-skinned ruling-class elites at the top, racially mixed middle sectors, and blacks and indigenous natives at the bottom. Even white elites from the economically vibrant and culturally sophisticated coastal port cities of Barranquilla and Cartagena have been tainted (in the eyes of their highland peers) by their association with the coast's racially mixed culture—especially its blackness.[7]

Each of Colombia's regions has its own distinctive musical genres, but few of these genres have been successful outside their region of origin, and fewer yet have made it to the United States, either before or after the first immigrant wave of Colombians began in the late 1940s. In the early twentieth century, the *bambuco* and *pasillo* from the Andean interior, based on stringed instruments and European harmonies, were being promoted by the interior's elites as a strategy for consolidating the country's various regions into a unified national culture reflecting their Eurocentric values.[8] Bambucos and pasillos were prominent in the repertoires of the first Colombian musicians who traveled to New York to record between 1910 and 1920, although in subsequent decades they did not evolve into commercially popular styles and nowadays are more akin to "folk" music.[9] Cali has achieved recognition as an important center for the production and consumption of salsa but not for a historically regional style. The Pacific Coast's traditional marimba-based *currulao* was too associated with poor blacks to be of interest outside its region of origin, and, despite the fact that its coastal port of Buenaventura has been an active site of popular musical production in recent decades (first salsa, then rap and *reggaeton*), the diffusion of music from the Pacific Coast has not been extensive, even within Colombia. The circulation of other regional styles, such as *joropo,* from the Orinocan lowlands plains have similarly remained confined within national boundaries.[10] Thus, despite the fact that the majority of Colombian migrants to the United States in later decades originated in the Andean interior, their regional styles have made little impression on the Latin/o American musical landscape outside Colombia. The same can be said for the guitar-based trios and quartets playing the Mexican *ranchera*-inspired *música carrilera* (also known as *música guasca*) popular among working-class folk in Colombia's interior in the mid– to late twentieth century.[11] In contrast, *música costeña,* especially cumbia, has wielded disproportionate influence not only in Colombia but also throughout the Americas.

The category referred to as música costeña includes a wide range of styles—such as *paseo, porro, gaita, merengue* (unrelated to the Dominican genre), *fandango, bullerengue,* and *mapalé*—but the most significant have been cumbia and its close relative, the vallenato. Like musics from the interior, coastal musics are the products of racial and cultural mixing but differ from their highland counterparts in the degree of their African-derived aesthetics and instrumentation.[12] Scholars describing the roots of coastal musics typically ascribe the wide variety of drums and their polyrhythmic musical structures to African influences, while the flutes (the *caña de millo* side flute and the *gaita* duct flutes) and the cane or wood *guacharaca,* scraped by a metal fork, are attributed to the region's original indigenous inhabitants.[13] European contributions are identified by instruments of European origin used to perform cumbia, such as accordions, guitars, and clarinets, as well as by the European forms of notation used in the compositions and arrangements of commercially recorded cumbias. In his groundbreaking book on Colombian popular music, Peter Wade has critiqued such tripartite explanations, because he believes they have encouraged ahistorical and simplistic accounts of how coastal genres developed, constructing them as the "authentic" musical practices of traditional (i.e., presumably unschooled and culturally insulated) black and indigenous musicians while downplaying or ignoring coastal musicians' musical cosmopolitanism and extensive dialogues with contemporary musical trends.[14]

Indeed, in contrast to their counterparts in Colombia's more remote interior regions, the coast's racially mixed population, located at the intersection of the Caribbean and Andean worlds, has always been relatively well connected to developments beyond Colombia, especially to the north. The port city of Barranquilla, until the 1940s second in size only to Bogotá, was particularly progressive, accustomed to the presence of foreigners and the ideals and practices of modernity. The arrival of recording and broadcast technologies to Barranquilla and the nearby port city of Cartagena in the first decades of the twentieth century only accelerated the ongoing circulation of styles from beyond the region. In short, while clearly discernable features of traditional African-derived and indigenous musical practices are present in coastal musics, they have been maintained, as Wade emphasizes, not as a result of isolation or some sort of "innate" conservatism but rather as deliberate choices.[15]

By the first decades of the twentieth century, cumbia was being performed throughout the coastal region, from the more indigenous and mestizo eastern sections to the western sabanas, which had a larger proportion of inhabitants of African descent. Early cumbias were performed by small ensembles consisting of gaita or caña de millo flutes, a variety of single- or double-headed drums,[16] and rattles (*guaches*) or maracas. Over time, cumbia came to be performed on many instruments—from guitars to large wind *orquestas*—but the accordion, which was portable and loud enough for dancing, became favored by rural and urban working-class musicians after the instrument arrived on the northern coast in the 1870s. One of cumbia's most salient characteristics—which distinguished coastal Colombian cumbia (and other related genres of coastal music) from other Spanish Caribbean genres—is its rhythm. A 2/4 meter with the accent on the upbeat of each beat, it is performed on a rasping idiophone, traditionally the bamboo/cane guacharaca but sometimes replaced by a metal güira. This particular rhythm, in which the offbeat is accented, was sometimes vocalized on early recordings as *chiquichá*. (Jorge Arévalo Mateus has diagrammed this rhythm; see Figure 6.1). While cumbias can be slow and melancholic, most of the time their rhythms are lively and danceable, and when sung (some cumbias are

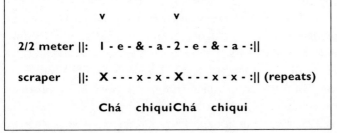

Figure 6.1. Cumbia rhythm diagram. *(Courtesy of Jorge Arévalo Mateus.)*

instrumental), the lyrics have characteristically employed the coast's rich vernacular to humorous effect (in this regard, much like the Cuban *guaracha* and Dominican merengue). Indeed, this quality of being *alegre*, or cheerful (which Wade links to related concepts of optimism and modernity), has contributed greatly to its popularity, not only in Colombia but everywhere it has spread as well.[17]

Although technically cumbia is a distinct rhythm that can be played by any instrument (which, as Héctor Fernández L'Hoeste argues, helps to explain its spread to so many different countries in the Americas),[18] it is often confused by nonspecialists with its proximate genres—gaita, porro, and vallenato—whose aesthetics share some of the same genealogical roots. For example, the porro, another close relative of the cumbia, developed primarily in the coast's western sabanas, emerging from the diverse local repertoires of mixed-race, village brass bands in the nineteenth century; the reedy sound of the clarinets introduced to these bands around 1850, however, point to porro's ancestral connections to indigenous gaita flute ensembles. Cumbia and the similarly upbeat porro were part of the rich musical matrix from which coastal musicians drew inspiration as they modernized their ensembles and repertoires in the early twentieth century, complicating efforts to construct neat, discrete genealogical histories for each of these overlapping styles. The confusion has been compounded by the fact that, even on the coast, cumbias from different microregions could sound quite different from one another. For example, traditional *conjunto de gaita* groups, who generally hailed from those parts of the coast where mestizos predominate, employed two gaita flutes, maracas, and the llamador drum, and their overall sound quality foreground cumbia's indigenous aesthetics. In contrast, the more complex and densely textured rhythms of the *conjunto de cumbia* groups from the areas around Barranquilla and Cartagena were produced by four different drums, guaches, and the caña de millo, producing a more distinctively Afro-Colombian sound.[19]

As Wade observes, between the 1920s and the 1940s, cumbia and porro, which had originated in more provincial areas of the coast, were adopted into the repertoires of the urban wind bands that entertained the cosmopolitan coastal elites, alongside then-popular international styles, such as U.S. fox-trots, Argentine tangos, and Cuban *danzones*. In their instrumentation and aesthetics, these bands were inspired not only by the international "Latin" (mostly Cuban) musics circulating at the time but also by U.S. big bands, such as Benny Goodman's, in which the clarinet was prominent.[20] (The importance of the clarinet distinguished Colombian big bands from most international Latin bands, in which trumpets, saxophones, and trombones were more common.) The most successful bandleaders, such as the Barranquilla-based Lucho Bermúdez and Pacho Galán, were white or light-skinned mestizos, although some of their musicians were darker.[21] Retaining the music's local character by employing the rich costeño vernacular in song lyrics, the sophisticated and modern-sounding arrangements of these band-leaders were highly regarded by coastal elites, who hired them to play in the region's most exclusive venues.

Despite its high-society success, the music of Bermúdez, Galán, and others like them was not limited to the elites; other social sectors consumed it as well via recordings released by costeño recording companies founded in the 1930s (among them the Cartagena-based Discos Fuentes and the Barran-quilla-based Discos Tropical) and disseminated on the coast's numerous radio stations.[22] These pioneering record companies operated in the freewheeling spirit of an emergent industry (much like ethnic recording in the United States in the 1920s; see Chapter 2), recording all sorts of coastal music from the cosmopolitan big bands to traditional flute and drum ensembles and accordion-based groups, all of which were released locally alongside music imported from other Latin American countries, especially Cuba, Mexico, and Argentina, being distributed by these same companies. In short, if cumbias and porros were the most popular and widespread genres of regional origins in those formative decades, they were only two among other local, national, and international styles swirling though the costeño musical landscape.

As Wade has extensively documented, big band–style cumbia and porro began spreading in the 1940s to elite venues in the interior sections of the country, where formerly only "respectable" musics, such as bambucos, pasillos, and Mexican boleros, had been heard. The coastal bandleader credited with popularizing porro and cumbia in the interior was the virtuoso clarinetist Lucho Bermúdez. As the demand for coastal music increased in the interior, other well-known costeño bandleaders, such as Antonio María Peñaloza, relocated to Bogotá, where they found ready work in high-society nightclubs and ballrooms. Many of the musicians hired to perform in these relocated bands were from Colombia's mestizo interior rather than the coast.[23] Ber-múdez retained the rasping sound produced by the guacharaca that was characteristic of cumbia and other coastal genres as well as the 2/4 rhythm with accented upbeats, but he reduced the number of drums, which had the effect of lessening the density of the rhythmic texture. Moreover, the slightly offbeat rhythms that had given coastal music its particular groove were aligned with the rhythms of other instruments, regularizing the rhythms in order to make it easier for highland dancers unfamiliar with coastal poly-rhythms and syncopation.[24]

After succeeding in Colombia's interior, costeño music spread beyond Colombia via recordings. Hit songs such as Bermúdez's "La Múcura" and "Salsipuedes," sung by his smoky-voiced singer and wife Matilde Díaz (a light-skinned mestiza from the interior region of Tolima),[25] generated invitations to perform (and in some cases to record) throughout the Americas, in Argentina, Chile, Ecuador, Cuba, Mexico, and the United States. As the coast's diverse styles began to travel beyond Colombia in the 1940s and 1950s, however, porro and other coastal styles were often subsumed under the term "cumbia" and even more often lumped together under the larger and even less-well-defined category *música tropical,* encouraging slippages between the boundaries of various coastal genres that have persisted to this day.[26] In the wake of cumbia's success beyond Colombia, other costeño bandleaders such as Pacho Galán began touring abroad as well, further familiarizing these styles to audiences throughout Latin America and making música costeña a source of national pride. Elaborating on why Andean Colombians who had long scorned coastal culture as too black, primitive, and plebian not only accepted coastal music but came to perceive it as a representative expression of Colombian national culture, Wade has suggested that big-band versions of música costeña, modeled on Cuban and other Latin American styles popular at the time, articulated Colombia's cosmopolitan modernity on national and international stages but without appearing to merely imitate foreign styles.[27]

As for the coastal vallenato, its origins are similarly located in the region's rich matrix of musical practices—although since it coalesced as a style later in the twentieth century, it is often considered to be an offshoot of cumbia. (Indeed, the geographical and aesthetic proximity of the two genres have produced some interesting overlaps in their international trajectories, which are discussed below.) Vallenato refers to a group of related styles said to originate in the valleys and savannahs of the coastal Valledupar region—hence the meaning of the term "vallenato," "from the valley";[28] the term, then, does not refer to a single rhythm but rather to a group of four rhythms from that region (*son,* paseo, merengue, and *puya*) although vallenato conjuntos often play cumbias as well. Originally referred to collectively as *música provinciana,* or music of the provinces, these styles were initially performed on the guitar and the accordion as well as with gaita flutes and maracas, all of which were also typical of cumbia and other coastal styles. The term "vallenato" to describe a particular genre of music did not come into use until the 1940s, after these regional styles were first recorded and marketed as a distinct genre defined by a particular combination of instruments: an accordion or guitar, *caja* drum, and guacharaca scraper (although other instruments were later added to this basic format).[29] While cumbia became a symbol of modernity after it was urbanized by the big bands, vallenato originated as and remains quintessentially a country music, strongly associated with rural coastal culture. Good accordion or guitar playing was appreciated, but, like the rural

Mexican *corrido,* vallenato was a primarily narrative music, valued for its rich vernacular language and colorful storytelling. It could be danced to, but no specific dance steps were associated with it; even as its rhythms have since become more prominent, vallenato has not been perceived as "dance music" in the same way cumbia and porro have been.

Like other forms of coastal music, each of vallenato's rhythms originated in the coast's rich polyracial musical matrix, expressing the particularities of local coastal locations in different combinations and proportions of African, indigenous, and European influences, layered by subsequent blends of traditional and newer aesthetics. The slow and somewhat melancholic 2/4-meter son, for example, is believed to express stronger indigenous sensibilities, while the more rhythmically complex 6/8-meter merengue, and its call and response between vocalist and chorus, is thought to foreground African influences.[30] As in the case of cumbia and porro, this sort of musical deconstruction provides insights into vallenato's multiple origins, although Wade's cautionary admonitions against unproblematically ascribing certain instruments and musical characteristics to different racial and cultural heritages must always be kept in mind. Moreover, despite the celebratory rhetoric regarding Colombia's cultural mestizaje that accompanied the earlier spread of porros and cumbias to the interior of the country, race- and class-based hierarchies continued to manifest themselves in the material conditions of vallenato's musical production and consumption. The accordion, notwithstanding its European origins, was widely considered to be a plebian instrument, so, as Wade notes, black or mulatto musicians, such as Alejo Durán, who performed vallenatos on the accordion were less successful in the interior than light-skinned musicians, such as Guillermo Buitrago and Julio Bovea, whose vallenatos were performed on guitars.[31]

From Chiquichá to Chucu Chucu: Racial and Aesthetic Considerations

The spread of coastal musics within Colombia in the 1940s and 1950s, and subsequently abroad, could not have happened without substantial efforts on the part of Colombia's music industry. Colombia's first recording companies were founded by costeños in the 1930s; in the 1940s, they began manufacturing records as well, but it did not take long before competitors, especially the famously entrepreneurial paisas from Medellín, emerged in the nation's highland cities. By the early 1950s, Medellín had become Colombia's recording center, and in 1954, even the seminal coastal recording company Discos Fuentes, seeking to position itself closer to the country's burgeoning national

music industry, moved there. Centralizing the industry in Medellín had profound effects on the commercial development of música costeña, because
it privileged the aesthetic preferences of the paisas running much of the
business and those of their highland consumers. Continuing the aesthetic
transformations begun by Bermúdez and other coastal bandleaders who
relocated to the interior, cumbia's original African-derived polyrhythms were
further regularized by the increasing number of paisa and cachaco musicians
recording música tropical in Medellín and Bogotá. Cumbia thus departed
not only from its original tri-ethnic birthplace but also from its signature
"polyrhythmic vigor"[32] as it acquired a more loping and regular 4/4 beat that
brought cumbia more in line with the musical sensibilities of the interior's
mestizo inhabitants. In addition to these rhythmic modifications, interior-
based songwriters abandoned the prominent vernacular orientation characterizing their coastal antecedents and adopted more generic song subjects,
especially love and romance. In an interview with Wade, a Bogotá-based
record company executive reflecting on these changes notes, "The way these
groups presented Costeño music, it was a lot easier to dance to. That is, us
people from the interior are not very good dancers, we don't dance Costeño
music very well. . . . But when new elements were introduced and perhaps
some rhythmic adjustments were made to the music and when the themes
became easier to understand for the people of the interior, I think that all
these things made us, the cachacos as they call us in La Costa, assimilate
this music more easily."[33]

In addition to recording and distributing existing Colombian bands, these
companies often established their own studio bands to increase production.
One of the most important of these was Los Corraleros de Majagual, a group
put together by Antonio Fuentes in the early 1960s that was originally composed of costeño musicians who had been recording cumbias, porros, and
other coastal genres with Fuentes for some time; later, non-costeño musicians were added to the band's roster. As Wade notes, Los Corraleros' most
important innovation was to incorporate new instruments, such as electric
bass, drum kits, or conga drums, with instruments associated with traditional
coastal music—such as the caja drum and, most significantly, the quintessentially working-class accordion—and to combine these with the wind instruments associated with urban *orquestas*. In addition to this instrumental (pun
intended) linking of city to country and traditional to modern, Los Corraleros
also introduced rhythms that had not previously been incorporated into larger
commercial ensembles—the rural paseo and merengue associated with the
accordion-based styles then coalescing as vallenato.[34] The rasping sound and
chiquichá cadence of the guacharaca, however, remained a signature feature
and mechanism for indexing música costeña. The result was a more modern-

ized yet still *típico* (folkloric) sound that appealed to Colombians throughout the country, including audiences in the interior. Los Corraleros then carried this new style abroad, touring successfully in Venezuela, Mexico, and even the United States. The international popularity of Los Corraleros was surpassed by the success of another group created by Discos Fuentes, La Sonora Dinamita, which similarly layered the sounds of modernity over a típico base and became immensely popular in Mexico.[35] Other groups, such as Los Teenagers, modernized their music by combining música tropical with the sounds of rock 'n' roll at a moment when it was sweeping through Latin America.[36]

These Medellín-based música tropical groups and their cumbias, however, did not fare well on the coast, where they were scorned as rhythmically inept and referred to by derogatory terms, such as *música gallega*[37] or *chucu chucu,* the latter a vocalization invoking the music's regular, repetitive rhythms. In the interior, chucu chucu–style cumbias continued to circulate, although without the symbolic resonances of national unity that big band–style cumbias and porros had indexed in the 1940s and 1950s. Record companies also continued to export chucu chucu–flavored cumbias to nations to the north (especially Mexico) and to the south (especially Ecuador and Peru), but they reached as far south as Argentina and Chile. By the 1970s, however, urban costeños had lost interest in the commercial cumbias being churned out of Medellín and Bogotá and instead embraced the Afro-Caribbean salsa that at the time was just beginning to spread throughout the Spanish Caribbean. Vallenato remained popular among rural costeños, but, being primarily narrative rather than rhythm oriented, it could not compete with urban costeños' desires for cosmopolitan and richly syncopated dance music. In Colombia's interior, in contrast, salsa was rejected because of its assertive tropical blackness, although later, after it became a symbol of pan–Latin American solidarity in the 1970s, salsa joined other international styles, such as *balada* (pop ballads) and rock, that were circulating through urban Colombia. Colombian dance-band musicians, who (like their U.S. counterparts) had long been familiar with salsa's antecedent (mostly Cuban) genres, began producing local versions of salsa that competed with the salsa being imported from New York, Puerto Rico, and Venezuela. Barranquilla and Cali, both of which had large black, working-class populations, became particularly active sites of salsa production and vied with one another to be recognized as Colombia's salsa capital.[38]

The salsa craze waned somewhat in the 1980s—challenged, as in the United States, by Dominican merengue—but commercial cumbia never regained its former popularity on the coast. In the 1990s, black Cartagena-born salsa star Joe Arroyo resuscitated cumbia to some extent by incorporating rhythmically dense and highly syncopated cumbias into his repertoires.

Other local revival bands, such as Son Cartagena, similarly generated cumbias with explicitly coastal aesthetics, which included the incorporation of gaita flutes and guache shakers into a big-band lineup. As these efforts demonstrate, some costeños still cherished the folkloric sounds of cumbia costeña, but the contemporary commercial cumbias produced in the interior, mostly for export, were seldom heard on the coast. The coastal vallenato, in contrast, began ascending in popularity in the 1970s, surpassing the sales of Colombia's most popular salsa performers, such as Arroyo and the Cali-based Grupo Niche.

Smaller, more roots-based costeño vallenato ensembles also followed the modernizing trajectory of Los Corraleros de Majagual by incorporating new instruments, such as the electric bass and conga drums, into the traditional lineup, greatly increasing vallenato's commercial appeal throughout Colombia, even among social classes formerly disinclined to embrace such a patently country style of coastal music. Vallenato's popularity was further accelerated when (not without controversy) groups such as El Binomio de Oro moved farther away from a folkloric sound and image toward a more international sound, with clothing styles and formal arrangements more reminiscent of pop salsa bands than grassroots ensembles.[39] In the 1990s, vallenato became even more pop oriented when photogenic young singers, such as Jean Carlos Centeno, who specialized in romantic songs (and correspondingly romantic videos), displaced the master accordionist as the center of attention. The lush strings and synthesizers layered over the once-central sound of the accordion furthered the move toward a pop aesthetic.

Other nonmusical factors intervened in vallenato's change in status as well. In 1967, costeño writer Gabriel García Márquez included famed vallenato composer Rafael Escalona as a character in his novel *One Hundred Years of Solitude* (the only real character to appear with his own name); later, when the book earned García Márquez a Nobel Prize for literature in 1982, he flew vallenato performers to Stockholm for his celebration party. These public displays of appreciation for vallenato as an authentic expression of Colombian regional character gave it a decided boost in status, particularly among intellectuals, artists, and students. It should be noted, however, that vallenato's ascent also owes a debt to less-distinguished supporters: Drug dealers from the eastern coast, enriched by marijuana production and trafficking, are widely believed to have promoted vallenato by using their profits to sponsor bands and their recordings and to ensure that they received airplay.

Unfortunately, the illicit drug business that helped capitalize vallenato's ascent also contributed to a surge of politically motivated violence that, over the next decades, would push hundreds of thousands of Colombians to migrate to the United States, bringing their musical preferences and practices with them. It is important to note that when the Colombian diaspora began to surge in the 1980s and 1990s, cumbia still retained its valence as an authentic form of folklore but was not significant commercially, including in the interior regions that were sending most migrants to the United States; indeed, by then it had lost its status as a symbol of the nation. Salsa remained popular among many urban Colombians, but its quintessentially pan–Spanish Caribbean (and New York) origins prevented it from serving as a uniquely Colombian symbol to nostalgic migrants. Vallenato, in contrast, despite its innovations, remained deeply associated with Colombian vernacular culture, replacing cumbia as the most potent symbol of Colombian national and cultural identity among most immigrants in the United States.

Routes: Cumbia's Mexican Connections

When Colombian immigrants began entering the United States in large numbers in the 1980s, cumbia was part of their cultural baggage, but it had a conspicuously low profile compared to that of vallenato. Paradoxically, cumbia had become Colombia's most internationally successful and well-traveled music, spawning an extraordinary range of musical permutations as it spread throughout the hemisphere. Beginning in the 1960s, cumbia styles, especially those descended from the chucu chucu style produced in Colombia's Andean interior, took root in Ecuador and Peru, eventually becoming closely linked to local cultures and identities in those nations. In Peru, indigenous migrants from the Andean highlands to urban centers combined Colombian cumbia with *huayno,* an older mestizo musical form, producing a new hybrid called *cumbia andina,* or *chicha.*[40] As Peruvian chicha evolved, Afro-Cuban percussion, such as congas, bongos, and timbales, added to the mix of indigenous and mestizo sensibilities. In the 1960s, chicha was further hybridized with elements of rock 'n' roll—for example, the accordion was replaced by the electric guitar, and traps and electric bass were added to the lineup—but it continued to be perceived as a form of tropical music. By the 1980s, thousands of working-class mestizo fans were flocking to dance halls called *chichódromos* on weekends; more recent variants, modernized by synthesizers and electronic percussion, are referred to as *tecnocumbia* (or *technocumbia*).[41]

Farther to the south, in Argentina, Colombian cumbia introduced in the 1960s had, by the 1990s, evolved into a lyrically aggressive variant called *cumbia villera,* associated with unemployed, displaced, and disgruntled urban working-class youths. Cumbia's richest and most complex development, however, has taken place in Mexico, where, since its introduction in the 1950s, it has been incorporated into a wide variety of ensembles, from the accordion-based norteño bands to Sinaloan brass-band *bandas-orquestas* to the more urban rock 'n' roll–inflected groups called *grupos* or *gruperos*. Contemporary cumbia's extraordinary multifaceted profile has led Fernández L'Hoeste to title his pioneering analysis of cumbia's multiple trajectories in Colombia, Argentina, Peru, and Mexico "All Cumbias, the Cumbia."[42]

Colombian cumbia was first popularized in Mexico in the 1940s and 1950s at a moment when big band–based Spanish Caribbean dance musics such as mambos and cha-chas—collectively known in Mexico as música tropical—were at the height of their popularity among urban dancers, in large part because of their perceived associations with Afro-Caribbean tropical festivity. Colombian big band–style cumbias and porros, whether heard on recordings or performed live by touring bandleaders such as Lucho Bermúdez, fit comfortably within the stylistic parameters of the international Latin dance styles then serving as hallmarks of urban Latin/o American cosmopolitan modernity, and they, too, arrived tinged with the exotic allure of Caribbean tropical blackness.[43]

José Juan Olvera, who has explored the proliferation of cumbia styles in Mexico, notes that as early as the 1950s, cumbias and porros were being recorded and performed by Mexican bands specializing in música tropical.[44] The first to incorporate these genres were large urban ensembles from Mexico City and its surrounding areas, inspired by the Colombian big-band sound of Bermúdez and La Sonora Dinamita. Porro faded into the background as the more versatile cumbia was incorporated into a range of instrumental ensembles, but, in the process, cumbia's rhythmic regularity was emphasized to suit local musical preferences. One Mexican observer cited by Olvera described the aesthetics of Mexican cumbia thusly: "Its rhythms without great complications (one-two, both stressed), its elemental melodic lines and harmonies, and the ingenuity of its lyrics . . . introduced a simplification that permitted any fan with minimum preparation to launch themselves in the musical arena."[45] These rhythmically regular cumbias, however, did not disrupt cumbia's associations with tropical blackness in the imaginations of most Mexicans.

As cumbia spread throughout Mexico, local variations began to appear. Some provincial ensembles, for example, could not afford the ten to twelve musicians typical of urban big bands, so they reduced their lineup to five to seven instruments for financial reasons, although they retained their identity as performers of música tropical. In northeastern Mexico, in contrast, where the accordion had long been central to local styles, the more traditional sounds of accordion-based cumbia took root, inspired by the recordings and tours of Los Corraleros de Majagual, who had performed in the Mexico-U.S. border region as early as the mid-1960s (and who continue to be more popular in northern Mexico than in Colombia). Structural commonalities between cumbia and norteño facilitated the adoption of cumbia in northeastern Mexico; as Alissa Simon has noted, "Since the cumbia is generally felt in two (arrangers will use 2/4 meter in their cumbia charts), it was easily adapted to the *norteño* ensembles' repertoire, which is dominated by the Mexican two-step."[46]

Olvera argues that the first accordion-based ensembles to incorporate cumbia were actually those living north of the Mexican border—Texas-based conjuntos El Conjunto Bernal, Valerio Longoria, and others who played border towns, such as Alice, Kingsville, and even San Antonio—and suggests that Mexican musicians learned the new style from them.[47] If tejano musicians were indeed the first to incorporate cumbia into their accordion-based ensembles (and U.S.-based scholars of Texas Mexican music, including Manuel Peña, do not make this claim), cumbia did not become well established in Texas until a decade later, when the musical preferences of the growing numbers of Mexican immigrants began making themselves felt. Instead, musicians from the Mexican side of the border, in the city of Monterrey and its nearby border towns, were responsible for developing the cumbia norteño style and making it the preeminent voice of working-class Mexicans—thousands of whom carried cumbia with them as they migrated to the United States in search of work.[48]

Olvera's analysis of Mexican cumbia styles emphasizes that the development of cumbia in Mexico cannot be separated from two parallel but distinct contextual factors: the rise of rock 'n' roll and the accelerating and expanding immigrant streams into the United States. Cumbia was introduced to Mexico in the 1950s at exactly the same moment rock 'n' roll was arriving from the north, and the subsequent trajectories of these two genres in Mexico became closely entwined. Both musical imports generated excitement in Mexico, although rock 'n' roll, with its assertive antiestablishment ethos, was far more controversial than the festive cumbia, and its fans were initially limited to urban and generally more affluent youths.[49] Some Mexican rock 'n' roll musicians, particularly those from central and southern regions of Mexico, were stimulated by the sounds of Colombian groups such as Los Teenagers, who had added tinges of rock 'n' roll into their music. Their Mexican admirers began incorporating cumbia into what was essentially a rock 'n' roll instrumental lineup—trap drums, electric guitar, bass, and keyboards—but adding cumbia's characteristic accordion and the rasping sound of the guacharaca or güira. The pioneer of this new style of Mexican cumbia was Mike Laure, a rock 'n' roller inspired by La Sonora Dinamita, which became hugely popular in central Mexico in the 1960s. Laure's cumbia and rock 'n' roll fusions were categorized as música tropical, and his numerous hits earned him the sobriquet "El Rey del Trópico."[50] (It is worth noting that Laure's concept of a "tropical" music combining Colombian cumbia and rock 'n' roll, mediated by Mexican sensibilities, was reminiscent of what Peruvian chicha groups were producing at approximately the same time, although the resulting sounds were very different.)

Laure exerted a major influence on Rigo Tovar, a younger Mexican musician whose highly romantic, rock-inflected cumbias made him a major star in the 1970s. Tovar and others like him were classified as gruperos, a loosely defined term derived from *grupo,* or "musical group," that emphasized the importance of the band itself as opposed to ensembles fronted and identified by an individual star. Gruperos, which ranged from large dance bands modeled after those specializing in música tropical and salsa to smaller rock 'n' roll–style ensembles, became ubiquitous in the 1970s. As Helena Simonett has pointed out, gruperos' repertoires were diverse and could include rancheras, baladas, rock, and cumbias, but the overall sound was pop oriented—what she calls a "bubblegum sound"[51]—and their characteristically overwrought romanticism often rendered their music more akin to baladas than to rock 'n' roll.[52]

Interestingly, although rock 'n' roll was embraced most avidly by urbanites in central Mexico, the development of the grupero style was very active in northeastern Mexico, where norteño groups were concurrently incorporating cumbias into accordion-based repertoires.[53] Olvera argues that even the most provincial residents of Mexico's northern border region were exposed to rock 'n' roll earlier and more intensively by the broadcasts that had been emanating from U.S.-owned radio stations located on the Mexican side of the U.S.-Mexican border since the 1930s. Many of these radio stations had immensely powerful transmitters, having been set up just south of the border by U.S. entrepreneurs trying to advertise and to sell medical remedies banned in the United States without being subject to U.S. regulatory agencies, such as the Federal Radio Commission. In the 1950s and 1960s, the musics broadcast by these border radio stations trying to entice U.S. listeners to tune in were R & B and rock 'n' roll.[54] While intended primarily for northern ears, U.S. rock 'n' roll quickly made its way into the repertoires of northern Mexican gruperos, whose styles then spread via their recordings to gruperos in more southerly regions of Mexico. Decades later, grupero pop- and rock 'n' roll–inflected cumbias had become part of Mexican immigrants' cultural baggage.

Mexican migration to the United States has always been steady, but in the wake of the North American Free Trade Agreement (NAFTA), which had the effect of displacing millions of Mexican workers, the Mexican-born population in the United States exploded between 1990 and 2000, increasing 52.9 percent, from 13.5 million to 20.6 million.[55] As the immigrant stream intensified, the wellspring of the Mexican diaspora expanded from the northern regions, which had traditionally sent most immigrants into the United States, into central and southern parts of the country. The string-based musical traditions typical of central and southern Mexico were profoundly different from the accordion-based norteño sound, but, as Olvera notes, migrants from these southerly regions passed through northeastern Mexico on their way to Texas (and beyond), picking up a taste for norteño along the way.[56] Once in the United States, surrounded by other homesick migrants seeking to combat the anxieties of displacement with music firmly anchored in Mexico, the accordion-based sounds of norteño, once associated primarily with northern Mexican working-class culture, became increasingly linked to the migratory experiences of all Mexican immigrants. Although polkas remained a staple of norteño repertoires, cumbia, along with the long-popular corrido, became norteño musicians' preferred idioms. Corridos retained their central role as the vehicle of choice for longer narratives about local concerns, celebrating smugglers' exploits, and lamenting the tribulations of migration, but the festive and humorous cumbia offered listeners a more "modern" and upbeat dance music, displacing (although not eliminating) the more traditional polkas, mazurkas, and schottisches that had once fulfilled this function.

In Texas in the 1960s, accordion-based cumbias were so closely associated with working-class Mexican immigrants that many tejano musicians avoided them, particularly those appealing to assimilating and upwardly mobile Mexican Americans. In the 1970s and 1980s, however, as the number of poor, undocumented Mexican migrants increased exponentially, Texas-based conjuntos hoping to increase record sales and performance opportunities were virtually obligated to incorporate cumbia into their repertoires. In a 1988 interview with Juan Tejeda, pioneering conjunto accordionist Narciso Martínez reflected on the increasing popularity of cumbia in Texas: "Today here . . . they are very enthusiastic about the *cumbia*. There's almost 60, 70 percent more on the side of the *cumbia* than on the polka."[57] Cumbia's reintroduction to Texas was not, however, limited to accordion-based cumbia norteña; as Peña notes, grupos tropicales, such as Rigo Tovar's, became so popular among working-class Mexican immigrants that they "altered the musical culture of Texas Mexicans."[58] In a later interview with Peña, major label producer Cameron Randle confirms the impact of cumbia on Tejano musicians: "The cumbia is an entry. . . . [I]t's not necessarily required for the Tejano world. It *is* required to get beyond Texas. . . . Cumbia's what opened the door for Selena. . . . And it's considered the musical passport to Latin America."[59] (Note: Capitalized, the term "Tejano" describes the eclectic, contemporary regional style of pop- and rock-inflected music produced by artists such as Selena that is popular among bicultural urban Texas Mexicans, contrasting to the more working-class orientation of accordion-based conjunto music.) Indeed, the deceased Tejana star Selena, who grew up a monolingual English speaker and rock 'n' roll fan, did not achieve fame and fortune until she turned to rock- and pop-inflected cumbias characteristic of the grupero sound, although her cumbia arrangements were more polished and eclectic in their sources (including hip-hop and R & B). Selena's cumbias would become closely identified with the Tejano sound that dominated the Texas Mexican musical landscape in the 1980s and 1990s and inspired countless other Texas-based groups that have since embraced cumbia, including her brother Abraham Quintanilla, cofounder of the Latin Grammy–winning group the Kumbia Kings.

In California, Mexican Angelenos, who historically have been more closely linked to developments in Mexico City than their Texas counterparts, would certainly have been familiar with Colombian cumbia when the recordings of internationally successful bandleaders Bermúdez and Galán were introduced to the Latin music mainstream. Historically, however, accordion-based music had not been a fundamental feature of the Mexican Angeleno soundscape, and the accordion, in combination with the cowboy-inspired costumes favored by norteño bands, was perceived as too "country." When the popularity of the norteño group Los Tigres del Norte mushroomed on U.S. soil in 1972, first in Texas and later wherever Mexican immigrants could be found, their stock-in-trade were corridos (many, but not all, of them the drug trade–oriented narcocorridos). But the cumbia norteña was among the boleros, waltzes, and other rhythms long popular among Mexicans that Los Tigres incorporated into their recordings, which helped spread the style to Mexican fans throughout the United States via their multiple platinum-selling records.

Mexican cumbia flowed into the United States in other musical garb as well, carried by immigrants whose preferences for particular styles of cumbia reflected their different regional and class backgrounds. The brass-band bandas-*orquestas* favored by more cosmopolitan urban Mexicans from Sinaloa, for example, had incorporated cumbias as far back as the 1950s and 1960s, when such bandleaders as Ramón López Alvarado and Cruz Lizár-raga were seeking to modernize their sounds. The newer *technobandas,* in contrast, which originated in the states of Jalisco and Nayarit, combined elements from acoustic banda, norteño, and grupero into a tropical-flavored style to which cumbia was central—although it is important to note that technobanda musicians' preferences for cumbias were influenced by the gru-peros rather than by the cumbias played by the elite-oriented urban Sinaloan bandas-*orquestas.*[60] In Los Angeles, technobandas (or tecnobandas) sought to increase their appeal to younger Mexican Angelenos in the 1980s by adding synthesizers and other modern accoutrements, such as smoke machines, light shows, and high-powered sound systems.[61] These technobandas, which were conceptually if not musically akin to Peruvian tecnocumbia, expanded and deepened cumbia's roots in Mexican Los Angeles. It is not surprising, then, that in the mid-1990s, when the multiethnic southern California–based rock fusion group Ozomatli began developing its signature blend of traditional and modern Mexican and Latin American sounds, cumbia rhythms featured prominently.

Another style of Mexican cumbia to arrive in the United States is known as *colombiana,* in which musicians try to replicate the "authentic" Colombian style of commercial cumbias still being exported by the Medellín-based music industry in Colombia. As Olvera notes, these Mexican colombiana groups emphasize their Colombian-ness by giving themselves names such as Los Guacharacos de Colombia (invoking cumbia's signature rasping sound produced by the guacharaca) or Los Nueve de Colombia and by incorporating Colombian place names and vernacular language into their lyrics.[62] Interestingly, cumbia's ascent in Mexico, facilitated by the appeal of its associations with a tropicalized Colombia, has paved the way for increased interest in cumbia's costeño relative, the vallenato. Olvera locates this development in Monterrey, the northeastern Mexican city that had previously nurtured the development of cumbia norteña and grupos.[63]

In the 1990s, Mexican accordionist Celso Piña, who began his career playing norteño, developed a *vallenato colombiana* style after he heard recordings by famed Colombian vallenato accordionists Aníbal Velásquez and Alfredo Gutierrez. Piña gave his group a name that would easily index Colombia— Celso Piña y Su Ronda Bogotá—although his choice of an indexical place name referred to Colombian's highland capital instead of vallenato's coastal birthplace. In 2002, Piña's recording *Barrio Bravo* included collaborations with major Mexican rock and hip-hop groups, Café Tacuba and Control Machete, respectively, who layered the cadences of the U.S. hip-hop then dominating the youth market onto Piña's vallenatos; the album was nominated for a Latin Grammy in the tropical music category.[64] Piña's incursions into the genre and his commercial success boosted vallenato's visibility in Mexico, although it also encouraged slippage in the boundaries between vallenato and cumbia.

Sonideros, mobile sound systems enhanced by high-tech light shows, smoke machines, and sonic special effects,[65] have been another key channel for disseminating cumbia throughout the United States and have been well documented by Cathy Ragland and Helena Simonett.[66] Sonideros, long popular among working-class Mexicans because they provided affordable dance venues with a veneer of modernity and glitz, first originated in Mexico City's poorest sectors around the 1970s and then spread to central and south-central Mexico, where for decades they have been key features of working-class Mexicans' musical life, particularly in the state of Puebla.[67] The music played by sonidero DJs in central Mexico has always been varied but typically has included the tropical-style cumbias recorded by gruperos. When norteño reached more southerly regions of Mexico in the 1980s, the sound of accordion-based cumbia may initially have been unfamiliar, but cumbia rhythms were not. As Mexican immigrants hailing from these central and south-central regions of Mexico fanned out to major cities throughout the United States, sonideros followed in their wake.[68]

The particular style of cumbias played at sonidero dances in the United States varies according to the musical preferences—linked to the regional backgrounds—of each DJ's audience, foregrounding high-tech or traditional aesthetics. The sonideros in Los Angeles observed by Simonett featured tech-nocumbias, which employed keyboard synthesizers rather than accordions. In contrast, the cumbias at sonidero dances observed by Ragland in New York and New Jersey, attended by immigrants from the central Mexican state of Puebla, were "largely instrumental, featuring a rootsy, Colombian vallenato-style sound, based on accordion and *guacharaca* scraper, often with distorted or electronically treated vocals unintelligibly punctuating the repetitive four-beat cumbia rhythm."[69] Ragland goes on to note that these Colombian-style cumbias, which are always recorded by Mexican groups, deliberately differ from commercially produced, mainstream-oriented cumbias and are recorded specifically for these sonidero dances. These various styles of cumbia are by no means the only music played on sonideros, which may also include salsa, rock, balada, and other styles in the course of a dance, but cumbia is at the sonic core of these events. As Simonett notes, "Overall, the sonideros share a common aesthetic that derives from a highly technologically produced music in a steady 4-beat rhythm (cumbia or more precisely Mexican cumbia)."[70]

As the stream of Mexicans to the United States has intensified, cumbia's role in Mexicans' musical imaginary has expanded beyond being simply a common feature of their popular culture, attaining its current valence as a powerful sonic symbol of the Mexican migration experience. The long-popular and indisputably Mexican corridos continue to narrate stories of border crossings in culturally relevant ways, but the humorous and upbeat cumbia, whose lyrics are less likely to articulate such serious subjects as displacement and alienation, has clearly become its rhythm and dance track. Indeed, with the exception of fans of the colombiana-style cumbia, who explicitly celebrate cumbia's Colombian roots, cumbia has become such an entrenched feature of Mexican musical practices that many Mexicans have come to believe that cumbia is of Mexican origin. Given the transformations in Mexican cumbia styles and its central role in contemporary Mexican musical practices, they are not entirely mistaken.

The cumbias circulating in the United States today, however, extend well beyond the already diverse range of Mexican and Colombian cumbias. In other parts of Latin America, cumbia's relationship to internal migration has continued to evolve as people experiencing the impacts of globalization have been drawn into powerful northward international migratory currents, bringing with them their own local versions of cumbia. Peruvian tecnocumbia and its Ecuadorian equivalents are now also circulating within the United States thanks to the growing numbers of immigrants from these Andean countries. Cumbia, which became entrenched in Central America decades ago, has been a feature of Central Americans' musical lives as well, although in the United States—where they have often ended up living side by side with Mexicans in such cities as Los Angeles—their connections to Mexican-style cumbia have been strengthened. Given the extensive interactions between immigrants from various Latin American countries sharing the same workplaces and neighborhoods, coupled with the ease with which cumbia can be reshaped and refashioned by musicians of dramatically different backgrounds and musical sensibilities, distinct national or regional cumbia variants will inevitably be cross-fertilized with one another as well as with other popular music forms circulating in the increasingly rich and complex U.S. Latino musical landscape. The recent incorporation of Puerto Rican reggaeton rhythms into Mexican pop cumbias indicates that this process is already well underway. Mexican rock and pop singer-songwriter Julieta Venegas, for example, employed locally rooted Mexican cumbia aesthetics in her reggaeton-inflected remix of the pop cumbia "Eres Para Mi (Sonidero Nacional Combow Remix)"—"combow" being a variant of "cumbow," a contraction between reggaeton's signature dembow rhythm and cumbia.

It is worth noting that, despite cumbia's extensive movements and commercial success throughout the hemisphere, Mexican cumbias do not seem to have captured the attention of Colombians. This does not mean that the direction of musical flow between Mexico and Colombia has been unidirectional; rather, cumbia has not been the sonic vehicle for such dialogues. As early as the 1930s, Mexican music (especially rancheras) propagated by Mexican films and recordings has been popular among working-class mestizo sectors of the interior of Colombia, spawning the música carrilera (mentioned earlier) in the 1940s. Colombia's urban elites at that time also embraced Mexican music, albeit the more polished versions of boleros and *canciones,* and Mexican-style mariachi ensembles can still be hired in cities and towns throughout the country to entertain at private parties. More recently, Mexican accordion-based narcocorridos have made their way into Colombia's interior regions, where they are listened to by thousands of Colombians who, like many of their Mexican counterparts, survive economically by participating in the illicit drug trade or know someone who does. A major point of connection between Colombia and Mexico appears to be the city of Monterrey, located close to the U.S. border, where smuggling has been a feature of that city's economy since colonial days. Trade connections with Colombia, which include the trafficking of illegal drugs, seem to have facilitated the exchange of accordion-based traditions in both locations.[71] Indeed, as Fernández L'Hoeste notes, colombiana-style cumbia and vallenato were originally associated with a particular subset of Monterrey's social hierarchy: drug dealers and users.[72]

Intriguingly, Mexican narcocorridos have moved into Andean Colombia largely intact, from their musical aesthetics (accordion and bass backed by highly regular rhythms played on trap-drums) down to the cowboy gear characteristically worn by Mexican norteño musicians (Stetson hats, fringed jackets, large silver or gold belt buckles, and cowboy boots) despite the fact that such outfits are not native to Colombia, even among those working in cattle ranching. Known in Colombia as *corridos prohibidos* (forbidden corridos), sound and video recordings are sold in *mercados* and thus are unknown to many Colombians who do not frequent such working-class markets. Many of the songs are direct copies of Mexican hits, although Mexican place names are sometimes changed to Colombian ones; original corridos about successful Colombian smuggling exploits are composed as well.[73] Like their Mexican counterparts, not all Colombian corridos are about drug smuggling; some are trenchant critiques of government corruption and state oppression. Two salient differences separate the Mexican and Colombian narcocorridos, however. First, migration is not a theme in Colombian corridos; and second, although Mexican norteño groups specializing in narcocorridos have included the more festive cumbia in their repertoires for variety, their Colombian counterparts do not favor cumbias.

Colombians and Their Music in the United States

In Colombia, the illicit drug business that accompanied the ascent of vallenato in the 1970s and 1980s, and later introduced Colombians to Mexican corridos prohibidos, was also responsible for creating intolerable levels of violence and social chaos, compelling hundreds of thousands of Colombians to leave their homeland for the United States in the last decades of the twentieth century. The Colombian diaspora contrasted notably to other migratory flows from Latin America not only in the speed of its expansion but in its class and racial composition as well, which, in turn, influenced the nature of the Colombian styles they transplanted to the United States.

The first noticeable ripple of immigration from Colombia, which antedated but set the stage for a later drug violence–related exodus, began during and after the murderous spasm of violence between Liberals and Conservatives known as *La Violencia*, which took over 200,000 lives between 1948 and 1958.[74] Although the socioeconomic backgrounds of these immigrants were diverse, the majority were working-class males from the mountainous interior of the country, where the violence was most intense. They subsequently brought their families to the United States, and by 1967 the number of Colombian immigrants had grown to approximately 32,000.[75] La Violencia subsided in the 1960s but was replaced in the 1970s with a rising tide of bloody conflict between government forces, drug traffickers, left-wing guerillas, and, increasingly in the 1980s, right-wing paramilitary forces. Despite relatively favorable economic conditions in Colombia at the time, the general climate of insecurity began to push Colombians into migration. By 1996, 3 million Colombians—a full 8 percent of that nation's 37 million citizens— had left the country. The tristate region of New York, New Jersey, and Connecticut received the largest number of the 370,000 Colombians counted in the 1990 census—40 percent of the total—followed by Miami (22 percent) and Los Angeles/California (11 percent).[76]

In the mid-1990s, intensifying violence coupled with a not-unrelated economic downturn expanded the number of Colombians joining the exodus: Between 1996 and 2002, over a million Colombians fled their country.[77] Like their predecessors, some sought refuge in Europe or in nearby Latin American countries, such as Venezuela, Ecuador, and Costa Rica, but many Colombians were able to obtain tourist visas to enter the United States and overstayed, increasing the number of Colombians in the United States by 60 percent in less than a decade. This immigrant wave was not only large; it was also socioeconomically diverse, because many of the country's most highly educated and accomplished elites were included in it.[78] Moreover, unlike most previous immigrants, many of whom had come from Colombia's interior regions and settled in the tristate area, this wave included people from throughout Colombia, and more of them settled in South Florida.[79]

Those able to reach the United States in the 1990s, a decade of already record-high levels of immigration from throughout the globe, found themselves less welcomed than those who had arrived earlier; indeed, with rising anxieties regarding the impacts of immigration, U.S. policy-makers were in no mood to facilitate the flow of another group of Latin Americans, particularly one stigmatized by their country's involvement with the international drug trade. Thus, unlike the undocumented Salvadorans who had begun arriving during their (U.S.-supported) civil war in the 1980s and were allowed to stay with Temporary Protected Status (TPS), Colombians found that, notwithstanding similar levels of violence in their homeland, their requests for TPS went unheeded. The result was that a large proportion of Colombian immigrants, including educated professionals, joined the ranks of the undocumented. In 2001, for example, almost half of South Florida's 250,000–350,000 Colombians, many of them from Colombia's middle and upper classes, were believed to be undocumented.[80]

Despite their legal obstacles, Colombians did enjoy the advantages of arriving in the United States at a moment when this country's Latino population was at record high numbers, growing rapidly, and much more internally diverse than in the 1960s and 1970s. Extensive and effective communications networks between the United States and Latin America (e.g., remittance services, accessible and affordable telephone contact, the Internet) were already in place, facilitating the creation of transnational fields allowing Colombians (like the Dominicans discussed in Chapter 5) to easily stay in close touch with kin and culture in the homeland. Well-established Spanish-speaking Latin/o American communities also offered Colombian newcomers an array of culturally appropriate goods and services—such as tropical foods and Spanish-language radio and television—that made it easy for them to maintain their language and culture. Today, Colombians—who now number well over three-quarters of a million[81]—are considered by scholars to be comparable to Dominicans and Salvadorans in their high levels of transnational activity.[82]

Given vallenato's ascending national popularity within Colombia in the 1970s, it is not surprising that it was transplanted in the United States by that decade's wave of Colombian working-class immigrants, particularly in New York and in adjacent areas of New Jersey and Connecticut, where most of them had settled. By the early 1980s, major Colombian vallenato groups, such as Biniomio de Oro, were being invited to perform in New York concerts, although the opening groups were often composed of U.S.-based immigrant musicians.[83] Jorge Arévalo, who conducted a two-year study documenting the activity of vallenato groups in New York City in 1997 and 1998, found that despite being in the minority relative to paisas and cachacos from the highland interior, costeño musicians enjoyed a special status, because they were believed to be uniquely capable of producing a more "authentic" vallenato sound.

Among the groups examined by Arévalo was Los Macondos, one of New York's first vallenato bands, led by Eugenio Ortega, a successful businessman in Bogotá for years (although born on the coast) before immigrating to the United States in 1971. Ortega had picked up the accordion as a hobby in Bogotá, but, within a few years of arriving in New York, he realized that the city's growing Colombian community offered economic opportunities for a vallenato group.[84] The name he gave the group referred to the fictional town featured in García Marquez's novel *One Hundred Years of Solitude,* although for many Colombians, including Ortega, the word "Macondo" has since become a metaphor for the coast and its culture in general and, within the U.S. context, for the Colombian nation as a whole. The group self-identified as a vallenato ensemble and employed vallenato's characteristic instrumentation—accordion, caja, and guacharaca—but they also incorporated cumbias into their repertoires.[85] Although Los Macondos and other groups like them found work in local cultural centers and social clubs, their professional development was hindered by a scarcity of experienced costeño musicians. They also found that New York's Latin music scene was dominated by more well-established nationalities and their musics. As one musician complained to Arévalo, "The opportunities exist, but they don't want to give the musicians a chance because New York is a monopoly of salsa and merengue."[86]

Until the 1990s, vallenato's trajectory within Colombia had been similar to that of other accordion-based musics, Dominican merengue típico and Texas-based conjunto: They had begun as low-status regional styles associated with rural folk; the styles had coalesced into distinct genres when they began to circulate commercially; and, despite their subsequent modernization with new instruments and infusions of nontraditional styles, they had retained their strong symbolic references to "authentic" regional and rural culture. Vallenato, however, benefited from the intervention of a Colombian musician who successfully translated this quintessentially country music into something more palatable to cosmopolitan audiences, much as Juan Luis Guerra had done for bachata in 1990. In 1994, vallenato exploded in the Colombian and international marketplaces when Carlos Vives, a white, middle-class costeño actor turned musician, had a smash hit with his recording *Clásicos de la Provincia,*[87] in which he reinterpreted legendary composer Rafael Escalona's most beloved vallenatos but modernized them with just enough rock and reggae influences (including their signature instrument, the electric guitar) to appeal to urban young people, while maintaining enough of vallenato's original folk aesthetics (especially its prominent accordion) to convey authenticity. Vives further foregrounded his regional roots by reincorporating cumbia into vallenato, adding the gaita flute, traditional cumbia's signature instrument, to his lineup. As Fernández L'Hoeste has noted, "Vives' great innovation was to more thoroughly fuse vallenato and cumbia, or rather to make cumbia's foundations for vallenato more explicit."[88]

It is not uncommon that first-generation immigrants become more receptive to popular music styles from the homeland that before migrating had been ignored or rejected as primitive or vulgar, so it is not surprising that one of Arévalo's narrators notes such a change in his musical practices after migrating to the United States: "When I was in Colombia, I don't think I appreciated vallenato music. . . . But when you're out of the country and you're, for example, in my case in the United States, I realized the value of Colombia . . . and one of them is the music. . . . The receptivity that Colombians here have for vallenato is a hundred percent positive."[89] Another of Arévalo's narrators, referring to Vives, illustrates the importance of vallenato's commercial success in establishing it as an icon of Colombian national culture within the United States: "One can say that vallenato music is the most important music of Colombia, the music that has given Colombia international fame."[90] Maria Elena Cepeda has observed that it is not coincidental that Vives's success happened in the 1990s, at the peak of the Colombian exodus, when so many Colombian immigrants in the United States of all social backgrounds were struggling with the intersecting traumas of violence, cultural dislocation, and the stigma of drug trafficking.[91] Clearly, with the success of *Clásicos de la Provincia* as well as subsequent recordings that similarly drew on vallenato, Vives vindicated the worthiness of Colombians' national culture (and, hence, their character); in doing so, he helped confirm vallenato as a powerful symbol of Colombian identity for Colombian immigrants regardless of their region of origin and class background.

If New York's vallenato scene was firmly rooted in a working-class Colombian community first established in the 1970s, in Miami, which received a larger proportion of the later migration waves, vallenato's circulation has been more recent and more influenced by the rock-tinged versions of vallenato associated with Vives than by more grassroots ensembles such as Los Macondos. Indeed, as a result of the large percentage of middle- and upper-class Colombians in Miami, Colombian music has been transplanted and nurtured in a very different, and in many ways more favorable, environment than in New York. The political and cultural inclinations of the numerically dominant Cubans in Miami exerted a powerful influence on that city's musical landscape (described further in Chapter 7), but, despite the successes of the pop rock "Miami Sound" pioneered by Gloria and Emilio Estefan, Miami was not dominated by a hegemonic style of Latin music (as New York was by salsa, merengue, and bachata), which provided more space for musical newcomers. Miami's Colombian immigrants did include those of both urban and rural working-class origins,[92] whose musical preferences mirrored the styles popular with their black, mulatto, and mestizo working-class cohorts at home—salsa or grassroots-style vallenato. But it was the sensibilities of the large number of young, urban, middle- and upper-class (and often light-skinned) Colombians, who had grown up embedded in a cosmopolitan musical culture that included domestic and international pop and rock, especially *rock en español,* that meshed perfectly with the interests of second- and third-generation Miami Cuban youths in pop and rock, including rock-inflected Latin American styles.[93] The rock- and reggae-tinged vallenatos and cumbias popularized by Vives fit right in.

Fortified by their significant social and cultural (and sometimes, economic) capital, well-educated and well-connected Colombian musicians such as Vives were able to make extraordinary inroads into a music industry dominated by Cuban Americans, especially media mogul Emilio Estefan, who had produced some of the Latin music industry's biggest stars (including Mexican superstars Alejandro Fernández and Thalia). Vives, whose two recordings released after the blockbuster *Clásicos de la Provincia* had not done well, teamed up with Estefan in 1999 to do another vallenato-inspired work, resulting in his hugely successful recording *El Amor de Mi Tierra,* which received a Latin Grammy nomination and several *Billboard* awards.[94] The career of Barranquilla-born Shakira similarly illustrates the powerful convergence of coastal Colombia's urban cosmopolitan (rock-oriented) sensibilities and the Estefan empire. Unlike Vives, however, the music that launched Shakira's career did not foreground her Colombian ethnicity by employing traditional Colombian styles—although later she did incorporate cumbia, salsa, and reggaeton rhythms into her 2006 megahit single "Hips Don't Lie," a remake of Haitian rapper Wyclef Jean's 2004 song "Dance Like This," which she coproduced with Jean. Other Colombian musicians with backgrounds in urban rock and pop were similarly able to establish careers in Miami, particularly those who formed a professional association with Estefan. As Cepeda has argued, these collaborations "Colombianized" Estefan's already successful pan-Latin "Miami sound."[95] Cali-born Kike Santander, for example, who had begun his career in Colombia as a songwriter and producer in 1993, arrived in the United States in 1995 and immediately landed a job as a coproducer and songwriter with Estefan. Santander collaborated on Gloria Estefan's Latin Grammy–winning recording *Abriendo Puertas,* whose songs drew on a variety of Latin American rhythms, including Colombian vallenato, cumbia, and currulao, and employed traditional coastal Colombian instruments, such as the caja drum and the guacharaca scraper.[96] Santander, whose sophisticated arrangements clearly appealed to the growing number of urban cosmopolatinos in the United States who understood and appreciated such musical mixings, similarly incorporated Colombian rhythms into the pop music of such other major Latin American musicians as Mexico's pop star Thalia, becoming what Cepeda calls "the Miami industry's premier hit-making songwriter and top producer."[97]

The Medellín-born Juanes (born Juan Esteban Aristizábal Vásquez) also merits mention as a highly successful Colombian cosmopolatino musician whose musical roots were in rock rather than traditional Colombian musical cultures, but whose career benefited from incorporating cumbia and vallenato aesthetics into his music. Juanes, originally a heavy-metal rocker, launched his career from Los Angeles rather than Miami, signing with noted Argentine producer Gustavo Santaolalla.[98] Juanes's recordings *Fíjate Bien* (2000), *Un Día Normal* (2002), and *Mi Sangre* (2004)[99] were eclectic blends of rock, Colombian coastal cumbia and vallenato as well as the highland working-class *guasca,* and other Latin American rhythms, and his lyrics—always in Spanish—were a mix of love songs and more serious reflections on violence and social injustice. Collectively, Juanes's recordings sold over 5 million copies internationally, while in the United States, his numerous Latin Grammy nominations and awards and sold-out tour dates gained the attention of the mainstream media, who heralded him as responsible for "help[ing] transform conventional Latin music, replacing the tuxedo-wearing crooner who once dominated the industry with the guitar-slinging singer-songwriter weaned on rock and wearing jeans."[100] Indeed, in 2005, Juanes was named by *Time* magazine as one of the one hundred most influential people in the world.

In summary, Colombian music and musicians managed to achieve remarkable success and visibility in the United States within a relatively short period of time. But these widely disseminated sounds have not been the organic voice of a mixed-race, working-class Colombian immigrant community as, for example, salsa was for Puerto Ricans in the 1970s, or bachata and merengue típico were for Dominican immigrants in New York in the 1980s and 1990s. The vallenatos and cumbias introduced to most non-Colombian listeners at the turn of the millennium were not those produced by U.S.-based grassroots ensembles, such as Los Macondos, or even the long-popular Colombia-based Binomio de Oro, who had a large fan base among Mexicans as well; instead, they were rock or rock-tinged interpretations by light-skinned, middle-class, well-educated, musically cosmopolitan Colombian musicians. These Colombian immigrant musicians have been able to parlay their cultural capital and musical compatibilities into access to key Miami-based Latin music business executives seeking "crossover" audiences of urban Latinos throughout the hemisphere. To be sure, as Arévalo's narrators demonstrate, Colombian immigrants of diverse backgrounds are proud of the success of musicians such as Shakira and Vives, but, the cumbias and vallenatos produced by these cosmopolatinos do not express the musical sensibilities and lived experiences of the majority of working-class Colombians at home or in the diaspora—in notable contrast to the cumbias performed by and for working-class Mexican immigrants.

Global Extensions

"Cumbia is arriving from all directions. And leaving." This observation made in 2008 by Jace Clayton (aka DJ Rupture) in the music magazine *Fader* neatly captured the latest phase of cumbia's continuing mobility and mutability as it began appearing more frequently in trendy cosmopolitan and cosmopolatino circuits.[101] In 2007, the Monterrey-based accordionist Celso Piña's "Cumbia Sobre el Rio" appeared on the soundtrack of the film *Babel*, introducing film audiences throughout the globe to Piña's eclectic style. (Interestingly, this song, performed by a Mexican accordionist known for his Colombian-style vallenatos, begins with the refrain *"cumbia colombiana!"*) That same year, a recording entitled "Heater," produced by the Swiss-Iranian DJ Samim, became a major international dance club hit, and its musical core was a sample directly lifted from a decades-old classic Colombian cumbia, "Cumbia Cienaguera," performed by Colombian accordionist Alfredo Pacheco.[102] The imagery of the video for "Heater," however, offered a thoroughly hip and internationalized vision of cumbia rather than one based in a folkloric Colombian (or Mexican) location: It opens with an image of an accordion case covered with baggage stickers moving through airports, followed by multiple shots of youthful dancers and individuals of all ethnicities (mock) playing the accordion, all of them situated in iconically global locations in Asia, Africa, Europe, the United States, and the Caribbean (e.g., downtown Tokyo, New York's Times Square, and the pyramids).[103] The following year, Pacheco's infectious accordion riff was resampled for Jamaican American dancehall artist DJ Shaggy in a soca-flavored version called "Feel the Rush," selected as the official song of the 2008 Euro soccer competition. This song's soccer-themed video, much of it shot in colorful, quintessentially Caribbean Jamaican settings, initially locates the groove in Jamaica, but it is subsequently moved visually across a map (by plane and then hot-air balloon) to the European Alps, the location of the games.[104] As DJ Rupture noted of the spreading cumbia phenomenon, "Cumbia is like 'rock'—it has escaped any retrospective cage of appropriateness and policing of influence; it is massive, fractal, varied."[105]

Despite the seeming novelty of cumbia's appearance in global cosmopolitan and cosmopolatino contexts, this most recent phase of cumbia's international travels began well over a decade ago. Vives's 1994 *Clásicos de la Provincia* clearly played an important role in introducing hip urban audiences to rock-tinged Colombian rhythms, but, as early as the mid-1990s, groups such as the eclectic Los Angeles–based Ozomatli, inspired by local sonorities of Mexican origin, were producing experimental cumbias for fans of diverse and mixed ethnic and racial backgrounds. In 1996, the New York–based Venezuelan and Latin ska band King Changó released an eponymous recording produced by David Byrne's label Luaka Bop that contained a song entitled "Revolution/Cumbia Reggae," which, as its name indicates, is a fusion of cumbia and reggae.[106] (Interestingly, the song includes snippets of the same accordion line from Pacheco's "Cumbia Cienaguera" that was more extensively sampled a decade later by DJs Samim and Shaggy.) That same year, an event called "Festicumex: El Primer Festival de Cumbias Experimentales" was organized in Honduras to celebrate cumbia's transcendence of existing commercial styles and categories. (It was described as an "event that unites friendship, music and new experiments, and that dares to ignore the music industry's laws.")[107]

At the turn of the millennium, the avant-garde Tijuana-based Nortec Collective was garnering attention from electronica fans throughout the globe for their combinations of the sounds and sensibilities of European electronica with the sounds of norteño, including its signature cumbia rhythms.[108] More recently, Argentina has become the source for experimental cumbias called *nueva cumbias* (new cumbias), based on the cumbia villeras that had been popular in that country's poor and working-class neighborhoods since the 1990s. Produced in trendy urban dance clubs, such as Zizek (named after Yugoslavian-born philosopher and cultural critic Slavoj Zizek), by local Buenos Aires DJs, these cumbias were thoroughly eclectic and self-consciously hybrid: As one DJ remarked, "When they ask me what type of music I play, I say bastard pop. It's not hip-hop, not electronica, not cumbia. It's more of a way of dealing with the music."[109] The cumbias created by Zizek's producers have been much remarked upon in blogs and online magazines, and their performances on their 2007 and 2008 international tours have drawn enthusiastic audiences of all ethnic, racial, and class backgrounds.[110] As one blogger noted, "Young but influential latino [sic] producers are rediscovering traditional cumbia songs, and mixing them up with all kinds of modern influences—from crazy electronics to hiphop [sic] beats, even dancehall. As long as it's rhythmic and mixable!"[111] Hip non-Latino musicians are also picking up on cumbia's possibilities for experimentation, such as the Brooklyn-based Chicha Libre, inspired, as the name indicates, by Peru's variant of cumbia.[112]

As cumbia moves beyond the confines of solidly working-class mestizo contexts into cosmopolitan and cosmopolatino dance-oriented settings around the globe, its already complicated genealogy and racial and cultural associations continue to shift, to twist, and to turn. Cumbia's original Afro-Colombian and Afro-Caribbean rhythmic sensibilities, for example, which were deemphasized in most Mexican-style cumbias, are being reemphasized in songs and videos such as DJ Samim's "Heater" and Shaggy's "Feel the

Move." More problematically, they are also being retropicalized with images of black festivity unconnected to any particular community and accessible to everyone around the globe. Cumbia's current novelty as a global viral phenomenon, of course, might not last long, and these changes in emphasis and iconography may be transient. If history can serve as an indicator of future trends, however, it seems quite certain that cumbia will remain deeply embedded in multiple working-class communities throughout the Americas, each characterized by its own distinct histories of migration and racial, ethnic, and class associations.

Final Reflections on Cumbia, Migration, Hybridity, and Identity

Given the complicated intersections between the musical practices and migrations of Colombians and Mexicans (and other Latin Americans) in recent decades, what conclusions can be drawn about the relationship between the movement of people and the movement of music—and, by extension, the relationship between migration, musical change, and identity? This final section explores a few salient issues raised by cumbia's long history of travel and transformation in the Americas and how these changes have been interpreted by musicians and fans as well as by scholars and other cultural observers.

Since migrants typically introduce musical practices from their homelands to their host societies, music and migration are generally directly linked. The literature is full of accounts of the many ways migrants use and transform their musics in new settings: as a link to home, as a form of cultural resistance, as a way of negotiating emergent identities, as a way of strengthening ethnic, racial, or class solidarities, and so on. Sometimes, however, musical genres move unaccompanied by migratory movements, as in the case of rock and hip-hop's global diffusion; the spread of cumbia to Mexico, Central, and South America; and the more recent movement of Mexican narcocorridos to Colombia. Musical dissemination disconnected from migratory flows has often been attributed to U.S. cultural and economic imperialism, whose internal logic demands creating new markets for its products by spreading (or imposing) them as widely as possible and, by extension, making U.S. popular culture hegemonic. But unlike rock 'n' roll and hip-hop's diffusion to all parts of the globe, cumbia's early movements throughout Latin America cannot be credited to a powerful U.S. music industry and its international subsidiaries. On the contrary, the Colombian cumbias that spread throughout the Americas in the 1960s were produced by relatively small Colombian record

.npanies such as Discos Fuentes. Eventually, domestic music industries in Mexico, Peru, Ecuador, Argentina, and other Latin American countries began recording and promoting their own local cumbia productions, but none of these enterprises had anywhere near the resources and international reach generally employed to explain the global diffusion of rock and hip-hop. Other Latin American musics, such as Mexican ranchera and Cuban son, have also circulated throughout the hemisphere without relying on the backing of a U.S.-based international music industry, but, with the arguable exception of salsa (first disseminated by the New York–based Fania label; see Chapter 2), none of these genres has spawned a range of distinct and locally entrenched offspring comparable to that of cumbia.

A related distinction between cumbia and other forms of traveling musics concerns cumbia's relationship to globalization. The diverse styles of Mexican cumbia now circulating within the United States are undeniably here because of economic globalization, as working-class Mexicans adversely affected by NAFTA and other globalizing processes (such as competition from cheap Chinese exports) have been streaming into the United States in search of employment and a future for their children. A similar analysis could be applied to the cumbias brought in by Colombian and Peruvian immigrants as a result of the international drug business that has generated much (although not all) of the violence that stimulated their diasporas. But cumbia's travels and permutations, which began in the 1950s and 1960s, were well underway before the impacts of globalization became widely felt in Latin America. In other words, if cumbia has migrated and resettled widely in Latin America, economic factors must be taken into consideration, but they alone do not suffice: Cultural explanations must also be taken into account.

The racial formations and imaginaries characterizing each of cumbia's relocations are particularly useful places to begin considering the cultural significance of cumbia's spread throughout the hemisphere. Wade and Fernández L'Hoeste have employed the lens of race to explain the spread of the tri-ethnic cumbia in and beyond Colombia, analyzing how cumbia's multiple roots in African, European, and indigenous cultural practices have been interpreted and manipulated by music industry personnel as well as by musicians and fans. In doing so, these scholars have challenged Latin Americans' celebration of their mestizaje because of the way this concept has historically been employed to subordinate and marginalize black and indigenous people and their cultural practices. As I discuss above (and in Chapter 1), for example, Wade argues that elite Colombians seeking to shape and to impose a unified national culture on a country deeply divided by geocultural differences employed stereotypical images of blackness that correlated cumbia and porro with tropical festivity and sensuality, while refusing to change the fundamental social relations that kept black Colombians disenfranchised and mired in poverty. Similar associations of blackness with festivity followed cumbia as it traveled north to Mexico and south to Ecuador, Peru, and Argentina, where, at least initially, it was received as an attractive novelty. Although these associations have persisted—Mexican cumbia, for example, is typically characterized by humorous, upbeat lyrics, while more serious subjects are articulated through corridos—cumbia's symbolic resonances have expanded well beyond notions of (black) tropical festivity. In many parts of Latin America, contemporary cumbia has instead become the voice of working-class people, especially migrants—most of whom are mestizos rather than Afrodescendants.

How do we interpret the significance of cumbia's shift away from its original tri-ethnic cultural matrix in coastal Colombia to its current associations with mestizo working-class people in the Americas? Historically, many Latin American mestizos have willfully ignored the cultural (and biological) legacies of the much larger number of blacks once residing in now predominantly mestizo parts of Latin America, such as Mexico City and Buenos Aires; by locating blackness in Caribbean tropical musics rather than their own musical practices, they disavow their own complicated histories of racial mixture. While it is important to recognize these historical realities, contemporary Mexican cumbia's association with blackness should not be overemphasized, because aesthetically Mexican cumbia has evolved into a musical style no longer characterized by one of the primary organizing principles of African-derived music—syncopated polyrhythms—but rather by its regular beats, foregrounded by the rasping sound of the indigenous ideophone, the guacharaca. Indeed, virtually all the scholarly literature on cumbia makes note of cumbia's rhythmic changes as it was adopted first in Colombia's mostly mestizo interior regions and later in other predominantly mestizo regions of Latin America.

The word most often used to describe these rhythmic changes in cumbia is "simplified." In Colombia, the term "simplified" has served as a veiled critique of the rhythmic changes made to cumbia as it was "whitened" in order to appeal to cachaco, paisa, and other audiences in Colombia's highland interior regions, but it has also been used to describe similar rhythmic changes in Mexico. This term is problematic, however, because it invokes cultural assumptions and valuations that the authors do not necessarily intend but that are latent in an implied binary—simple/complex—in which "complex" suggests a more advanced and sophisticated form of development. The term "regular," in contrast, does not similarly imply lack of development or complexity but rather a different organizing principle more characteristic of indigenous musical practices, which may have carried over into contemporary musics in similar ways that African-derived syncopation is widely recognized as doing. European musical sensibilities could also be said to include a preference for regular beats, but, given the ubiquity of European influences throughout Latin America, including regions where Afrodescendants predominate, they do not adequately account for the rhythmic changes in cumbia as it moved beyond Colombia. In the Spanish Caribbean, in contrast, where African-derived aesthetics have always been stronger, cumbia has not been comparably adopted and resignified as an identifiably local expression as it has been in Mexico or Peru. Recent fusions of reggaeton and cumbia by the likes of Calle 13 (e.g., in "Atrévete-te-te" and "Cumbia de los Aburridos") more likely represent attempts to infuse reggaeton with novelty (and, in the latter case, with humorous references to working-class Mexican immigrants) rather than a signal of a new Spanish Caribbean style of cumbia grounded in local grassroots culture.

It is also worth noting that the distinct aesthetic sensibilities characteristic of tri-ethnic and mestizo musics in Colombia have been quite apparent to citizens of that nation, although, because these differences (like other differences, such as skin color) have historically been valued hierarchically, they have often been perceived and described in racist as well as racial terms. An example can be found in the recollections of the dark-skinned costeño musician Antonio María Peñaloza quoted by Wade, in which Peñaloza describes how in 1940 a musician from Bogotá responded when Peñaloza suggested making changes to a bambuco: "Listen *negrito,* you should know that in order to play bambuco you have to eat *chunchullo, sobrebarriga,* and chicha."[113] Wade observes, "His [Peñaloza's critic's] implication was that to have the embodied capacity to play the music correctly, a person had to have physically absorbed the characteristics of its region of origin. . . . All of these had their racial associations: the highlands, with its food, music and people, were non-black, the coast black." In other words, Peñaloza, whose coastal cultural practices did not include eating foods and drinks of indigenous origins, such as chunchullo and chicha, that were characteristic of the mestizo highlands, was believed to be incapable of understanding bambuco's aesthetics.[114] The mestizo bandleader's churlish attempt to put Peñaloza in his place for having the audacity to question him clearly revealed his racist attitudes toward a dark-skinned costeño, but his belief that costeños and cachacos have different aesthetic sensibilities is simply the flip side of similar sentiments regarding racially inflected aesthetic differences underlying costeños' disparaging terms—música gallega and chucu chucu—for the unsyncopated cumbias produced by mestizos in the interior. The value placed on costeño musicians by New York–based vallenato groups similarly expresses such beliefs, as does Mexicans' belief in the greater "authenticity" of cumbias produced in Colombia.

I am not advocating an essentialist view that only triethnic costeños are capable of producing *real* cumbia. Some cumbias performed by Mexicans (or other nationalities) may be indistinguishable from cumbias produced by costeños, just as African American or Latin/o American music performed by non–African Americans or non-Latinos can be indistinguishable from that produced by African Americans and Latinos themselves. Moreover, it would be simply wrong to suggest that African-derived aesthetics are entirely absent in highland Colombian, Mexican, Peruvian, and Ecuadorian cumbias. Rather, I observe that essentialist ideas about the relationship between race and culture in Latin/o America, which (as I discuss in Chapter 1) go back centuries, are still widely held, and still influence the way different styles of cumbia have been received and interpreted in different locations.

A related point, regarding the way valences are ascribed to the constituent parts of hybrid musical aesthetics and practices, is that scholars have long acknowledged and extensively documented the influence of African organizing principles in the trajectories of aesthetically mixed Afro-Latin musics of all sorts, but the indigenous organizing principles that just as surely have shaped musics associated with mestizos, including Mexican-style cumbias, have not received comparable attention. (Indigenous influences have been acknowledged more widely in Peruvian chicha.)[115] Although there may be good explanations for why one ancestral organizing principle and not another predominates in a particular style of music or why one cultural heritage might be more influential than others present at the same time and place, these questions have not yet been fully explored. In the absence of more systematic analyses of this question by trained musicologists, I can only speculate that at least some of the transformations in the sounds of cumbia as it traveled throughout working-class sectors of the Americas, as well as its persistent popularity in so many different locations, might be attributed to organizing principles and aesthetic sensibilities deriving from Latin/o American mestizo communities' indigenous cultural heritage.

7

Marketing *Latinidad* in a Global Era

When immigration from Latin America to the United States exploded in the 1980s and 1990s, music industry personnel in the United States began to listen: Realizing that far-reaching demographic and cultural shifts were permanently transforming the U.S. popular music landscape, they needed to find out how to profit from these changes. In 1999, the Recording Industry Association of America (RIAA) commissioned a study of Hispanic music consumers, "because our Latin labels wanted a meticulous profile of Hispanic consumers of music." The study, which employed the term "Hispanic" in order to differentiate them from Latin American *latinos,* concluded that, "not surprisingly, Hispanic consumers are also purchasers of English language music," and that, although their favorite genre was Latin, they also consumed hip-hop, pop, and R & B."[1] To anyone familiar with the half-century of U.S. Latino rock 'n' roll, disco, freestyle, hip-hop, and other blended styles that had been produced since the 1950s, nothing was new in this description of Latinos' linguistic and musical fluidity.

As discussed in Chapter 2, in the 1960s, the major record companies (Sony, Warner, Universal, EMI, and BMG) began losing interest in Latin music when its profitability was dwarfed by the rising tide of rock 'n' roll. In the 1990s, in response to changing demographics driven by high rates of immigration, the majors established new Latin music divisions, whose purpose was to prepare for and to profit by the changes brewing in the popular music marketplace. The conceptual underpinnings of these Latin music divisions, however, were unclear and unstable from the start, as they targeted groups of consumers with profoundly different cultural preferences and outlooks: well-established bicultural and often (but not necessarily) bilingual U.S.-born Latinos; monolingual new immigrants from Latin America; Latin American nationals in their home countries (confusingly referred to in Spanish shorthand as *latinos*); and, it was hoped, non–Latino consumers in the United States who might once again be enticed into crossing aesthetic and linguistic boundaries, as had occurred during the mambo boom of the 1940s.[2] The distinctions between these groups, in particular U.S.-born Latinos and new immigrants from Latin America, were as elusive as they were perplexing. Moreover, the increasing number of Latino children born to parents of more than one national, ethnic, and racial background has further blurred and destabilized the boundaries between Latino groups (e.g., Mexicans and Puerto Ricans) formerly perceived to be culturally homogeneous. As *Billboard* acknowledged in its end-of-year summary of trends in 2004, "OK. The new Latino generation is out there. It primarily speaks English but supposedly 'feels' Latin (according to many published studies). Why then, isn't it buying the alternative, edgier Latin music that should appeal to it? Perhaps because it's in Spanish. Whoever resolves this riddle will make a bundle."[3]

To a music industry that had historically constructed its marketing categories on assumed racial and cultural essentialisms, these new demographic and cultural mixings and layerings represented profound challenges as well as opportunities. The industry's responses as it attempted to position itself to "make a bundle" from the promises of an expanding and increasingly globalized popular music landscape, and the corresponding responses of U.S. Latino musicians and fans, are the subject of this chapter. My analysis begins, however, a decade before the demographic and cultural impacts of spiking immigration rates had made themselves fully felt, although the impact of economic and cultural globalization was already becoming audible on the U.S. musical landscape as "world beat." Not surprisingly, the vexing location of U.S. Latinos within the United States' long-standing racial imaginaries profoundly shaped the outcome.

Latino Music in (and out of) the International World Beat Industry

In the early 1980s, the global circulation of so-called "world beat" musics originating in economically underdeveloped but musically rich regions beyond the Anglophone U.S. and U.K. orbit brought an array of new artists and styles into the U.S. popular music arena. "World beat" was an industry term for the highly hybridized products of cross-fertilization between third-world aesthetics and first-world technologies and styles, particularly R & B, funk, and rock. Unlike the more geographically inclusive and folk-oriented category of "world music," world beat musics were intended for urban dance floors, and most of them were being produced in areas where highly syncopated percussion has been most consistently and successfully cultivated over time—Africa and its diaspora. At the same time that world beat groups such as Nigeria's King Sunny Adé and Fela Kuti were attracting the attention of U.S. audiences, U.S. rock musicians such as David Byrne and Paul Simon also began introducing African and Afro–Latin American sonorities into their music.

While the increasing circulation of world beat musics within the United States was made possible by economic and cultural globalization, these musical developments were not directly tied to immigration, as world beat's primary promoters and consumers were not from the musics' various regions of origin but rather members of the better-educated, primarily white, middle-class U.S. (and European) sectors. Many world beat performers hailed from non-English-speaking nations, so their lyrics were not responsible for their appeal: What mattered were their highly danceable rhythms. This is not to say that world beat performers were apolitical—some, such as Fela Kuti and Haiti's Boukman Experyans, were active in antiracist movements and liberation struggles in their homelands—but what caught the attention of mainstream consumers throughout the developed world were their fresh and innovative sonorities. The images of exotic difference perceived by world beat audiences also offered alternative constructions of blackness more palatable to the eyes and ears of consumers uncomfortable with the aggressiveness of the urban African American hip-hop then in ascent.

The new aesthetic and commercial spaces created by the fledgling world beat industry in the 1980s made non-English-language dance music viable for the first time since Latin music had declined and then virtually disappeared from the mainstream popular music landscape in the 1960s and 1970s. The salsa and merengue being produced in New York and the Spanish Caribbean in the 1970s and 1980s, respectively, were aesthetically analogous to other world beat musics: They were sophisticated, modern, mass-mediated dance musics underpinned by complex rhythms originating in Afro-Caribbean traditions. Nonetheless, one of the more curious features of salsa's meteoric rise in the 1970s and merengue's in the 1980s was that, despite their remarkable success among U.S. Latinos and throughout Latin America, they were largely ignored by the world beat industry and its consumers.[4] The world beat–oriented *Beat* magazine, for example, which included regular columns on African, Brazilian, and Haitian musics, rarely even mentioned salsa or merengue, nor were these genres heard on world music radio shows or invited to the stages of world-music festivals.[5]

The invisibility of Spanish Caribbean musics in the U.S. world beat arena in the 1980s can be attributed to the racial imaginaries of both mainstream and Latino musicians and audiences. Despite their clearly African-derived percussion sections, salsa and merengue in the 1980s lacked the explicit references to African roots foregrounded by most world beat groups (e.g., dreadlocks and brightly colored African or African-inspired clothing) and therefore failed to meet northern expectations of racial authenticity. The fact that many salsa and merengue performers were light- or white-skinned and dressed in elegant suits visually conveyed and confirmed the identification of these musics as "not black." More importantly, since the 1960s, Spanish Caribbean Latinos (especially Puerto Ricans) had been routinely stereotyped in the media as greasers or gangsters, and their culture was depicted as flashy and vulgar—that is, manufactured rather than authentic (the quintessential example being the Puerto Rican gang members in *West Side Story*). In Europe, which had not received major waves of Spanish Caribbean immigrants, salsa and merengue were incorporated into world beat networks, but in the United States, where these musics were associated with a racially and culturally ambiguous population whose rapid growth was creating anxieties among their non-Latino neighbors, salsa and merengue remained confined within the Latino-oriented music-industry circuits described in Chapter 2.

The conflicts and contradictions produced by a U.S. music industry structured on essentialist notions of ethnicity and race were dramatized in the 1985 film *Crossover Dreams,* directed by Cuban American filmmaker Leon Ichaso and starring *salsero* Rubén Blades. The film narrates the story of a fictional New York salsa musician, Rudy Veloz, who fleetingly achieves mainstream success after abandoning salsa aesthetics in favor of a more eclectic and world beat–inflected style. (These changes are represented cinematically when Rudy replaces his original Puerto Rican trumpet player with a non-Latino saxophone player and his dress suits with colorful flowered shirts and casual pants more characteristic of the tropical imagery found on world beat CDs.) Despite being fully bilingual, bicultural, and bimusical (Rudy's record collection pointedly contains rock 'n' roll records), he is unable to sustain his mainstream success and ends up returning to the barrio and his musical roots, a culturally wiser, if economically poorer, man. While the primary theme of *Crossover Dreams* was the importance of maintaining connections to one's ethnic community and cultural identity, it raises the question of why Rudy believes he has to alter his musical and performance style at all to gain mainstream acceptance at a time when so many non-Latino consumers were favorably disposed to dance musics of diasporic origins.

As Rudy's ambitions suggest, New York Latino musicians, mindful of the successes of their predecessors during the Latin music and mambo boom in the 1940s and 1950s, were well aware of the economic benefits of "crossing over" to wider audiences—as well as its dangers. Indeed, Spanish Caribbean musics were already circulating within a well-established and self-contained Latino-owned music industry (described in Chapter 2). From the perspective of Latinos attempting to control the production and marketing of their own cultural resources, it may have been more advantageous to maintain distance between their own well-defined musical domain and the ethnically and racially diffuse domain of world beat, particularly since it was so closely associated with and dominated by non-Latinos.

Spanish Caribbean music's uneasy relationship to world beat can also be attributed to the region's history of ambivalence toward its own darker-skinned population, making participation in the explicitly racialized world beat arena less attractive to Latino audiences. Indeed, even salsa was initially rejected among elite and middle-class Puerto Ricans and other Latin Americans because of its associations with prominent black working-class aesthetics. If world beat promoters were relying on exotic images of black diasporic authenticity to market their music, the increasingly internationally oriented Latin music industry in the 1980s, aware of the cultural preferences and social aspirations of its own middle-class consumers, was promoting images of a whiter, culturally homogenized pan-Latino identity.

In the 1990s, the boundaries between the domains of Latin music and world beat became more permeable, due in large part to the reappearance of Cuban music in the United States after decades of exclusion. Afro-Cuban music, the aesthetic backbone of mambo, cha-cha, and then salsa, had all but disappeared from the mainstream arena after the 1960s thanks to the Cold War barriers impeding the free flow of people and culture from Cuba (although Cuban aesthetics continued to infuse some R & B and rock 'n' roll throughout the 1950s and 1960s).[6] When restrictions on the exchange of cultural materials between the United States and Cuba were temporarily relaxed in the early 1990s, Cuban dance musics reentered the U.S. marketplace—but not, as might have been expected, via Latin music industry networks. Instead, the U.S.-based Latin music industry declined to promote music from Cuba. This resistance to Cuban music can be partly credited to the political passions of anti-Castro Cuban Americans, who at the time were becoming increasingly influential in the Latin music industry as it began relocating to Miami and who refused to promote any music originating on the island while Castro was still in power. But New York–based Latin music industry personnel have also been accused (by island-based Cubans) of deliberately ignoring Cuban music in order to protect their domestic Latino musicians from competition.

The outcome of these intersecting ethnic, racial, economic, and political realities was that, when Cuban music began trickling into the United States in the 1980s and then flowing in the 1990s, it did not enter via Latino-owned industry circuits; instead, it was diverted into the domain of world beat labels, such as Ned Sublette's Qbadisc, David Byrne's Luaka Bop, and Island Records' imprint Mango, whose audiences were attracted to Cuban music precisely because of the degree to which its Afro-Cuban aesthetics were foregrounded.[7] Mainstream interest in Afro-Cuban music culminated in 1997 with the wildly successful release of the Ry Cooder–produced CD *The Buena Vista Social Club*[8] and the subsequent 1999 film of the same name by Wim Wenders. Throughout the 1980s, then, New York's Latin music scene remained largely independent from and marginal to the world beat and mainstream music industries. It should be noted, however, that world beat and Latin music did intersect aesthetically within Latin America, where various diasporic musics were increasingly being drawn upon by (often non-Afrodescendant) musicians eager to experiment with the vibrant musical resources then in circulation—and also interested, no doubt, in gaining access to the northern world beat marketplace. The Dominican Republic's Juan Luis Guerra and Colombia's Carlos Vives, for example, ventured well beyond the formerly well-defined boundaries of Latin musics, such as merengue, salsa, and vallenato, hybridizing them with diasporic genres from Africa and the English and French Caribbean and stimulating another round of musical exchange and another layer of Latin/o American musical hybridity.[9]

The 1990s and Beyond: The Impact of Immigration on the Latin Music Industry

In the 1980s alone, the U.S. Latino population increased by 53 percent, propelling the annual growth of Latin music to more than 20 percent annually. By this time, several subcategories were recognized by the music industry, including tropical (salsa, merengue, and bachata), regional Mexican and Tejano, and Spanish-language rock and pop. Nationally, over half the sales of Latin music were regional Mexican styles that appealed to the proportionately larger Mexican and Mexican American market, although tropical Latin still represented a healthy 23 percent.[10] Despite the promising numbers, the mainstream music industry exhibited little interest in Latin musics; as producer Ralph Mercado recalls of this period, "When it came to getting major record labels to sign these artists, forget it. . . . They didn't think there was a Latin market. Or if they did, they didn't know how to treat the artists."[11] Nevertheless, the decade witnessed the germination of seeds that would burst into florescence in the 1990s; some of these seeds were demographic, some were economic, and some were cultural.

Frustrated with his inability to get his artists signed to labels with promotional clout and national distribution, Mercado founded his own label, RMM Records, in 1986. He already owned a major management company with a roster containing the country's top Spanish Caribbean artists, a concert production company, and a number of smaller related enterprises, such as a film company and nightclubs, making Mercado uniquely situated to promote his artists. More importantly, he was fully bicultural and open to musical innovations of all sorts, even if it meant going beyond what had formerly been considered Latin music. Mercado was the New York–born son of a Dominican dockworker and Puerto Rican factory worker, who had grown up listening to salsa and merengue, but, having promoted the likes of James Brown and the Temptations, he was also familiar with the African American musical arena. Recognizing the economic potential of the diversifying U.S. Latino population, he actively produced and promoted merengue as well as salsa, even putting merengue bands on the stages of his annual Madison Square Garden Salsa Festival.[12]

Well attuned to the aesthetic sensibilities of young bicultural Latinos, Mercado also hired producer Sergio George, one of the pioneering innovators in the bilingual, bicultural Latin freestyle music genre described in Chapter 4. Unlike the more roots-oriented salsa that made Fania famous, the salsa produced by George with former freestyle musicians such as La India and Marc Anthony was a more deliberately cross-cultural, sometimes bilingual salsa, which music critic Peter Watrous describes as "more inclusive and more representative of the hybrid lives most of its consumers lead, part in the Hispanic world, part in the international world of New York."[13] Other innovative groups produced by RMM included the salsa-rap group DLG (Dark Latin Groove, discussed in previous chapters). Mercado's attention to the nuances of the domestic market paid off: If initially RMM's sales were stronger in Latin America (80 percent of its revenues in 1991), by the end of the 1990s, most of its sales were from within the United States.[14]

In the early 1990s, Latin music began to resurface on the radar screens of the mainstream music industry—but, unlike in the 1940s, this time its perceived market strength was based not on crossing over to non-Latino audiences but rather on the sheer numbers of U.S. Latino consumers nationwide. Recognizing the potential of the growing U.S. Latino market, the major recording companies—Sony, Warner, Universal, EMI, and BMG—established Latin music divisions. (Interestingly, these divisions sometimes employed the English term "Latin," as in EMI Latin or BMG U.S. Latin, and sometimes its Spanish equivalent "latino," as in WEA Latina and Universal Music Latino.) Although based in the United States, these divisions were designed to simultaneously promote Latin music domestically (within the

United States), south into Latin America, and to other regions of the globe, especially wealthy ones such as Western Europe and Japan, where Latin music has always had an audience. For years, Mercado's RMM held its own, accounting for 40 percent of all tropical music sales in the United States in 1998.[15] The remaining 60 percent, however, were primarily the products of the major labels. With the entrance of these powerful players into the Spanish Caribbean Latino music arena, RMM began losing its dominance; in 1998, Mercado told the *Miami Herald* he was considering selling off some of his assets: "Right now I'm in competition with all the major labels because suddenly everyone is interested in tropical music. . . . And we're competing with deep pockets."[16]

Ironically, what brought Mercado's RMM to its knees was not competition from the majors but the unanticipated outcome of a project in which he attempted the culturally significant but politically risky move of reconnecting New York and Puerto Rican salsa with its Cuban roots. In 1996, RMM Filmworks released a feature-length documentary called *Yo Soy, del Son a la Salsa,* which included interviews and performance footage filmed in New York, Puerto Rico, and Cuba—the latter guaranteed to outrage anti-Castro Miami Cubans. Amazingly, despite her persistent and vocal anti-Castro sentiments, salsa diva Celia Cruz agreed to participate, and her interviews appeared side by side with interviews of Cuban-based musicians. The film opened to critical acclaim in New York and Canada[17] but was quickly pulled from circulation when Puerto Rican composer Glenn Monroig sued RMM for changing the lyrics to his song "Yo Soy" and including it in the film without his permission. In 2000, Monroig won the suit and received an award of $7.7 million, the largest award ever associated with a tropical Latin song.[18] Mercado declared bankruptcy and was forced to begin selling off his assets. In 2005, after receiving bids from Sony Discos and Universal Music, his entire back catalogue was sold to Universal Music.[19] That same year, Fania's back catalogue (which included recordings from the influential Tico, Alegre, and Cotique labels discussed in Chapter 2) was also sold to a Miami-based company, Emusica.[20] Spanish Caribbean Latino musics continue to be produced in New York, but, with Miami emerging as the capital of the Latin/o American entertainment and media industries, New York lost its long-standing position as the undisputed center of the Latin music industry.

Spanish Caribbean tropical music, which had long been perceived as practically synonymous with Latin dance music and as the core of the Latin music industry, also lost its position of centrality as sales of regional Mexican styles surged in tandem with the post-NAFTA increases in Mexican immigration to the United States. In the early 1990s, the major labels opened up divisions specifically focusing on Texas Mexican music or signing distribution deals with independent labels; Arista/Latin, for example, signed established artists Freddy Fender (born Baldemar Huerta) and Flaco Jiménez as well as more modernized accordion-based groups, such as La Diferenzia, La Mafia, and Tropa F. Collectively, the more contemporary styles produced in Texas (often in *cumbia* rhythm), which included accordion-based groups such as La Mafia, the more eclectic pop-oriented Selena, and other more ballad-oriented groups such as Mazz, were referred to as "Tejano" (in order to distinguish it from the more vernacular and rural-oriented conjunto music).[21] The expected profits from the Tejano market did not materialize, however, and by 1998 Arista abandoned the venture; as one executive noted, "We had aspirations for the Tejano market growing more quickly than it did."[22] Industry-oriented periodicals speculated on why sales of Tejano music had fallen. One observer, for example, suggested that "the traditional Tejano market is shrinking in part because so many of the big names play the same cities so often. The big bands need to do their part to expand the market by touring beyond Texas."[23] Another complained, "There's too many Tejano bands working in Texas."[24] The decline in Tejano sales was also attributed to the death of Selena in 1995 and the subsequent move of Tejano music's other star, Emilio Navaira, to country and western. Almost everyone agreed, however, that the primary challenge was competition from Mexican *norteño,* whose consumer base was being bolstered by the steady influx of new Mexican immigrants.[25]

Indeed, by the end of the 1990s, sales of Mexican regional musics, especially norteño, were dwarfing the more regionally specific Tejano as well as tropical Latin.[26] In the wake of these demographic and cultural transformations, Mexican regional became "an attractive genre to the majors right now for the same reasons it has always been attractive. The music is popular with Mexican immigrants, who account for . . . 60% to 65% of the Hispanic population in the country. . . . And the continuous flow of immigrants from Mexico who are fiercely protective of their cultural roots assures an ever-enlarging, enthusiastic—and loyal—base of consumers. Further, these immigrants are spreading beyond their traditional bases such as California to nearly every corner of the U.S., to any place there is agriculture."[27] As discussed in Chapter 6, cumbia and norteño had, in fact, become virtually required in the repertoires of musicians with ambitions of succeeding in Texas and the Southwest.

These developments brought the mainstream music industry around full circle, recalling the early days when the U.S. music industry recognized the value of marketing culturally relevant music to recent immigrants (as discussed in Chapter 2). The multilayered nature of the U.S. Latino cultural landscape in the 1990s, however, did not much resemble conditions in the early twentieth century, when the majority of the proportionately small

Spanish-speaking population in the United States was foreign-born or strongly oriented to their home countries and cultures. By the 1990s, the differences between well-established Latinos and new immigrants were apparent, and the language used to compare them was distinctly contemporary, often employing the sort of critiques surfacing in current debates about immigration and trade policies. One commentator, for example, trying to explain why Tejano musicians did not tour more widely, pointed to the stronger work ethic—and compliance—of their competitors from Mexico: "[Regional Mexican recording artists] are down-to-earth, hard gigging performers who draw huge crowds and high marks for good behavior. . . . They don't complain and they are open to play anytime, anywhere."[28] Abraham Quintanilla, Selena's father and manager and owner of the Corpus Christi–based Q Productions, similarly pointed to the impact of competition, but especially the protectionist practices of the Mexican music industry, which refused to give the same level of airplay in Mexico to Tejano acts that Mexican acts enjoyed in Texas.[29]

Quintanilla was correct in noting the advantages enjoyed by Mexican groups backed by Mexican-owned media, whose deep pockets and cross-border distribution networks were beyond the reach of most Texas-based independent labels. After Sony Mexico, the most powerful player in Mexican regional music was Fonovisa, Mexico's largest record company, founded under the aegis of the Mexican media and entertainment conglomerate Televisa. Fonovisa also had access to the television networks owned by Univision, Mexico's even larger and more formidable media conglomerate, of which Televisa was part owner in 1996.[30] In addition to the benefits of enjoying access to Mexican radio stations in Mexico that collectively reached half the Mexican population, Fonovisa was also able to develop significant distribution networks in the United States, which included a U.S. record division able to attract top artists, including norteño superstars Los Tigres del Norte and pop icon Enrique Iglesias. Indeed, Fonovisa's U.S. division had more artists on its roster than its Mexican division did, and a catalogue twice as extensive.[31]

In 2002 (around the same time Fania and RMM's catalogues were being sold off), Fonovisa was acquired by Univision. With this acquisition, Univision Music Group (UMG), which already owned 50 percent of Disa, Mexico's most important independent Mexican regional label, became "a Latin music mammoth," the largest distributor in the United States and Mexico.[32] The advantages of these media conglomerates and their distribution networks were considerable. UMG's artists had access to Univision's major television shows, such as *Sabado Gigante,* as well as guaranteed advertising spots on Univision's television and radio networks. It also used its clout to gain access for Mexican regional music in major U.S. retail chains, such as Walmart. In

2004, Fonovisa and Disa together accounted for a full 33 percent of the U.S. Latin music market.[33]

As the distinctions between Tejano and norteño became blurred, Tejano artists who turned to the norteño style found they could gain access to Mexican radio and audiences,[34] but even this development could not compensate for the competition they encountered within the increasingly dominant Mexican regional market in the United States, which had become larger than Mexico's. One Mexican musician who immigrated to the United States to pursue his career notes the changes: "Mexican regional music used to be based in Mexico. But that's all changed now. It's all about Southern California. Mexican artists know that they have to be heard here in order to become successful. The market is too big to ignore. . . . The music is only popular in Mexico after it is popular here. We focus on the U.S. market because we know it will soon cross back into the market in Mexico."[35]

Despite the powerful competition from Mexican-based companies, Southwest-based independent labels continued to survive, and some even thrived, particularly those that embraced Mexican regional musicians and styles. Discos Freddie, for example, profited from the increasing popularity of Mexican acts, winning multiple Latin Grammy nominations and awards in both Tejano and Mexican regional categories.[36] Nonetheless, it became harder for small Texas-based companies to gain access to the Spanish-language radio and television stations owned by their larger rivals, limiting them to whatever visibility they could obtain from local radio stations and Internet radio.[37] These developments—the increasing influence of Mexican regional music and the ascendance of a Mexican company in the Latin music industry, coupled with the fact that none of the major music companies are now U.S. owned—necessarily call for replacing the long-standing U.S. cultural imperialism thesis with a more multilateral transnational model.

Naming Rights (and Wrongs): Language, Culture, and Identity in the Latin Music Construct

In the wake of the rapidly expanding Mexican regional market, coupled with the increasing numbers of immigrants and musical styles originating in other parts of Latin America such as the Dominican Republic and Colombia, the U.S. music industry has had to come to grips, conceptually and structurally, with the unwieldy heterogeneity of the Latin music construct. Changes, however, have generally been slow and fitful, in large part because of the ambivalent position of Latinos within the U.S. racial imaginary. Despite the long-term presence of Latinos in the United States, their musical practices were routinely excluded from what was considered "American" music; indeed, when the National Academy of Recording Arts and Sciences (NARAS) was founded in 1957 to focus public attention on its products via its annual Grammy Awards ceremony, no categories for Latin music existed. For years thereafter, even as sales of music made by and for U.S. Latinos surpassed those of jazz and classical music—both of which were recognized with Grammys—Latin musics were lumped into an "ethnic and traditional" music category, which confined fully urbanized and cosmopolitan Latinos in a category suggesting unchanging and premodern musical practices.

In response to these exclusions, in 1975—at the apogee of salsa's international success—salsa musicians in the New York chapter of NARAS organized a protest at the Grammy Awards ceremony, demanding that Latin music be acknowledged with its own Grammy categories.[38] NARAS complied with a single award for Latin music, but it rejected the protesters' requests for multiple categories that would accommodate the diversity of Latino musical practices. Eight years later, after complaints from Mexican American musicians that the Latin music award was being dominated by tropical music, three new categories were created to recognize Best Mexican American, Best Tropical, and Best Latin Pop.[39] In subsequent years, other categories were added or renamed. In 1995, the Mexican American Performance category was renamed Best Mexican American/Tejano Performance, recognizing that Tejano should not simply be subsumed under the Mexican American rubric; in 1998, this category was split into separate Tejano and Mexican American categories; and in 1997, a Latin Rock/Alternative category was added. In short, it took almost twenty-five years for the mainstream music industry to recognize with individual awards the various styles performed and consumed by U.S. Latinos, most of which had been in circulation since the founding of NARAS.

By the time the majors began establishing Latin divisions in the 1990s in response to changing demographics, the U.S. Latin music landscape had become vexingly complicated. Unlike most of the Latino-owned independent labels (described in Chapter 2), which had limited themselves to locally relevant styles, the "Latin" music handled by the majors and their Latin music divisions included a wide range of styles with geographically and culturally distinct audiences, including such genres as merengue, tango, samba, and mariachi, identified as the "national" musics of the Dominican Republic, Argentina, Brazil, and Mexico, respectively; regionally or class-oriented styles, such as norteño and bachata, with roots in Latin America but that were increasingly being produced and consumed in the United States; styles developed by and primarily for Latinos within the United States, such as New York salsa and Tejano; and international styles not connected to any particular place of origin, such as *salsa romántica, balada,* Latin pop, and *rock en español*.[40] The only thing these "Latin" musics had in common was that their lyrics were in Spanish or Portuguese.

Although on the surface the organizational strategy of combining U.S. Latino and Latin American musics into one category might have made cultural and economic sense in the context of late-twentieth-century migrations and diasporas, this decision had the potential to profoundly impact U.S. Latino artists whose musical practices and marketing needs were not identical to those of their Latin American counterparts. As Keith Negus has astutely observed, the Latin music industry became subject to the contradictions of being at once a U.S. (domestic) industry, producing and marketing a variety of regional styles by and for U.S. Latinos, and at the same time an industry with important historical and economic connections to Latin America. As a result, Latinos were lumped with Latin Americans in companies' international rather than domestic divisions.[41] More insidiously, U.S. labor standards did not apply in the companies' international divisions, where wages and benefits were significantly inferior. Tejano musicians recording for the Latin music divisions of Sony, EMI Latin, and WEA, for example, did not receive the same union-scale wages and protections, as, say, musicians who were recording country music or other "American" niche musics, such as Christian music.[42]

For purposes of distributing Latin music within the United States, however, the majors assigned this responsibility to the companies' domestic divisions; thus, as Negus observes, U.S. Latino musical productions often ended up in the hands of people with little knowledge of Latin music, who did not understand the crucial distinctions between Latin American *latinos* and U.S. Latinos and who lacked the cultural competence to effectively negotiate the complexities of the United States' language- and culture-specific media and distributions networks.[43]

Negus's observations about industry perceptions of U.S. Latinos as being alien to the cultural fabric of the United States were confirmed in statements made by an EMI Latino executive to a reporter in San Antonio in 1999: "The Latin music business, specifically Tejano music, is significantly different—certainly in the way we do it—from the way that traditional, for lack of a better term, anglo [*sic*] business is done."[44] As Henry Brun, a percussionist who had played with the likes of Marc Anthony and Tito Puente, noted caustically to another reporter about how they were treated by non-Latino music industry personnel, "They look at musicians down here as second-class citizens who just came out of the barn."[45] Without competent promotion, U.S. Latino musicians remained marginalized from the mainstream media, but, at the same time, excluded from the Spanish-language media if their music was in English or if their aesthetics were not clearly associated with Latin American origins.

The growing Latin American orientation of the Latin music industry became even more apparent in 1997, when a new organization complementary to NARAS was established: the Latin Academy of Recording Arts and Sciences (LARAS).[46] While the U.S.-based NARAS eventually came to include seven Latin music categories in its Grammy Awards, LARAS is an international organization—voting members can live either in the United States or abroad—and it recognizes forty categories for recordings released not only in the United States but also in any Spanish- or Portuguese-speaking market.[47] In 2001, LARAS began hosting an annual stand-alone gala ceremony to award Latin Grammys, which was broadcast on CBS, signaling the network's interest in reaching mainstream as well as Latino audiences. Although in some respects a separate awards ceremony represented progress because it opened up many more award categories, it also meant that U.S. Latinos (if their music was in Spanish) would have to compete more directly for LARAS votes with major artists from throughout Latin America as well as Spain, such as the Madrid-born Alejandro Sanz, who sold millions of records abroad.[48] Some U.S. Latino observers also perceived that the Latin Grammys ran the danger of perpetuating the segregation of Latin music from the industry mainstream. As journalist Fernando González asked, "Will Latin music in the United States gain visibility in exchange for a separate-but-equal arrangement?"[49] Indeed, no Latin acts performed or appeared on air at the mainstream Grammys between 2002 and 2005, when the ceremonies included a duet sung by Marc Anthony and Jennifer Lopez, who at the time were constantly in the tabloid news thanks to Lopez's well-publicized romantic entanglements with Ben Affleck and then Anthony. The fact that they sang in Spanish was highly unusual for the Grammys and might have been received favorably as a milestone were it not for the pair's overwrought performance style and gaudy stage setting: Invoking stereotypical images of Latin Americans featured in the melodramatic *telenovelas* that are staples on more immigrant-oriented Spanish-language television, these bicultural U.S. Latino icons' on-stage personas did not correspond to the duo's cosmopolitan urbanity familiar to their Latino fans.

The Latin Grammys did provide national visibility for U.S. Latino and Latin American musicians, but the fact that the ceremony was broadcast to mainstream television viewers exposed some of the faults in the Latin music construct. Artists whose Spanish lyrics were their very reason for being included in the Latin music category were pressured to make their speeches in English in order to keep non-Spanish-speaking U.S. viewers tuned in. Moreover, although the largest-selling category of Latin music in the United

States was regional Mexican, far surpassing sales of the tropical styles most people equated with Latin music, regional Mexican acts were consistently underrepresented in the first televised Latin Grammy performances. To Mexicans and Mexican Americans, the show's Miami Cuban producer, Emilio Estefan, seemed to have concluded that mainstream audiences tuning in and expecting to hear the hot, urban Afro-Caribbean sounds historically imagined as "Latin music" would be turned off by the unfamiliar sounds and images (such as the fringed and sequined cowboy garb) of the rural-oriented norteño and conjunto music being purchased by millions of working-class Mexicans and Mexican Americans. As Abraham Quintanilla notes, Mexican Americans were being slighted by "the Caribbean people" from the power centers of the Latin music industry, particularly Miami.[50] Subsequently, under pressure from the regional Mexican music industry, Mexican music became more prominent in the televised ceremonies.

The relocation of the Latin music industry to Miami from its former epicenters, New York and Los Angeles, was directly tied to the increasing Latin Americanization of the concept of Latin music and the globalizing structures of the music industry. The reasons for Miami's growing centrality to the Latin music industry were multiple, beginning with Miami's strategically crucial position as the trade gateway between Latin America to the south and the huge and relatively more affluent Latino market to the north.[51] Miami's bilingual Latino community was also well educated, economically and politically well organized, and demographically dominant. Miami's Latino population, originally primarily Cuban, was also being diversified not only by new immigrants from throughout Latin America and the Caribbean but also by U.S. Latinos of all national backgrounds who were attracted to the professional opportunities offered by the city's bilingual and bicultural character. The headquarters of related Spanish-language entertainment media were also concentrated in Miami for the same reasons. Even smaller Latino-owned independent labels, such as the Dominican-owned and Dominican-oriented J&N, moved their main offices from New York to Miami, despite the fact that the city lacked the same sort of community base for Dominican music the company had enjoyed in New York.

The emergence of Miami as the capital and linchpin of a hemispherically oriented Spanish-language entertainment industry began to challenge long-standing structural hierarchies characterizing the U.S. music industry, in which the domain of Latin music had always been considered subordinate (and inferior) to the English-only mainstream arena. As one music business expert noted in 1997, "The development of a separate but parallel universe that consists of recording studios, rehearsal studios, personal and project studios, pre-mastering houses, pressing plants for vinyl, CDs—and even some DVD-ready facilities—in all of which there may be no English language spoken, is viewed with some confusion amongst the mainstream record community. . . . Most are surprised to find a second tier or, if you prefer, 'shadow empire' of firms that provide similar services but operate almost totally within the Spanish language and remain less visible to the English-speaking mainstream of record production and replication. The labels are not totally unaware of the size and power of this emerging marketplace but service it with varying degrees of success. And much of that effort is also focused on Miami!"[52]

Miami's ascent also had the effect of overshadowing those regionally oriented ethnic music businesses remaining in New York and Los Angeles, increasing the influence of Miami-based Cuban Americans. As the primary power brokers in Miami's powerful Spanish-language entertainment and communication industries, Cuban American music-industry personnel acquired the ability to project Latin music to the world, but their conceptions of what Latin music is and how it should be promoted were not necessarily shared by other U.S. Latinos. After the 2000 Latin Grammy Awards ceremony, Mexican American and Puerto Rican producers and musicians complained bitterly that their communities' musics were not adequately represented in the on-air television extravaganza, and they accused the Cuban American organizers of using the event to promote their own products. New York salsero Willie Colón went further, charging producers Gloria and Emilio Estefan with usurping the very definition of Latin music itself.[53] According to Colón, "The new trend was to define everything Latin as Cuban. . . . Just to be able to control everything that is Latino, once again we have been plundered by the Miami mafia."[54] Ironically, Miami's fanatically anti-Castro Cuban American community impeded the process of centralizing the Latin music business in Miami: Their intransigence on the issue of allowing island-based Cubans to perform in Miami (even those winning Grammys, such as the group Buena Vista Social Club) forced the Latin Grammy ceremonies to subsequently be moved to Los Angeles and Las Vegas.

The increasing commercial dominance of Mexican norteño, coupled with the rising popularity of musics from other Spanish-speaking countries (e.g., Dominican bachata and Colombian vallenato, Spanish pop ballads, and the eclectic hybrids produced by the likes of the Colombian Juanes and the Mexican group El Gran Silencio), thoroughly disrupted the former primacy of New York–based Latino musical productions in the Latin music arena. Even Cuban Miami's centrality to the Latin music industry has been vulnerable to challenges from those promoting Mexican-origin music. In 2002, when Univision Music Group purchased Fonovisa and became the biggest player in Latin music, they moved their offices from Miami to Woodland Hills,

California.[55] In 2005, the Latin Grammy Awards ceremony, which since 2000 had been aired in English on CBS, moved to the Spanish-language network Univision—and, as *Billboard* noted, "Univision's broadcast was more successful than any other on CBS since the inaugural Latin Grammys in 2000."[56] That same year, the Latin Grammys collapsed the two categories for Spanish Caribbean dance music—Salsa/Merengue and Traditional Tropical—into only one Latin Tropical category, while the number of regional Mexican categories increased from two to four, with new categories for what had been essentially Mexican genres (norteño and *banda*) added to the existing Mexican American and Tejano categories.[57]

In short, the Latin music industry, which has been growing hand in hand with the comparably expanding Spanish-language television, radio, and advertising industries (including those owned by Mexican interests), has increasingly been promoting products and images reflecting the tastes and attitudes more characteristic of recent immigrants, whose language and cultural preferences are not identical to those of U.S.-born Latinos. Indeed, as Arlene Dávila has noted, the Spanish-language media's conflation of *latinidad* with being foreign-born and Spanish-dominant is quite deliberate and self-interested, since they understand that Latinos who are bicultural and bilingual are more likely to be drawn to their competitors in the mainstream media.[58] If such equations strengthen the long-standing tendency of U.S. Latinos to be imagined as foreign rather than "American," they even more effectively serve to exclude newer immigrants from belonging to and within a nation that has always imagined itself as monolingual.

One incidental but telling example demonstrates how linguistically and ethnically essentialist marketing categories reinforce such exclusions. At the end of 2008, a blogger published his analysis of record sales, gleaned from *Billboard* charts, in order to construct a better picture of who we are as a nation:

> When future pointy-headed academics are scouring data in attempts to better understand America in 2008, might it not be instructive to offer a snapshot of a different sort, one that attempts to explain the People and their mindset from a quasistatistical/analytical ethno-musicosociological [sic] perspective? Specifically, let's address the population in a head and/or heart space it cares deeply about: through its music. How does it sing and dance? Who does this singing? Who best moves our collective booty and tugs at our heartstrings? I've been crunching *Billboard* album and singles chart data in order to better understand Who We Are in 2008. I've compiled information on every artist who cracked the Top 10 album chart and the Hot 100 singles

chart this year. I've researched each artist and tallied the lot of them based on a number of factors, including gender, ethnicity, nationality, state of origin (if American) and record label. I've then analyzed these numbers.[59]

The blogger's goals are laudable, and his methods appropriately break down the artists by race, region, gender, and ethnicity, but, by making the superficially logical choice to take into consideration only *Billboard* top album and singles charts, he effectively eliminates from his consideration of "how do we sing and dance" the musical preferences of millions of U.S. Latinos—new immigrants and bilingual, bicultural Latinos alike—who purchase music sung in Spanish. Sales of Spanish-language musics in the United States have always been far smaller than mainstream English-language musics, such as hip-hop and rock,[60] but the tiny percentage of "Latinos" identified by the blogger's analysis—1 percent—would surely have been larger had he devised a way to factor into his portrait of "who we are" the musical practices of the over 44 million Latinos reported by the 2007 American Community Survey to be living in the United States.[61]

In summary, historically the music industry's way of understanding U.S. Latinos and their musical practices has changed continuously in response to demographic, cultural, economic, and political transformations within the United States. But as the Latin music construct continues to evolve, it is important to remain vigilant regarding how the term used to define it correlates with the musical practices and cultural identities of communities whose musics are corralled within this term. These cultural industries, in which music plays a central role, yield immense influence over how people (especially, but not exclusively, non-Latinos) conceptualize not only *latinidad*—what it is that makes someone or something "Latino/a"—but also how latinidad itself is positioned within the broader U.S. cultural landscape.

Concluding Thoughts on Hybridity, Identity, and Latino Popular Music in the New Millennium

As the preceding chapters in this book have made clear, music industry personnel have always simultaneously acknowledged, resisted, and adapted to the hybridity and layered-ness of U.S. Latino musical practices. Indeed, even strongly rural-oriented regional Mexican musics have been fused with hip-hop and rock and have incorporated English—for example, the group Akwid, discussed in Chapter 4, whose 2004 highly successful banda-rap recording was entitled *Hoy, Ayer and Forever*—spawning the curiously contradictory but appropriately hybrid marketing category "urban regional Mexican." When the mainstream entertainment corporation Clear Channel began flipping formerly English-language radio stations over to Spanish in 2004 in order to target bicultural urban Latino youths whose musical tastes include hip-hop (in both languages), *reggaeton,* and pop music, they began describing their lineups as "Hurban Top 40," a contraction of "Hispanic" and "urban."[62] Clearly, language-based constructions of latinidad employed by the Latin and mainstream music industries had proven inadequate to describe the multidimensional experiences of U.S. Latinos.

The explosion of reggaeton in the United States in 2005 provides a particularly vivid contemporary case study of how Latinos' multiple, intersecting, and overlapping boundary crossings have further destabilized the industry's long-standing musical categories and upset their terminological applecarts. As discussed in Chapter 4, reggaeton's multiple roots are in Jamaican dancehall reggae, Panamanian *reggae en español,* and hip-hop (in English and Spanish), complicated by infusions of Puerto Rican and Latin American styles, particularly salsa, merengue, and bachata. As reggaeton emerged in Puerto Rico, however, it was almost entirely in Spanish, and its Jamaican dancehall *dembow* beat distinguished it from hip-hop, so even as it became immensely popular on the island and among young Spanish Caribbean Latinos on the East Coast, it could not penetrate the English-only mainland U.S. media. Nonetheless, reggaeton's aesthetic roots in hip-hop provided a sonic bridge to mainland hip-hop audiences, especially urban Latinos/as born and bred in the United States who had grown up embedded in U.S. hip-hop culture.

In 2004, two major events converged that pushed reggaeton into the English-language media arena. One was Daddy Yankee's release of his all-Spanish recording *Barrio Fino* containing the song "Gasolina," which went on to become an international megahit.[63] Reversing the usual pattern of radio play pushing sales and media attention, it was Daddy Yankee's exploding sales numbers that got him radio play and lots of attention from the press.[64] That same year, the established rapper N.O.R.E. (born in New York to African American and Puerto Rican parents), who had recognized reggaeton's potential to cross musical and linguistic boundaries, released his highly successful song and video "Oye Mi Canto," which has been credited with opening the doors of the English-language media to reggaeton. In 2005, *Billboard* noted the impact of reggaeton's access to the domestic English-language media: "The year before, reggaeton was on the map, but it wasn't embraced by a lot of the domestic accounts. And little by little, they've been opening up to it. Yankee's sales rose dramatically once the single 'Gasolina' garnered airplay on English language stations and the album gained broader distribution."[65] The Colombian singer Shakira, it should be noted, benefited from similarly

atypical access to the English-language market. In an extraordinarily reveal-
ing moment, a 2005 article in *Billboard* notes that her recording *Fijación Oral*
"has been marketed and promoted *as a major release instead of as a Latin title,
with all the effort that implies*" (emphasis mine).[66]

The impact of such border-breaching developments was not lost on the
music industry, which quickly sought to capture two previously underserved
market segments: (1) bilingual and bicultural Latino youths of all ethnicities
eager to embrace a music that fused hip-hop with Spanish lyrics and aesthetics and (2) for the first time since the mambo craze in the 1940s (see Chapter 2), mainstream English-speaking fans, black and white, gravitating to a
music whose Spanish lyrics they might not understand but whose rhythms
and attitudes they understood perfectly. In the wake of these developments,
a number of radio stations across the country, English and Spanish, began
to flip to the bilingual "hurban" format, and even English-language hip-hop
stations and MTV began giving airplay to reggaeton hits.[67] All the existing
Latin music labels created new "urban" divisions, but even more notably,
English-language hip-hop labels, such as Wu Tang and Bad Boy, created
Latino divisions.[68] The RIAA added a new "urban" subgenre to its Latin
music shipment report, which included reggaeton, rap, banda-rap, and hip-
hop. Interestingly, in 2006, sales of Mexican regional dropped for the first
time in years, from 60 percent to 48 percent, although it still remained the
bedrock of the Latin music industry.[69]

In 2006, the much-hyped and overinflated reggaeton bubble burst, with
Billboard reporting huge numbers of unsold urban recordings returned to
the shippers by year's end.[70] Reggaeton began appearing less frequently on
hip-hop stations, and dire predictions of reggaeton's demise were not long in
following. Language was cited as the primary reason: Non-Latino listeners
simply would not stick with music whose lyrics they could not understand.
Few English-speaking fans, I might note, questioned the naturalness of U.S.
popular musics being routinely embraced in non-English-speaking countries
around the world.

Whether or not reggaeton's mainstream visibility survives, the demographic realities of the growing U.S. Latino population, the majority of whom
(as I discuss in Chapter 5) will be U.S. born, will continue to present a
quandary to the media and, by extension, to the nation whose imaginations it
nurtures. By 2007, the dilemma of what to do with the "urban Latino" market was producing a series of remixes and collaborations between reggaeton
artists and musicians already well established in English-language markets;
well-known examples include Miami Cuban rapper and *reggaetonero* Pitbull's
remix with hip-hop star Lil John and reggaeton stars Wisin y Yandel's col-
laboration with R & B artist R. Kelly, in which English and Spanish lyrics

appear. Such recordings were clearly intended to increase Latino musicians' access to the English-language media while at the same time increasing English-language hip-hop and pop stars' access to the bilingual and Spanish markets—although the results were often unsatisfying to fans of both genres. These efforts may be optimistically interpreted as welcome and long-overdue cross-cultural collaborations, but it worries me that the implicit message may be that Spanish-speaking Latino artists require English-speaking escorts in order to penetrate the inner circles of the mainstream market, where the money is to be made.

As the industry continues to grapple with the confusion caused by the coexistence of "urban" Latinos of so many different national backgrounds and so many culturally dissimilar newcomers (many of them as racially and culturally mixed as long-established U.S. Latinos) it has become clear even to the music industry that language-based constructions of latinidad are inadequate for capturing the multidimensional experiences of U.S. Latinos. In July 2005, *Billboard* came up with a new definition for Latin music: any album that was at least 51 percent in Spanish.[71] Acknowledging that Latin music need not necessarily be entirely in Spanish indicates progress of sorts, because it expands the industry's concept of latinidad in order to include bilingual (but not monolingual English-speaking) U.S. Latinos. Yet, as groundbreaking and paradigm-shaking as these developments have been, they have not yet disrupted the conflation of U.S. Latinos with Latin Americans—that is, as racially and culturally distinct foreigners. Indeed, the questions of who would calculate these percentages and how were not specified, so the decision as to what is Latin music and what is not will almost certainly continue to conform to Negus's observation (discussed in Chapter 2) that the cultural predispositions and ethnoracial imaginaries of music industry personnel, not observable sociocultural and demographic realities, will overdetermine the industry's economic decisions.[72] Hopefully, the U.S.-born Latino population, which continues to grow by leaps and bounds, will push the United States to overcome its historically erroneous image of itself as a solely black-and-white, English-only nation and will begin accepting bicultural and bilingual Latinos and their musics on their own terms.

Notes

PREFACE

1. George Lipsitz, *Dangerous Crossroads: Popular Music, Post-Modernism and the Poetics of Place* (New York: Verso, 1994).

2. Juan Flores has been analyzing musical dialogues between New York Puerto Ricans and African Americans since the 1980s. See, for example, "'Qué Assimilated, Brother, Yo Soy Assimilao': The Structuring of Puerto Rican Identity," in *Divided Borders: Essays on Puerto Rican Identity* (Houston: Arte Público Press, 1993), 182–195; "'Puerto Rican and Proud, Boyee!' Rap, Roots and Amnesia," *Boletín del Centro de Estudios Puertorriqueños* 5, no. 1 (1992–1993): 22–31; and "'Cha-Cha with a Backbeat': Songs and Stories of Latin Boogaloo," in *From Bomba to Hip-Hop: Puerto Rican Culture and Latino Identity* (New York: Columbia University Press, 2000), 79–112. See also George Lipsitz, *Footsteps in the Dark: The Hidden Histories of Popular Music* (Minneapolis: University of Minnesota Press, 2007), and Luis Alvarez, "From Zoot Suits to Hip Hop: Towards a Relational Chicano/a Studies," *Latino Studies* 5 (2007): 53–75.

3. Regarding the proper spelling of the song and this book title, an Internet search found that the Tito Puente and Santana versions of "Oye Como Va!" sometimes use the ending exclamation point but never seem to use the accent over the "o" or the opening (upside-down) exclamation point. I follow this convention.

4. Available at http://www.kevinjohansen.com/2007/en/bio.html (accessed February 2009).

5. As I discuss at length in later chapters, Cuban music has been an integral feature of New York's Latin music landscape, while Cuban Americans have made their mark primarily on Miami.

CHAPTER 1

1. See Eric Zolov, *Refried Elvis: The Rise of the Mexican Counterculture* (Berkeley: University of California Press, 1999).

2. David Welna, "NPR 100: 'Oye Como Va,'" available at http://www.npr.org/templates/story/story.php?storyId=1111466 (accessed February 2009).

3. In a review of Huntington's book *Who Are We? The Challenges to America's National Identity* (New York: Simon and Schuster, 2004), for example, Harrison repeats Huntington's argument that large-scale immigration from Latin America is threatening the fabric of U.S. life, because "all cultures are not equal when it comes to promoting progress, and very few can match Anglo-Protestantism in this respect." Lawrence E. Harrison, "The End of Multiculturalism," *Christian Science Monitor,* February 26, 2008, available at http://www.csmonitor.com/2008/0226/p09s01-coop.html.

4. See, for example, Faye V. Harrison, "Introduction: Expanding the Discourse on 'Race,'" *American Anthropologist* (New Series) 100, no. 3 (September 1998): 609–631.

5. See, for example, Herbert S. Klein, *African Slavery in Latin America and the Caribbean* (New York: Oxford University Press, 1986).

6. Martha Ellen Davis, for example, defines "creole" as "a cultural conglomerate born of Old World parentage and tempered by New World circumstance and creativity," while Kenneth Bilby defines "creolization" as the "meeting and blending of two or more older traditions on new soil, and a subsequent elaboration of form." See Martha Ellen Davis, "Music and Black Ethnicity in the Dominican Republic," in *Music and Black Ethnicity: The Caribbean and South America,* ed. Gerard H. Béhague (New Brunswick, NJ: Transaction Publishers, 1994), 120; and Kenneth M. Bilby, "The Caribbean as a Musical Region," in *Caribbean Contours,* ed. Sidney W. Mintz and Sally Price (Baltimore: Johns Hopkins University Press, 1985), 182. Other terms used to describe such cultural mixtures include "syncretism," in which European forms and meanings have been layered over African or Amerindian ones in order to avoid censure by officials seeking to ban supposedly primitive behaviors and practices.

7. Scholars using the term "mestizaje" to describe racial and cultural blending in areas of Latin America where African/European mixtures predominate often insert in parentheses the term *"mulataje"* or *"mulatez"* to clarify that the mixture they are referring to is European/African, not European/native. See, for example, Lourdes Martínez-Echazábal, "Mestizaje and the Discourse of National/Cultural Identity in Latin America, 1845–1959," *Latin American Perspectives* 25, no. 3 (May 1998): 21–22.

8. I use the term "Afrodescendant" as employed by Helen Safa to refer to both mulattos and blacks. She notes that Afrodescendants, who constitute 30 percent of the population of Latin America, outnumber indigenous peoples fivefold. Helen Safa, "Challenging *Mestizaje*: A Gender Perspective on Indigenous and Afrodescendant Movements in Latin America," *Critique of Anthropology* 25, no. 3 (2005): 307–330. However, if a comparable category of "Indo-descendants" were employed—that is, if mestizos were counted collectively with indigenous peoples, as Safa counts mulattos and blacks together—the relative size of both groups would be quite different.

9. Examples of the arguments made for and against the term "black music" can be found in Reebee Garofalo, "Black Popular Music: Crossing Over or Going Under?" in *Rock and Popular Music: Politics, Policies, and Institutions,* ed. Tony Bennett, Simon Frith, Lawrence Grossberg, John Shepherd, and Graeme Turner (New York: Rout-

ledge, 1993): 231–248; Stuart Hall, "What Is This 'Black' in Black Popular Culture?" in *Black Popular Culture*, ed. Gina Dent (Seattle: South Bay Press, 1992): 255–263; Phillip Tagg, "Open Letter about 'Black Music,' 'Afro-American Music' and 'European Music,'" *Popular Music* 8, no. 3 (1989): 285–298. In *The Black Atlantic: Modernity and Double Consciousness* (Cambridge: Harvard University Press, 1992), Paul Gilroy offers slightly differently inflected observations on the relationship between race, culture, and identity in his chapter "'Jewels Brought from Bondage': Black Music and the Politics of Authenticity" (72–110).

10. In brief, "Latin" music conflates Latin American and U.S. Latino musical productions. The term "Latino" is often misinterpreted as shorthand for Latin American and hence presents the same problem as "Latin." The term "U.S. Latino" does properly situate its subjects in the United States, although it also conflates profoundly different populations and styles, many of which are not considered "Latin." See Deborah Pacini Hernandez, "The Name Game: Locating Latinas/os, Latins, and Latin Americans in the US Popular Music Landscape," in *A Companion to Latino Studies*, ed. Juan Flores and Renato Rosaldo (Malden, MA: Blackwell Publishing, 2007), 49–59.

11. George Lipsitz, "Cruising around the Historical Bloc: Postmodernism and Popular Music in East Los Angeles," *Cultural Critique* 5 (Winter 1986–1987): 157–177.

12. Raquel Z. Rivera, "Between Blackness and Latinidad in the Hip Hop Zone," in *A Companion to Latino Studies*, ed. Juan Flores and Renato Rosaldo (Malden, MA: Blackwell Publishing, 2007), 351–362.

13. Ibid., 351.

14. See, for example, George Reid Andrews, *Afro-Latin America* (New York: Oxford University Press, 2004); Anani Dzidzienyo and Suzanne Oboler, eds., *Neither Enemies nor Friends: Latinos, Blacks and Afro-Latins* (New York: Palgrave, 2005); and Helen Safa's Introduction to "Race and National Identity in the Americas," a special issue of *Latin American Perspectives* 25, no. 3 (1998).

15. See Peter Wade, *Music, Race, and Nation: Música Tropical in Colombia* (Chicago: University of Chicago Press, 2000).

16. Miriam Jiménez Román, "Looking at That Middle Ground: Racial Mixture as Panacea?" in *A Companion to Latina/o Studies*, ed. Juan Flores and Renato Rosaldo (Malden, MA: Blackwell Publishing, 2007), 329.

17. See, for example, Ian F. Haney Lopez, "Colorblind to the Reality of Race in America," *Chronicle of Higher Education* 53, no. 11 (November 3, 2006). Unfortunately, in such constructions, Latinos' hybridity is believed to render them particularly prone to "buying in" to the United States' racial hierarchy, because they can "pass." Although there is certainly some truth to this analysis, the inability to imagine Latino hybridity as a progressive force in U.S. race relations means that all but the darkest-skinned Latinos are relegated to being "whites in waiting" or "honorary whites."

18. Peter Wade, "Rethinking Mestizaje: Ideology and Lived Experience," *Journal of Latin American Studies* 37, no. 2 (May 2005): 239–257.

19. Jacques Audinet, *The Human Face of Globalization: From Multicultural to Mestizaje* (Lanham, MD: Rowman and Littlefield, 1999), 51.

20. Ibid., 100.

21. Jiménez Román, "Looking at That Middle Ground," 330.

22. For further discussions about why so many popular musics have originated in marginalized communities, see Charles Keil, "People's Music Comparatively: Style

and Stereotypes, Class and Hegemony," *Dialectical Anthropology* 10 (1985): 119–130; and Peter Manuel, *Perspectives on the Study of Non-Western Popular Musics* (New York: Oxford University Press, 1988), 18–19.

23. Raquel Z. Rivera, personal communication, 2008; see also Raquel Z. Rivera, *New York Ricans from the Hip Hop Zone* (New York: Palgrave, 2003).

24. See, for example, Nina Glick Schiller, Linda Basch, and Cristina Blanc-Szanton, *Towards a Transnational Perspective on Migration: Race, Class, Ethnicity, and Nationalism Reconsidered* (New York: New York Academy of Sciences, 1992); Peggy Levitt, *Transnational Villagers* (Berkeley: University of California Press, 2001); Alejandro Portes, "Introduction: The Debates and Significance of Immigrant Transnationalism," *Global Networks* 1, no. 3 (2001): 181–193.

25. See, for example, Roger Waldinger and Mehdi Bozorgmehr, eds., *Ethnic Los Angeles* (New York: Russell Sage Foundation, 1996).

26. See, for example, Reebee Garofalo, "Culture Versus Commerce: The Marketing of Black Popular Music," *Public Culture* 7, no. 1 (Fall 1994): 275–287.

27. Arlene Dávila, *Latinos, Inc.: The Marketing and Making of a People* (Berkeley: University of California Press, 2001).

CHAPTER 2

1. "Mainstream" is an imprecise but often-used shorthand term for those musics receiving more financial resources, media exposure, and critical attention than those "marginal" musics located along the periphery of the nation's popular music landscape. Although to many people the term "mainstream" might invoke cultural expressions associated with the Eurocentric "core culture" of the United States, since the emergence of rock 'n' roll in the 1950s, African American musicians and styles have figured prominently in the U.S. musical mainstream, complicating clear-cut associations of "mainstream" with the musical practices of Euro-descendants. Latin American and Latino musics have also influenced various mainstream styles, although they have not received recognition commensurate with their contributions. Nevertheless, while mainstream popular music may be quite diverse in terms of origins, content, and styles, its language has always been English-only: Other than a few novelty songs that have occasionally appeared on hit-parade lists, music in any language other than English has yet to achieve sustained visibility in the mainstream arena.

2. Keith Negus, *Music Genres and Corporate Cultures* (London: Routledge, 1999), 14–30.

3. Keith Negus, "La cultura, la industria y la matriz de la salsa: El negocio de la música en los Estados Unidos y la producción de la música Latina" [Culture, Industry and the Salsa Matrix: The Music Business in the United States and the Production of Latin Music], *Revista de Ciencias Sociales* 4 (1998): 27–52.

4. Pekka Gronow, "Ethnic Recordings: An Introduction," in *Ethnic Recordings in America: A Neglected Heritage* (Washington, DC: American Folklife Center, 1982), 6.

5. Ibid., 3.

6. Ibid.

7. Richard K. Spottswood, "Commercial Ethnic Recordings in the United States," in *Ethnic Recordings in America: A Neglected Heritage* (Washington, DC: American Folklife Center, 1982), 55.

8. Alan Sutton, "The Origins of Okeh," available at http://www.mainspringpress. com/okeh.html (accessed November 17, 2007).

9. Ibid.

10. Chris Strachwitz and Cristóbal Díaz Ayala, liner notes to *Lamento Borincano: Early Puerto Rican Music: 1916–1939* (Arhoolie 7037–38). See also Ruth Glasser, *My Music Is My Flag: Puerto Rican Musicians and Their New York Communities, 1917–1940* (Berkeley: University of California Press, 1995), 133–135.

11. Within a few decades, most Latin American nations established their own domestic music industries, which allowed Latin American musicians to develop their careers without traveling abroad, at which point U.S.-based companies simply bought the rights to proven hits or signed successful musicians.

12. Strachwitz and Díaz Ayala, liner notes to *Lamento Borincano*, 7.

13. Manuel Peña, "The Emergence of Conjunto Music, 1935–1955," in *Puro Conjunto: An Album in Words and Pictures*, ed. Juan Tejeda and Avelardo Valdez (Austin: Center for Mexican American Studies and Guadalupe Cultural Arts Center, 2001), 16–17.

14. Jukeboxes played an important role in disseminating music to poor and working-class listeners unable to purchase record players in Latin America as well; I document the role of jukeboxes in the Dominican Republic in *Bachata: A Social History of a Dominican Popular Music* (Philadelphia: Temple University Press, 1995), 54–55.

15. See George Sánchez, *Becoming Mexican American: Ethnicity, Culture and Identity in Chicano Los Angeles, 1900–1945* (New York: Oxford University Press, 1993), 182–183. One indication of the freewheeling nature of the ethnic music business at this early stage was that one of the earliest recordings made in Los Angeles, the song "El Lavaplatos," was recorded in 1930 by no fewer than three groups on three different labels. The song was recorded by its composer Jesús Osorio and Manuel Camacho for Victor, by Los Hermanos Bañuelos for Brunswick/Vocalion, and by Chávez y Lugo for Columbia; see Steven Loza, *Barrio Rhythms: Mexican American Music in Los Angeles* (Urbana: University of Illinois Press, 1993), 22.

16. For more on Pedro González and Los Madrugadores, see Loza, *Barrio Rhythms*, 33–34; and Chris Strachwitz and Zac Salem, "Pedro J. González y los Madrugadores," liner notes to *Pedro J. González y los Madrugadores, 1931–1937* (Arhoolie Folklyric CD 7035, 2000). See also *Break of Dawn*, Isaac Artenstein's fine 1988 biopic based on González's musical career and political activism in Los Angeles, and Paul Espinosa's 1983 documentary, *Ballad of an Unsung Hero*.

17. Steve Traiman, "What a Difference a Song Makes (100th Anniversary Edward B. Marks Music Company)," *Billboard* 106, no. 41 (October 8, 1994): 8.

18. In 1925, Peer left Okeh and signed on to work with the Victor Recording Company, which later agreed to allow his publishing company, Southern Music, which he founded in 1928, to retain the publishing rights to the music recorded by the musicians he had signed to Victor. Peer, it should be noted, did not own the rights to "El Manisero," which became the first authentically Latin music song to become a top hit nationally after it was recorded in New York in 1931 by Cuban bandleader Don Azpiazú's orchestra with singer Antonio Machín. The rights to "El Manisero" had been acquired by the other major non-Latino holder of publishing rights to Latin American music, E. B. Marks, who released a version of the song, with English lyrics written by Louis Rittenberg, as "The Peanut Vendor." The song received additional mainstream

exposure when it was included in the 1931 Hollywood musical *Cuban Love Song*, sung by Lawrence Tibbet. See Ned Sublette, *Cuba and Its Music: From the First Drums to the Mambo* (Chicago: Chicago Review Press, 2004), 399. Another English-language version was written by Azpiazú's sister-in-law, Marion Sunshine, and Wolfe Gilbert; see Gustavo Pérez Firmat, "Latunes: An Introduction," *Latin American Research Review* 43, no. 2 (2008): 185.

19. Richard M. Sudhalter, "Ralph S. Peer: A Life of Infinite Variety and Many Achievements," available at http://www.peermusic.com/aboutus/rsp01.cfm (accessed July 2007).

20. For an extensive discussion of how Latin American music influenced the U.S. mainstream popular music landscape in the 1930s, 1940s, and 1950s, see Pérez Firmat, "Latunes," 180–203.

21. John Storm Roberts, *The Latin Tinge: The Impact of Latin American Music on the United States* (1979; repr. New York: Oxford University Press, 1999), 45.

22. Glasser, *My Music Is My Flag,* 111.

23. Christopher Washburne, *Sounding Salsa: Performing Latin Music in New York City* (Philadelphia: Temple University Press, 2008), 12. See also Glasser, *My Music Is My Flag,* 107–109.

24. Virginia E. Sánchez Korrol, *From Colonia to Community: The History of Puerto Ricans in New York City* (1983; repr. Berkeley: University of California Press, 1994), 80–81.

25. Glasser, *My Music Is My Flag,* 107–109, 143–144.

26. Max Salazar, interview with Gabriel Oller, in *Mambo Kingdom: Latin Music in New York* (New York: Schirmer Trade Books, 2002), 19–23.

27. Chris Strachwitz with James Nicolopulos, *Lydia Mendoza: A Family Autobiography* (Houston: Arte Público Press, 1993), 356–358; Loza, *Barrio Rhythms,* 78.

28. Strachwitz with Nicolopulos, *Lydia Mendoza,* 357. Another Los Angeles–based company specializing in Mexican music that also recorded in Texas was Globe Records, but Strachwitz reports that otherwise little is known about it, including the ethnicity of its original owners.

29. In spite of the linguistic similarities between their names, there appears to be no relationship between Ralph Peer's Peer Music and the Mexican company Peerless, one of the most important Mexican-based music labels. The likeliest explanation for the similarity is that the owners of the Mexican company were trying to replicate the branding success of the well-known U.S.-based company. Peer Music, it should be noted, has continued to be a powerhouse in Latin music publishing, holding the rights to hit songs by such major Latin/o artists as Mark Anthony, Julio Iglesias, Paulina Rubio, and Thalia (not to mention hits by English-language superstars, such as Frank Sinatra, Johnny Cash, and the Beatles). See "Company History," available at http://www.peermusic.com/aboutus/companyhistory.cfm (accessed July 2007).

30. Josh Kun, "Bagels, Bongos, and Yiddishe Mambos, or the Other History of Jews in America," *Shofar* 23, no. 4 (Summer 2005), 50–68. See also "The Mamboniks," a Web site archiving information on the history of Jews in the Latin music businesses, available at http://mamboniks.blogspot.com (accessed January 2009).

31. See Roberta L. Singer and Elena Martínez, "A South Bronx Music Tale," *Centro Journal* 16, no. 1 (Spring 2004): 177–201.

32. For more on Jewish interest in Latin music, see Ralph J. Rivera's fine docu-

mentary, *Through the Eyes of Larry Harlow: El Judio Maravilloso* (Tropical Visions Entertainment Group, 1998).

33. Kun, "Bagels, Bongos."

34. Stuffed Animal (pseudonym), "Mambo USA, Morris Levy and Rhythm 'n' Blues," 4 (pt. 2 of "Mambo Gee Gee: The Story of George Goldner and Tico Records"), available at http://www.spectropop.com/tico/index.htm (accessed February 2009).

35. See Don Charles, "The Seeco Records Story," in "Seeco Album Discography," by Don Charles, David Edwards, and Mike Callahan, available at http://www.bsnpubs.com/latin/seeco.html (accessed February 2009).

36. "Sidney Siegel and Seeco Records," posted by The Snob, January 11, 2007, available at http://mamboniks.blogspot.com/2007/11/sidney-siegel-and-seeco-records.html (accessed February 2009).

37. Steven Loza, *Tito Puente and the Making of Latin Music* (Urbana: University of Illinois Press, 1999), 9.

38. Vernon Boggs, *Salsiology: Afro-Cuban Music and the Evolution of Salsa in New York City* (New York: Excelsior Music Publishing, 1992), 214. See also Washburne, *Sounding Salsa,* 41.

39. Ibid., 203–227; see also John Child, "Profile: Al Santiago," February 23, 1999, available at http://www.descarga.com/cgi-bin/db/archives/Profile36 (accessed January 5, 2009).

40. Boggs, *Salsiology,* 212.

41. Stuffed Animal, "Mambo Gee Gee." For more on boogaloo, see Juan Flores, "'Cha Cha with a Backbeat': Songs and Stories of Latin Boogaloo," in *From Bomba to Hip-Hop: Puerto Rican Culture and Latino Identity* (New York: Columbia University Press, 2000), 79–112.

42. In an interview with Steven Loza, former Imperial artist Lalo Guerrero expressed resentment at Chudd for this change in direction: "They cancelled all of us Chicanos out. They threw the Chicanos out because they were making too much money off the blacks." Loza, *Barrio Rhythms,* 77.

43. David Reyes and Tom Waldman, *Land of a Thousand Dances: Chicano Rock 'n' Roll from Southern California* (Albuquerque: University of New Mexico Press, 1998), 58.

44. There were some exceptions, however, such as the Texas-born Chelo Silva, who, in the 1940s, recorded with the powerful Mexican company Peerless (no relationship to Ralph Peer) and later with Columbia. Manuel Peña, *Música Tejana: The Cultural Economy of Artistic Transformation* (College Station: Texas A&M University Press, 1999), 65.

45. Reyes and Waldman, *Land of a Thousand Dances,* 37–38.

46. Ibid., 56. See also Mark Guerrero, "Billy Cardenas: East L.A. Manager and Record Producer of the 60s," available at http://markguerrero.net/misc_48.php (accessed February 2009).

47. Peña, *Música Tejana,* 97.

48. A poignant scene in the film *Selena* dramatizes the dilemma for aspiring Texas Mexican rock 'n' rollers. As a youth, Selena's father, who played in a rock 'n' roll band, was hired to play in a club, but when the owners saw that the band members were Mexican, they canceled the contract. When they attempted to play rock 'n' roll in a Mexican venue, the patrons booed and threw bottles at them.

49. In 1965, Meaux scored another hit with a Texas Mexican group, but not until he had hidden its identity with a faux-British name: the Sir Douglas Quintet. See Joe

Nick Patosky, "Huey P. Meaux: The Crazy Cajun" (excerpt from "Sex, Drugs, and Rock and Roll," *Texas Monthly* 24, no. 5 [May 1996]: 116), available at http://www.laventure. net/tourist/sdq_meaux.htm (accessed February 2009).

50. Peña, *Música Tejana,* 162.

51. Ibid., 163–175.

52. Jennifer LeClaire, "Latin Music Mecca Freddie's Stars Continue to Shine a Spotlight on Tejano Music," available at http://www.hispaniconline.com/trends/2004/ sep/briefcase/trendsetters.html (accessed November 21, 2007).

53. The Italian American Masucci, a lawyer and personal friend of Pacheco's, had no prior interest in or knowledge of Latin music, but he agreed to handle the business end of the company. Izzy Sanabria, "The World's Greatest Force in Latin Music," liner notes to *Fania: 1964–1994* (Musicrama/Koch B000008UGE, 1994).

54. For a full description and analysis of Fania's emergence, see Washburne, *Sounding Salsa,* 15–23. For more on Operation Bootstrap, see, for example, Edna Acosta-Belén and Carlos E. Santiago, *Puerto Ricans in the United States: A Contemporary Portrait* (Boulder, CO: Lynne Reiner Publishers, 2006); and César J. Ayala and Rafael Bernabé, *Puerto Rico in the American Century: A History since 1898* (Chapel Hill: University of North Carolina Press, 2007).

55. Stuffed Animal, "The Last Gasp, Fania, and the Death of George Goldner," 5 (pt. 5 of Stuffed Animal, "Mambo Gee Gee"), available at http://www.spectropop.com/ tico/TICOpart5.htm (accessed April 28, 2009).

56. John Lannert, "Salsa Pioneer Jerry Masucci, 63, Dies, Fania Records Co-Founder Made Latin Style a Hit," *Billboard,* January 10, 1998.

57. J&N Records, for example, was established in New York and later expanded, with offices in the Dominican Republic; Karen Records, in contrast, originally established in the Dominican Republic, later opened up offices in Miami.

58. Quoted in Alisa Valdes, "The Berry Gordy of Tropical Latin Music," *Boston Globe,* June 21, 1998.

59. Judy Rosen, "The Return of Fania, the Record Company That Made Salsa Hot," *New York Times,* June 4, 2006.

60. See Robert Suro and Jeffrey Passel, "The Rise of the Second Generation: Changing Patterns in Hispanic Population Growth," a study published by the Pew Hispanic Center, October 14, 2004, available at http://pewhispanic.org/files/reports/22.pdf (accessed August 12, 2007).

CHAPTER 3

1. I employ the term "rock 'n' roll" (as sparingly as possible) as a *generic* term for the continuum of mainstream U.S. popular musics that dominated the airwaves in the 1950s and that has subsequently included styles associated with and produced by African Americans (such as soul and funk), with the understanding that scholars and fans often distinguish rock 'n' roll from styles developed later on, referred to as "rock." Despite strong African American aesthetics in guitar-led rock, including the influence of seminal guitar players Carlos Santana and Jimi Hendrix, rock has been coded as white, distinct from styles such as hip-hop and R & B that are coded as black.

2. An earlier version of this chapter appeared as "A Tale of Two Cities: A Com-

parison of L.A. Chicano and New York Puerto Rican Engagement with Rock and Roll," *Centro: Journal of El Centro de Estudios Puertorriqueños* 11, no. 2 (2000): 71–93.

3. Ricardo Romo, *East Los Angeles: History of a Barrio* (Austin: University of Texas Press, 1983), 11.

4. Alejandro Portes and Rubén G. Rumbaut, *Immigrant America: A Portrait* (Berkeley: University of California Press, 1990), 227.

5. While people of Mexican descent still constitute the majority of the Latino population in Los Angeles, the proportional size of New York's Puerto Rican community has diminished as immigrant populations from other Latin American countries in that city have grown; see Juan Flores, "Pan-Latino/Trans-Latino: Puerto Ricans in the 'New Nueva York,'" in *From Bomba to Hip-Hop: Puerto Rican Culture and Latino Identity* (New York: Columbia University Press, 2000), 141–165.

6. Mexico also received enslaved Africans in the colonial period, although they never exceeded 2 percent of the total population. In 1810, Mexico had ten thousand slaves, although its free colored population is estimated to have been sixty thousand to seventy thousand, plus a population of Afro-mestizos, whose numbers are disputed. Herbert S. Klein, *African Slavery in Latin America and the Caribbean* (New York: Oxford University Press, 1986), 222.

7. See, for example, Martha Menchaca, "Latinas/os and the *Mestizo* Racial Heritage of Mexican Americans," in *A Companion to Latina/o Studies,* ed. Juan Flores and Renato Rosaldo (Malden, MA: Blackwell Publishing, 2007), 313–324; George Martinez, "Mexican Americans and Whiteness," in *The Latino/a Condition: A Critical Reader,* ed. Richard Delgado and Jean Stephanic (New York: New York University Press, 1998), 175–179; and Arturo F. Rosales, *Chicano! The History of the Mexican American Civil Rights Movement* (Houston: Arte Público Press, 1997), 95–96.

8. See Juan Flores, "'Qué Assimilated, Brother, Yo Soy Assimilao': The Structuring of Puerto Rican Identity," in Juan Flores, *Divided Borders: Essays on Puerto Rican Identity* (Houston: Arte Público Press, 1993), 183–195.

9. George Lipsitz, "Land of a Thousand Dances: Youth, Minorities, and the Rise of Rock and Roll," in *Recasting America: Culture and Politics in the Age of Cold War,* ed. Larry May (Chicago: University of Chicago Press, 1989), 269.

10. See Eric Zolov, *Refried Elvis: The Rise of the Mexican Counterculture* (Berkeley: University of California Press, 1999); and Javier Santiago, *Nueva ola portoricensis: La revolución musical que vivió Puerto Rico en la década del 60* (Santurce, Puerto Rico: Editorial del Patio, 1994).

11. In the 1980s, these perceptions were articulated in the rockero/cocolo (rockers versus salseros) debates; see Ana María García's documentary *Cocolos y Rockeros* (Pandora Films, 1992). The equation of electric guitar, rock, and U.S. imperialism by island-based Puerto Rican nationalists has lasted until recently: Ángel Quintero Rivera, for example, describes a 1993 concert in which salsero Gilberto Santa Rosa, acting out a mock discussion with a young (female) rocker, asserted that it was impossible for an electric guitar to appear in a salsa concert because it was so closely identified with rock; see Quintero Rivera, *Salsa, sabor y control! Sociología de la música "tropical"* (Havana, Cuba: Casa de las Américas, 1998), 195–196. See also Frances R. Aparicio, *Listening to Salsa: Gender, Latin American Music, and Puerto Rican Cultures* (Middletown, CT: Wesleyan University Press, 1998), 69–73.

12. See, for example, Rubén Guevara, "The View from the Sixth Street Bridge:

The History of Chicano Rock," in *The Rock History Reader,* ed. Theo Cateforis (New York: Routledge, 2007), 37–42; George Lipsitz, "Cruising around the Historical Bloc: Postmodernism and Popular Music in East Los Angeles," *Cultural Critique* 5 (1986–1987): 157–177; Lipsitz, "Land of a Thousand Dances"; Steven Loza, *Barrio Rhythms: Mexican American Music in Los Angeles* (Urbana: University of Illinois Press, 1993); David Reyes and Tom Waldman, *Land of a Thousand Dances: Chicano Rock 'n' Roll from Southern California* (Albuquerque: University of New Mexico Press, 1998); Jim McCarthy with Ron Sansoe, *Voices of Latin Rock: The People and Events That Created This Sound* (Milwaukee: Hal Leonard Corporation, 2004); Matt Garcia, "The 'Chicano' Dance Hall: Remapping Public Space in Post–World War II Greater Los Angeles," in *Sound Identities: Popular Music and the Cultural Politics of Education,* ed. Cameron McCarthy, Glenn Hudak, Shawn Miklauic, and Paula Saukko (New York: Peter Lang Publishing, 1999), 317–341; Roberto Avant-Mier, "Latinos in the Garage: A Genealogical Exploration of Latino/a Influence in Garage Rock, Rock and Pop Music," *Popular Music and Society* 31, no. 5 (2008): 555–574.

13. Lipsitz, "Land of a Thousand Dances," 272.

14. See Garcia, "The 'Chicano' Dance Hall," 324–333.

15. Testifying to the close relationship between the two communities is a three-volume set entitled *Brown Eyed Soul: The Sounds of East L.A.* (Rhino R2 72868, R2 72869, R2 72870; 1997) that chronicles the music popular in East Los Angeles in the 1950s, 1960s, and 1970s, which includes as many songs by African American musicians as by Mexican Angeleno groups.

16. Reyes and Waldman, *Land of a Thousand Dances,* 118.

17. See Michelle Habell-Pallán, *Loca Motion: The Travels of Chicana and Latina Popular Culture* (New York: New York University Press, 2005), 151; and Ed Morales, *The Latin Beat: The Rhythm and Roots of Latin Music from Bossa Nova to Salsa and Beyond* (Boston: DaCapo Press, 1999), 289–290.

18. Reebee Garofalo believes Chicano rockers' preference for the sound of the organ may also be indebted to the music of Cuban-born, Mexican-based bandleader Pérez Prado, who was wildly popular in Los Angeles in the 1950s. Prado's earlier mambos did not use the organ, but his late 1950s and 1960s pop- and rock 'n' roll–inflected mambos, which often used an organ, might well have inspired Chicano rockers (pers. comm., 2007).

19. Guevara, "The View from the Sixth Street Bridge," 118.

20. Garcia, "The 'Chicano' Dance Hall," 330.

21. Lipsitz and others have linked West Coast Chicanos' love of rock 'n' roll to California's teenage car culture, in which the experiences of cruising—roaming widely through the extensive urban landscapes of Los Angeles—and listening to rock 'n' roll on the car radio have been seamlessly woven together into a single experience of freedom and pleasure. See Lipsitz, "Land of a Thousand Dances," 277; and Garcia, "The 'Chicano' Dance Hall," 324–325.

22. Lead singer Sam the Sham (Domingo Samudio) was born and raised in Dallas, Texas.

23. The Sir Douglas Quintet was from central Texas, and some of its members were Latinos; the group's lead singer, Doug Sahm, was not of Mexican descent, but he was so thoroughly immersed in Texan styles that he later recorded an album under the name of Doug Saldaña. Despite the musicians' efforts to make the group appear to be a part of the wildly popular British Invasion, scholars have noted the group's clear Tejano

influences in their accordion-based melodies and "slowed down polka rhythm" (Peter Manuel, pers. comm.); see also Avant-Mier, "Latinos in the Garage," 563–564.

24. Freddy Fender, interview with Davia Nelson, liner notes to Fender's *Canciones de Mi Barrio* (Ideal/Arhoolie CD 366).

25. Lead singer Rudy Martinez and several of the band members were born in Texas but raised in Saginaw, Michigan.

26. For example, when I first arrived at the University of Wisconsin–Madison in 1967, the freshman mixer featured ? (Question Mark) and the Mysterians, whose song "96 Tears" had become a major national hit in 1966. Neither I nor any of my new acquaintances had any idea they were of Mexican descent.

27. Reyes and Waldman, *Land of a Thousand Dances,* 118–119.

28. Interestingly, Chuy Varela's liner notes for Volume 4 of the CD set *The West Coast East Side Sound* (VSD 6020) state that the idea for the name change originated not with the band but with producer Eddie Davis, who released the song "Viva Tirado" under the new name without the band's permission; the band did not accept the name until "Viva Tirado" became a national hit.

29. *Malo* (Warner Brothers 2584-2, 1995; original release date 1972).

30. Estevan César Azcona, liner notes to *Rolas de Aztlán: Songs of the Chicano Movement* (Smithsonian Folkways CD40516, 2005).

31. Any musical development of significance coming out of the Spanish Caribbean or New York, from mambo to cha-cha to salsa, also made it to Los Angeles, in part because of the latter city's pivotal importance in the U.S. entertainment industry but also because of the city's large population of cosmopolitan musicians and fans eager to participate in and contribute to whatever cultural fashions were currently in vogue. See Loza, *Barrio Rhythms*. In "The 'Chicano' Dance Hall," Garcia similarly notes that the music played on Spanish-language radio and the musicians playing in Mexican American dance halls included those of Spanish Caribbean origins.

32. It is noteworthy that, although Carabello was of Puerto Rican origins (but raised in San Francisco's Mission District), the other seminal percussionists responsible for infusing Chicano Latin rock with its distinctively Afro-Cuban sounds were not of Spanish Caribbean origins: The Escovedos were of Mexican descent, and Areas was Nicaraguan. After playing with Santana's band, the Escovedos formed the group Azteca in the early 1970s. See McCarthy with Sansoe, *Voices of Latin Rock*.

33. Rubén Guevara, telephone interview by the author, March 3, 2008.

34. Reyes and Waldman, *Land of a Thousand Dances,* 145–154; Loza, *Barrio Rhythms,* 233–254.

35. El Vez, *Fun in Español* (SFTRI 234-S, 1994).

36. For more on El Vez, see Habell-Pallán, "Bridge over Troubled Borders," 181–204; Marjorie Chodorov's fine documentary on El Vez, *El Rey de Rock 'n' Roll* (Soap Box Films, 2000).

37. Ruth Glasser, for example, has documented the interactions between African American and Puerto Rican musicians as far back as World War I, when black Puerto Rican musicians were recruited for James Reese Europe's all-black regimental band, many of whom ended up in New York, playing in Harlem jazz clubs after the war. See Glasser, *My Music Is My Flag: Puerto Rican Musicians and Their New York Communities, 1917–1940* (Berkeley: University of California Press, 1995).

38. Blanca Vázques, Juan Flores, and Pablo Figueroa, "Interview with KMX

Assault: The Puerto Rican Roots of Rap," *Boletín del Centro de Estudios Puertorriqueños* 1, no. 1 (1992–1993): 39–51.

39. Flores, "Qué Assimilated, Brother."

40. For more on the tensions between Puerto Ricans' racial, cultural, and national identities, see, for example, Piri Thomas, *Down These Mean Streets* (1967; repr. New York: Vintage Books, 1991); and Raquel Z. Rivera, *New York Ricans from the Hip Hop Zone* (New York: Palgrave, 2003).

41. For musical examples, see *Vaya!!!! R & B Groups Go Latin* (Relic 7098, 1995) and relevant commentary in the liner notes by Donn Fileti.

42. The popularity of doo-wop among New York Puerto Rican teens explains why several of the songs in Paul Simon's ill-fated 1998 musical *Capeman*, about a young New York Puerto Rican in the 1950s, were in the doo-wop style.

43. Frankie Lymon and the Teenagers were signed by George Goldner, founder of the legendary Latin music label Tico, whose roster boasted New York's most successful Latin musicians, including superstars Machito and Puente; see Stuffed Animal (pseudonym), "Mambo Gee Gee: The Story of George Goldner and Tico Records," available at http://www.spectropop.com/tico/index.htm (accessed February 2009).

44. Max Salazar, "Afro-American Latinized Rhythms," in *Salsiology: Afro-Cuban Music and the Evolution of Salsa in New York City,* ed. Vernon W. Boggs (New York: Excelsior Music Publishing, 1992), 241.

45. Dorin Fileti, liner notes to *Vaya!!!!*; Tony Orlando also started his career singing doo-wop in the 1950s with a group called the Five Gents. Santiago, *Nueva ola portoricensis,* 196.

46. The dance music scene in Cuba also suffered from the rupture of interactions from New York, worsened by the postrevolutionary fervor that stigmatized musical forms perceived to be foreign to Cuba. When Havana's dance music scene began to regroup and recuperate in the 1970s, it did so with few direct contacts with musicians in New York. See Robin Moore, *Music and Revolution: Cultural Change in Socialist Cuba* (Berkeley: University of California Press, 2006); see also Deborah Pacini Hernandez and Reebee Garofalo, "Between Rock and a Hard Place: Negotiating Rock in Revolutionary Cuba, 1960–1980," in *Rockin' Las Américas: The Global Politics of Rock in Latin/o America,* ed. Deborah Pacini Hernandez, Eric Zolov, and Héctor Fernández L'Hoeste (Pittsburgh: University of Pittsburgh Press, 2004), 43–67.

47. Audiences were already familiar with the term "watusi" from the Orlons' 1962 hit song "The Wah Watusi," although there were no aesthetic or commercial connections between the two songs.

48. Stuffed Animal, "Mambo Gee Gee."

49. For an extensive discussion of boogaloo's development, see Juan Flores, "'Cha Cha with a Backbeat': Songs and Stories of Latin Boogaloo," in *From Bomba to Hip-Hop,* 79–112.

50. Ibid., 81.

51. Matt Garcia gives a slightly different spin to the party sounds in some Chicano rock 'n' roll, explaining that the "hoots and hollers" reflected the close contact between bands and their audiences; see Garcia, "The 'Chicano' Dance Hall," 330.

52. Vernon W. Boggs, "Johnny 'Mr. Boogaloo Blues' Colon," in *Salsiology: Afro-Cuban Music and the Evolution of Salsa in New York City,* ed. Vernon W. Boggs (New York: Excelsior Music Publishing, 1992), 272.

53. Steven Loza, *Tito Puente and the Making of Latin Music* (Urbana: University of Illinois Press, 1999), 41–42.

54. Elsewhere in Latin America, salsa was similarly embraced by nationalists as the authentic voice of the hemisphere's urban working classes and as a bulwark against rock and other styles of U.S. popular music perceived as manifestations of U.S. cultural imperialism. For a more extensive analysis of widespread Latin American perceptions of rock as a form of U.S. cultural imperialism that needed to be actively resisted, see Deborah Pacini Hernandez, Eric Zolov, and Hector Fernández L'Hoeste, eds., "Mapping Rock Music Cultures across the Americas," in *Rockin' Las Américas: The Global Politics of Rock in Latin/o America,* ed. Deborah Pacini Hernandez, Eric Zolov, and Héctor Fernández L'Hoeste (Pittsburgh: University of Pittsburgh Press, 2004): 1–21.

55. See Quintero Rivera, *Salsa, sabor y control!* 204. The appeal of brass-based bands, such as Chicago, was not limited to New York Puerto Ricans—they were also popular among dance bands in Cuba at the time. See Pacini Hernandez and Garofalo, "Between Rock and a Hard Place," 62.

56. For more on such musical fusions, see the liner notes to *Nu Yorica!* (Soul Jazz Records CD29, 1996).

57. John Storm Roberts, *The Latin Tinge: The Impact of Latin American Music on the United States* (1979; repr. New York: Oxford University Press, 1999), 187.

58. Stuart Baker, liner notes to *Chicano Power! Latin Rock in the USA 1968–1976* (Soul Jazz Records CD39, 1998).

59. Averne also started his own record company, Toro Records, and released (and sometimes produced) influential pieces of Latin rock/jazz fusions, such as Rafael Cortijo's *Time Machine* (Musical Productions, 1974), Machito's *Fireworks* (Timeless, 1977), and Eddie Palmieri's *Sun of Latin Music* (Musical Productions, 1973). Ibid.

60. Jason Ankeny, "Biography of Jose Feliciano," http://www.allmusic.com/cg/amg. dll?p=amg&sql=11:wifoxqw5ld6e~T1 (accessed April 29, 2009).

61. Donald Clarke, ed., *The Penguin Encyclopedia of Popular Music* (New York: Viking Books, 1989), 877.

62. Linda Ronstadt is a comparable example of a mainstream pop star with Mexican American ancestry whose musical success in the 1970s was not linked to her ethnic roots; indeed, most mainstream audiences did not even know she was of Mexican descent until well after her career was firmly established, when she recorded an album called *Canciones de Mi Padre* (*Songs of My Father*) in 1988, whose cover pictured her in traditional Mexican garb. The father referenced in the album title was actually her paternal grandfather, Fred Ronstadt, a German-born Mexican rancher and inventor (*Rolling Stone,* October 19, 1978). In 1992, she recorded two more albums of Mexican songs.

63. See Reyes and Waldman, *Land of a Thousand Dances,* 103–109.

64. Lipsitz, "Cruising around the Historical Bloc," 164.

65. See Pacini Hernandez and Garofalo, "Between Rock and a Hard Place," 43–67.

66. Cf. Mike Davis, *City of Quartz: Excavating the Future in Los Angeles* (New York: Vintage Books, 1992); and David Rieff, *Los Angeles: Capital of the Third World* (New York: Simon and Schuster, 1991).

67. Rubén Guevara, liner notes to *Ay Califas! Raza Rock* (Rhino R2 72920, 1998).

68. As with any generalizations, there are some exceptions; for examples of songs with more positive views of New York City, see Peter Manuel, "Representations of New York City in Latin Music," in *Island Sounds in the Global City,* ed. Ray Allen and Lois

Wilken (New York: New York Folklore Society and the Institute for Studies in American Music, Brooklyn College, 1998), 23–43.

69. Cf. Thomas, *Down These Mean Streets*; and Frances Negrón-Muntaner's semi-autobiographical documentary *Brincando el Charco: Portrait of a Puerto Rican* (National Latino Communications Center and Independent Television Service, 2000).

70. Quintero Rivera, *Salsa, sabor y control!* 212.

CHAPTER 4

1. I borrow the term "sociosonic circuitries" from Wayne Marshall, who develops the concept in his essay "From Música Negra to Reggaeton Latino: The Cultural Politics of Nation, Migration, and Commercialization," in *Reggaeton,* ed. Raquel Z. Rivera, Wayne Marshall, and Deborah Pacini Hernandez (Durham, NC: Duke University Press, 2009), 19–76.

2. Peter Shapiro, *Turn the Beat Around: The Secret History of Disco* (New York: Faber and Faber, 2005), 258.

3. Marshall Berman, "View from the Burning Bridge," *Dissent* 46, no. 3 (Summer 1999): 79.

4. Shapiro, *Turn the Beat Around,* 239.

5. The Puerto Rican contributions to early hip-hop can be seen in *Wild Style,* a 1983 film on early hip-hop culture by Charlie Ahern that features Puerto Rican DJ Charlie Chase, Puerto Rican break-dancers the Rock Steady Crew, and graffiti artists Lee Quiñonez and Sandra Fabara.

6. See Juan Flores, "Wild Style and Filming Hip-Hop," *Areito* 10, no. 37 (1984): 36–39; Flores, "'Puerto Rican and Proud, Boyee!' Rap, Roots and Amnesia," *Boletín del Centro de Estudios Puertorriqueños* 5, no. 1 (1992–1993): 22–31; Flores, *From Bomba to Hip-Hop: Puerto Rican Culture and Latino Identity* (New York: Columbia University Press, 2000); Raquel Z. Rivera, "Boricuas from the Hip Hop Zone: Notes on Race and Ethnic Relations in New York City," *Boletín del Centro de Estudios Puertorriqueños* 8, nos. 1–2 (1996): 202–215; and Rivera, *New York Ricans from the Hip Hop Zone* (New York: Palgrave Macmillan, 2003). See also the documentary *From Mambo to Hip Hop: A South Bronx Tale,* directed by Henry Chalfant and produced by Elena Martínez and Steve Zeitlin (New York: City Lore, 2006).

7. Chalfant, *From Mambo to Hip Hop.*

8. Ibid.

9. The success of these bilingual West Coast rappers was later surpassed by the thoroughly multiethnic and multiracial group Cypress Hill, comprised of a Mexican/Cuban American lead singer, an Afro-Cuban (Mellow Man Ace's brother), and an Italian American. Los Angeles also produced dozens of Chicano and Latino rap groups, such as Proper Dos, Fifth Sun, and Delinquent Habits, that did not chart nationally but had local followings.

10. John Storm Roberts, *The Latin Tinge: The Impact of Latin American Music on the United States* (1979; repr. New York: Oxford University Press, 1999), 169.

11. Alan Jones and Jussi Kantonen, *Saturday Night Forever: The History of Disco* (Edinburgh: Mainstream Publishers, 1999), 28.

12. "This Is a Tribute to Salsoul Records," available at http://www.disco-disco.com/labels/salsoul.shtml (accessed May 2009).

13. Shapiro, *Turn the Beat Around,* 146–147.

14. Tim Lawrence, *Love Saves the Day: A History of American Dance Music Culture* (Durham, NC: Duke University Press, 2003), 170.

15. See "This Is a Tribute to Salsoul Records."

16. Andy González is primarily known as a bassist, although he also played percussion, for example, with Conjunto Libre in 1977; see César Miguel Rondón, *The Book of Salsa: A Chronicle of Urban Music from the Caribbean to New York City* (Chapel Hill: University of North Carolina Press, 2008), 248; translated by Frances R. Aparicio, with Jackie White, from the original *El libro de la salsa: Crónica de la música del Caribe urbano* (Caracas, Venezuela: Editorial Arte, 1980).

17. A number of inconsistencies in the history and chronology of the founding of the Caytronics, Mericana, and SalSoul labels are reported in three recently published books on disco and dance music (Jones and Kantonen's *Saturday Night Forever,* Shapiro's *Turn the Beat Around,* and Lawrence's *Love Saves the Day*). I rely here on an extensive interview with Ken Cayre reproduced online, trusting that, as Cayre was one of the principal players in these events, his version is accurate. See "This Is a Tribute to Salsoul Records."

18. For more on Grupo Folklorico y Experimental Nuevayorkino and Conjunto Libre, see Roberta L. Singer, "Tradition and Innovation in Contemporary Latin Popular Music in New York City," *Latin American Music Review* 4, no. 2 (1983): 183–202; and Rondón's *The Book of Salsa,* 238–248.

19. See Richard Pierson's biography of Joe Bataan, available at http://www.allmusic.com/cg/amg.dll?p=amg&sql=11:hzftxqw5ldse~T1 (accessed May 2009).

20. "This Is a Tribute to Salsoul Records."

21. See Shapiro, *Turn the Beat Around,* 188. See also an online article on the history of the hustle, in which Billy Fajardo elaborates on the origins of the Latin hustle: "In the Latin discotheques of that day, including 'The Corso,' 'Barney Goo Goo's' and 'The Ipanema,' disco music was used as a bridge between live band sets. In these clubs, touch dancing had always been present in the form of Mambo, Salsa, Cha Cha and Bolero. As a result of this fusion, the simple 6-count dance began to incorporate the 'ball change' action of the Mambo. The count of the dance now became 1-2-3 & 4-5-6. The dance, although a touch dance, was now performed mostly side-by-side. It also began to incorporate a lot of the intricate turn patterns of the Mambo. The dance began to include multiple turns and hand changes with a ropey feel to the arm movements. Hence the danced [sic] was now referred to as the 'Rope Hustle' or 'Latin Hustle.'" Fajardo, "The History of Hustle," available at http://www.seattlehustleclub.com/about_hustle.htm (accessed May 2009).

22. Shapiro, *Turn the Beat Around,* 186.

23. Chalfant, *From Mambo to Hip Hop.*

24. Unfortunately, none of those describing the development of the hustle discusses whether its "aerials" and acrobatics were connected to similar developments on break-dance floors.

25. Jones and Kantonen, *Saturday Night Forever,* 37–41.

26. Shapiro, *Turn the Beat Around,* 189.

27. In an uncharacteristically antiracist cinematic gesture, Travolta's character actually presents the Puerto Rican couple with his first-place trophy and cash prize.

28. See Lawrence, *Love Saves the Day,* 384.

29. Shapiro, *Turn the Beat Around,* 242–243.

30. See Rivera, *New York Ricans,* 79–96.

31. Shapiro, *Turn the Beat Around,* 321–322.

32. A more electronic sound imported from Europe further complicated disco's genealogical mix. See Reebee Garofalo, *Rockin' Out: Popular Music in the U.S.A.* (Upper Saddle River, NJ: Pearson/Prentiss Hall, 1997), 312–319.

33. Lawrence, *Love Saves the Day,* 221.

34. Shapiro, *Turn the Beat Around,* 186–187.

35. These lyrics, however, were not necessarily sung as complete songs—producers would often sample particular vocal lines and manipulate them in the studio.

36. Shapiro, *Turn the Beat Around,* 273.

37. Rivera, *New York Ricans,* 89.

38. Quoted in Cristina Verán, "Let the Music Play (Again)," *Village Voice,* April 11, 2006.

39. Quoted in ibid.

40. See d. u. proserpio, "Freestyle: How Can We Be Wrong?" (unpublished manuscript).

41. See Jennifer Parris, "Freestyle Forum," *Urban: The Latino Magazine* 2, no. 1 (1996): 30–31; also Verán, "Let the Music Play (Again)."

42. proserpio, "Freestyle."

43. La India's powerful voice in her early freestyle recordings has since been sampled by countless DJs.

44. George Rivera, "Dicen Que Soy . . . All That and More: The India Interview," available at http://www.jazzconclave.com/i-room/india.html (accessed May 2009).

45. Roberta Morgan's 1979 book *Disco,* a history and "how to" book on disco dancing targeting general audiences, contains a list of discos in major U.S. and Canadian cities; with eighteen listings, Los Angeles was second only to New York in the number of its disco clubs (New York: Bell Publishing, 1979). Disco's popularity on the West Coast accounts for the 1978 film *Thank God It's Friday,* a commercially and critically less-successful follow-up to *Saturday Night Fever* about Los Angeles nightlife, featuring disco legends Donna Summer and the Commodores.

46. The numerous and thorough accounts of Mexican American engagement with rock 'n' roll and its multiple offshoots virtually ignore disco. Stephen Loza's *Barrio Rhythms: Mexican American Music in Los Angeles* (Urbana: University of Illinois Press, 1993) and David Reyes and Tom Waldman's *Land of a Thousand Dances: Chicano Rock 'n' Roll from Southern California* (Albuquerque: University of New Mexico Press, 1998), for example, do not even have an entry for disco in their indexes.

47. Telephone interview by the author, March 3, 2008. One of disco's biggest critics was Frank Zappa, who produced two antidisco songs in the 1970s, "Disco Boy" and "Dancin' Fool." Rubén Guevara, who collaborated with Zappa in the 1970s, did not share these views.

48. Los Angeles's promoter/party crew scene has only recently been documented systematically. Gerard Meraz, who participated in the scene as a DJ, later wrote a master's thesis on the subject entitled "An Oral History of East Los Angeles DJ Culture" (California State University, Northridge, December 2004; also available online at http://www.lulu.com). See also the proceedings from a July 2, 2008, panel discussion entitled "Anatomy of the North-

east L.A. Backyard Party," moderated by Raúl Báltazar with Willie (DJ Guilty), Karen Salgado (Divine Dolls), Gerard Meraz (Wild Boyz, Brat Pack), Miguel (DJ Reckless, Anti Socials), and Chris Gutiérrez (Anti Socials, Jam Packed Productions), available at http://sicklyseason .com/dialogo/g727/g727dj.htm (accessed May 2009). The panel discussion was part of Gallery 727's exhibit "Featuring the Lightz and Soundz of: A 30-Year Survey of DJ Culture from East L.A." Thanks to Rubén Guevara for bringing these materials to my attention.

49. DJs purchased their records at record stores or obtained them through record pools. Well-known DJs also received free promotional copies from record labels.

50. Meraz, "An Oral History of East Los Angeles DJ Culture."

51. Ibid.

52. Ibid.

53. Robert Karimi, "Wax Alchemists," *Frontera* 1, no. 4 (1996): 28.

54. See James Clifford, "Traveling Cultures," in *Cultural Studies,* ed. Lawrence Grossberg, Cary Nelson, and Paula Treichler (New York: Routledge, 1992), 96–112.

55. Karimi, "Wax Alchemists," 29.

56. Ibid.

57. Yvette C. Doss, "Choosing Chicano in the 1990s: The Underground Music Scene of Los(t) Angeles," *Aztlán: A Journal of Chicano Studies* 23, no. 2 (Fall 1998): 192. It is important to note that Mexican American rock, even when in Spanish, was not coterminous with *rock en español.* As discussed in Chapter 3, Chicano rockers' musical roots were in U.S. rock 'n' roll, not Mexican, and they always used English freely and without apology, reaching out not only to their own bilingual community but also to mainstream audiences—and, more recently, to international audiences as well. In contrast, the *rock en español* emerging from Latin America at the time was, by definition, only in Spanish and in the United States was more closely associated with newer immigrants from Latin America (the majority of whom have been Mexican) who had grown up listening to it prior to coming to the United States. See Deborah Pacini Hernandez, Eric Zolov, and Héctor Fernández L'Hoeste, eds., *Rockin' Las Américas: The Global Politics of Rock in Latin/o America* (Pittsburgh: University of Pittsburgh Press, 2004).

58. Quoted in Melissa Castillo-Garstow, "Latinos in Hip Hop to Reggaeton," *Latin Beat Magazine* (March 2005), available at http://www.brownpride.com/latinrap/latinrap. asp?a=hiphoptoreggaeton/index1 (accessed January 15, 2009).

59. The document from which this citation was taken was sent to me by Elijah Wald, who downloaded it from Universal Records' Web site in 2006. The document is no longer available online.

60. Ibid.

61. Ibid.

62. Quoted in Ramiro Burr, "Urban Regional Sound Pays Off for Mexiclan," *Houston Chronicle,* February 20, 2004.

63. Juan Flores discusses Latin Empire, another equally talented, bilingual, bicultural group whose music fused hip-hop and a variety of Latin styles, in "Puerto Rocks: Rap, Roots and Amnesia," from his book *From Bomba to Hip-Hop,* 115–139. See also the documentary *The Americans,* part 10 of the *Americas* series (WGBH Boston and Central Television Enterprises, United Kingdom, 1993), which contains excellent interviews and performance footage demonstrating Latin Empire's fluid biculturalism.

64. Marshall, "From Música Negra to Reggaeton Latino," 19–76.

65. In the Caribbean port city of Cartagena, Colombia, for example, styles from

Africa and its diaspora had been circulating in the city's poor black community since the 1960s; see Deborah Pacini Hernandez, "Sound Systems, World Beat and Diasporan Identity in Cartagena, Colombia," in *Diaspora: A Journal of Transnational Studies* 5, no. 3 (1996): 429–466. As I note in this essay, Jamaican popular musics were introduced to Cartagena's black population by sailors working the maritime trade between that city and the Colombian-owned island of San Andrés, whose black, Protestant, English-speaking population has always been culturally closer to Jamaicans than to the more recently arrived Spanish-speaking, Catholic Colombians who have come to dominate the island's economy.

66. See Christoph Twickel, "Reggae in Panama: *Bien* Tough," and "Muévelo (Move It!): From Panama to New York and Back Again, the Story of El General," both in *Reggaeton*, ed. Raquel Z. Rivera, Wayne Marshall, and Deborah Pacini Hernandez (Durham, NC: Duke University Press, 2009), 81–88 and 99–108, respectively.

67. For more on dembow, see Wayne Marshall, "Dembow, Dem Bow, Dembo: Translation and Transnation in Reggaeton," *Song and Popular Culture* 52 (2008): 131–151.

68. For more on the circulation of diasporic musics in the Caribbean in the 1980s and early 1990s, see Deborah Pacini Hernandez, "A View from the South: Spanish Caribbean Perspectives on World Beat," *World of Music* 35, no. 2 (1993): 40–69.

69. See, for example, Sujatha Fernandes, *Cuba Represent! Cuban Arts, State Power, and the Making of New Revolutionary Cultures* (Durham, NC: Duke University Press, 2006); Wayne Marshall, "Routes, Rap, Reggae: Hearing the Histories of Hip-Hop and Reggae Together" (Ph.D. diss., University of Wisconsin, Madison, 2007); and Deborah Pacini Hernandez and Reebee Garofalo, "Hip Hop in Havana: Rap, Race and National Identity in Contemporary Cuba," *Journal of Popular Music Studies* (1999–2000): 18–47.

70. They did not, however, necessarily give up their attachment to salsa, which, as the raging *cocolo* versus *rockero* (salseros versus rockers) controversies in the 1980s demonstrate, remained a powerful symbol of Puerto Rican working-class identity as well as of the resistance to U.S. cultural imperialism perceived to be encoded in rock. See, for example, Ana María García's documentary *Cocolos y Rockeros* (Pandora Films, 1992), in which some of the young cocolos she interviews are also listening and dancing to hip-hop.

71. See Raquel Z. Rivera, "Policing Morality, *Mano Duro Stylee*: The Case of Underground Rap and Reggae in Puerto Rico in the Mid-1990s," in *Reggaeton*, ed. Raquel Z. Rivera, Wayne Marshall, and Deborah Pacini Hernandez (Durham, NC: Duke University Press, 2009), 111–134.

72. Marshall, "From Música Negra to Reggaeton Latino," 42.

73. Jorge L. Giovannetti, "Popular Music and Culture in Puerto Rico: Jamaican and Rap Music as Cross-Cultural Symbols," in *Musical Migrations: Transnationalism and Cultural Hybridity in Latin/o America,* ed. Frances R. Aparicio and Cándida F. Jáquez (New York: Palgrave Macmillan, 2003), 89.

74. Christian Capellan, interview by the author and Raquel Z. Rivera, May 9, 2005.

75. Raquel Cepeda, "Riddims by the Reggaetón: Puerto Rico's Hip-Hop Hybrid Takes Over New York," *Village Voice*, March 28, 2005.

76. Jose Davila, "You Got Your Reggaetón in My Hip-Hop: Crunkiao and 'Spanish Music' in the Miami Urban Scene," in *Reggaeton*, ed. Raquel Z. Rivera, Wayne Mar-

shall, and Deborah Pacini Hernandez (Durham, NC: Duke University Press, 2009), 200–213.

77. George Lipsitz, *Dangerous Crossroads: Popular Music, Postmodernism and the Poetics of Place* (New York: Verso, 1994), 4.

CHAPTER 5

1. Fulanito, *El Hombre Mas Famoso de la Tierra* (Cutting Records R 330447, 1997).

2. The metal "güira," also called a *"guayo,"* is related to but distinct from the gourd, "güiro."

3. The term "guallando" refers to the act of scraping the güira/guayo but serves as a double entendre for the close body rubbing that can take place in merengue dancing.

4. The exact figure cited by the 2007 American Community Survey is 1,183,365 (available at http://www.census.gov/acs/www/index.html [accessed February 2009]).

5. Suro and Passel support this argument with the following statistics: "Young adults have dominated most migrant streams in modern times, and that is certainly true of Latino immigrants who are concentrated in the child-bearing years. . . . In 2000 the first generation totaled 14.2 million people, or 40 percent of the Latino population, while the second generation counted 9.9 million, or 28 percent. The third-plus generation numbered 11.3 million and made up 32 percent of the Hispanic population. The growth of the second generation accelerated in the 1990s and reached 63 percent for the decade, up from 52 percent in the 1980s, surpassing the growth due to immigration (55 percent in the 1990s and 78 percent in the 1980s) even as the nation experienced a record influx from Latin America." Robert Suro and Jeffrey Passel, *The Rise of the Second Generation: Changing Patterns in Hispanic Population Growth*, Pew Hispanic Center, Washington, D.C., October 14, 2004, p. 3, available at http://pewhispanic.org/files/reports/22.pdf (accessed January 23, 2009).

6. Ibid.

7. See Juan Flores, "'Qué Assimilated, Brother, Yo Soy Assimilao': The Structuring of Puerto Rican Identity," in *Divided Borders: Essays on Puerto Rican Identity* (Houston: Arte Público Press, 1993), 183–195.

8. See, for example, Gustavo Pérez Firmat, *Life on the Hyphen: The Cuban American Way* (Austin: University of Texas Press, 1994).

9. Peggy Levitt, *Transnational Villagers* (Berkeley: University of California Press, 2001).

10. The literature on transnationalism is extensive, but for a sample of early influential work, see Nina Glick Schiller, Linda Basch, and Cristina Blanc-Szanton, eds., *Towards a Transnational Perspective on Migration: Race, Class, Ethnicity, and Nationalism Reconsidered* (New York: New York Academy of Sciences, 1992); Ulf Hannerz, *Transnational Connections: People, Cultures, Places* (London: Routledge, 1996); and Alejandro Portes, Luis Guarnizo, and Patricia Landholt, "The Study of Transnationalism: Pitfalls and Promise of an Emergent Research Field," *Ethnic and Racial Studies* 22, no. 2 (March 1999): 217–237.

11. For centuries, Rio Grande Valley tejanos, for example, kept in regular touch with friends and family just across the border; Cubans around the turn of the nineteenth century routinely shuttled between Tampa and Cuba; and the cultural interac-

tions between island- and mainland-based Puerto Ricans have been constant for well over a century.

12. Alejandro Portes, "Introduction: The Debates and Significance of Immigrant Transnationalism," *Global Networks* 1, no. 3 (2001): 189. For more thorough discussions of transnational theory's utility in understanding the second generation, see Peggy Levitt and Mary C. Waters, eds., *The Changing Face of Home: The Transnational Lives of the Second Generation* (New York: Russell Sage Foundation, 2002); and Phillip Kasinitz, John H. Mollenkopf, Mary C. Waters, and Jennifer Holdway, *Inheriting the City: The Children of Immigrants Come of Age* (Cambridge, MA: Harvard University Press, 2008; New York: Russell Sage Foundation, 2008).

13. Levitt and Waters, *Changing Face of Home,* 2. The simultaneity of the relationship between assimilation and transnationalism is explored further in Peggy Levitt and Nina Glick Schiller, "Conceptualizing Simultaneity: A Transnational Social Field Perspective on Society," in which the authors note that "it is more useful to think of the migrant experience as a kind of gauge, which while anchored, pivots between new land and a transnational incorporation. Movement and attachment is not lineal or sequential but capable of rotating back and forth and changing direction over time. The median point on this gauge is not full incorporation but rather simultaneity of connection." *International Migration Review* 38, no. 3 (Fall 2004): 1011.

14. Nineteenth-century musical exchanges between the islands produced variations on the European contredanse that developed into the *danzón* in Cuba, *danza* in Puerto Rico, and merengue in the Dominican Republic; see Paul Austerlitz, *Merengue: Dominican Music and Dominican Identity* (Philadelphia: Temple University Press, 1997), 15–18.

15. The same group of Dominican and Puerto Rican musicians recorded as Trio Quisqueya for the Dominican market and as Trio Borinquen for the Puerto Rican market, each name referencing the indigenous name for the island of Hispaniola and of Puerto Rico, respectively.

16. Exiled Dominican accordionist Dioris Valladares estimated that in the mid-1930s, only one hundred Dominicans lived in New York, including consular personnel; see Thomas van Buren and Leonardo Ivan Dominguez, "Transnational Music and Dance in Dominican New York," in *Dominican Migration: Transnational Perspectives,* ed. Ernesto Sagas and Sintia E. Molina (Gainesville: University Press of Florida, 2004), 248.

17. See Deborah Pacini Hernandez, *Bachata: A Social History of a Dominican Popular Music* (Philadelphia: Temple University Press, 1995), 35–61.

18. See Austerlitz, *Merengue,* 73–75.

19. See van Buren and Dominguez, "Transnational Music and Dance in Dominican New York," 250.

20. Austerlitz notes, citing Dominican singer Joseíto Mateo, that many of Viloria's fans were Puerto Ricans; see "From Transplant to Transnational Circuit: Merengue in New York," in *Island Sounds in the Global City: Caribbean Popular Music and Identity in New York,* ed. Ray Allen and Lois Wilken (New York: New York Folklore Society and the Institute for Studies in American Music, Brooklyn College, 1998), 47.

21. Pacini Hernandez, *Bachata,* 45.

22. Vernon W. Boggs, ed., *Salsiology: Afro-Cuban Music and the Evolution of Salsa in New York City* (New York: Excelsior Music Publishing, 1992), 214. See also van Buren and Dominguez, "Transnational Music and Dance in Dominican New York," 250.

23. "Mambo Gee Gee: The Story of George Goldner and Tico Records," an online history of Tico Records by the pseudonymous author Stuffed Animal, notes that the Latin musicians signed by Tico Records owner George Goldner in the 1950s included Dominican Ricardo Rico and his merengue band, but the author later in the article refers to the Rico recordings as "folk" music, suggesting that the band was an accordion-based conjunto rather than an *orquesta*. Available at http://www.spectropop.com/tico/TICOpart3.htm (accessed November 15, 2007). Rico does not, however, seem to have been a significant figure in the development of Dominican merengue in New York.

24. Austerlitz, *Merengue*, 74.

25. Max Salazar, *Mambo Kingdom: Latin Music in New York* (New York: Schirmer Trade Books, 2002), 160. In this same book, however, Salazar writes that it was the popular Dominican merengue vocalist and bandleader Joseíto Mateo, whose song "El Negrito del Batey" had made him a major star in the Dominican Republic, who performed at the Palladium in 1947 (p. 89). Given the difficulty of leaving the Dominican Republic, it seems more likely that it was Josecíto Ramón whose orchestra played the Palladium, since Austerlitz suggests he played routinely in New York. It should be noted, however, that Mateo was given permission to perform in Cuba in 1954, although after he returned to the Dominican Republic he was denied a visa to leave again to fulfill a contract he had gotten with a recording company in Havana. See http://www.grandesestrellas.com/j/joseito-mateo-biography.html (accessed October 25, 2007).

26. In an interview with Vernon Boggs, musician and later record-label owner Al Santiago recalled that during the mambo period, maybe one merengue a night might be played. Boggs, *Salsiology*, 205. Merengues were incorporated into bands via arrangements by non-Dominicans as well. Max Salazar, for example, notes that Tito Puente included a song called "Merengue Pa' Tí" in a 1947 recording; see Salazar, *Mambo Kingdom*, 113.

27. See Silvio Torres-Saillant and Ramona Hernández, *The Dominican Americans* (Westport, CT: Greenwood Press, 1998), 59–60.

28. Gabriel Haslip-Viera, "The Evolution of the Latino Community in the New York Metropolitan Area, 1810 to the Present," in *Latinos in New York: Communities in Transition,* ed. Gabriel Haslip-Viera and Sherri Baver (Notre Dame, IN: University of Notre Dame Press, 1996), 14–15.

29. See, for example, Christopher Washburne, *Sounding Salsa: Performing Latin Music in New York City* (Philadelphia: Temple University Press, 2008), 153–154.

30. Merengue's ascent generated hostility from some Puerto Rican musicians, who perceived merengue as a threat to their livelihoods, particularly since Dominican musicians were willing to accept lower performance fees than those commanded by more well-established *salseros*. See Pacini Hernandez, *Bachata*, 109–110; and Austerlitz, *Merengue*, 128.

31. The category referred to as "música tropical" includes dance musics of Spanish Caribbean origin, such as salsa, merengue, and cumbia; the term distinguishes these genres from Mexican regional music, *rock en español*, and international pop *baladas*.

32. Interestingly, many of the Puerto Rican musicians making names for themselves with merengue were women, although most of them reproduced the masculinist perspectives of merengue sung by their male counterparts. See Jorge Duany, "Lo tengo dominao: El boom de las merengueras en Puerto Rico," *Diálogo* (October 1998): 28–29.

33. Ben Ratliff, "Flash and Discipline in the Art of Salsa," *New York Times*, September 14, 1999.

34. Austerlitz, *Merengue*, 94–95.

35. Sydney Hutchinson, *"Merengue Típico* in Santiago and New York: Transnational Regionalism in a Neo-Traditional Dominican Music," *Ethnomusicology* 50, no. 1 (Winter 2006): 59.

36. As elsewhere in Latin America, the Spanish term "popular" refers to its association with ordinary folk rather than to the extent of its commercial success.

37. Pacini Hernandez, *Bachata*, 153–184.

38. In the mid-1980s, I looked for bachata recordings in Inwood, a solidly Dominican neighborhood in upper Manhattan, but I could find only a handful, hidden away in the back of the one or two stores I located that carried them. In a recent interview with bachata guitarist Edilio Paredes, he recalled that bachata was discriminated against by Dominican immigrants in the 1980s—but interestingly, he noted, not by Puerto Ricans, for whom the genre's disreputable reputation was of no concern. Telephone interview, February 1, 2008.

39. Juan Luis Guerra, *Bachata Rosa* (Karen Records KCD 136/BMG 3230, 1990).

40. The 2000 U.S. Census Bureau report indicates that 53.8 percent of the Dominican population in the United States was female.

41. Marti Cuevas, interview by the author, February 4, 2001; see also J&N Records, available at http://www.jnrecords.com/jnstore/about_jn.php (accessed January 23, 2009).

42. Quoted in Anjelina Tallaj, "'A Country That Ain't Really Belong to Me': *Dominicanyorks*, Identity and Popular Music," *Phoebe* 18, no. 2 (Fall 2006): 4.

43. For example, "She left in the early morning without reason, without a *cartita* [letter] or a clue where she might be at." *Generation Next* (BMG 70318, 1999).

44. K.O.B. stands for "Kings of Bachata." *K.O.B. Live* (Premium 0560, 2006).

45. David Wayne, "Aventura," available at http://www.iasorecords.com/aventura.cfm (accessed January 23, 2009).

46. Tallaj, "'A Country That Ain't Really Belong to Me,'" 11.

47. Hutchinson, *"Merengue Típico,"* 37–72.

48. Ibid., 37–41.

49. Ibid., 51.

50. Tallaj recalls her family's response when she first returned to the Dominican Republic: "When my mother saw me, she screamed: 'Ah, you look like a *Dominicanyork.*'" Tallaj, "'A Country That Ain't Really Belong to Me,'" 3.

51. Ibid.

52. Marti Cuevas, interview. Cuevas also informed me that in an effort to attract more Mexicans to their product, J&N released a CD of Mexican narcocorridos (corridos with lyrics about the drug trade) played bachata-style and titled the recording *Narco-bachata.*

53. See, for example, Jorge Duany, "Reconstructing Racial Identity: Ethnicity, Color and Class among Dominicans in the United States and Puerto Rico," *Latin American Perspectives* 25, no. 3 (May 1998): 147–172.

54. See, for example, Martha Ellen Davis, "Music and Black Ethnicity in the Dominican Republic," in *Music and Black Ethnicity: The Caribbean and South America,*

ed. Gerard H. Béhague (New Brunswick, NJ: Transaction Publishers, 1994), 121–122; and Pacini Hernandez, *Bachata,* 127–136.

55. Pacini Hernandez, *Bachata,* 132.

56. "Congos" are traditional drum and percussion ensembles associated with particular religious brotherhoods in Villa Mella and Baní. The African-derived *gaga* is practiced more widely, in the nation's extensive sugarcane planting zones; but, despite its long-term presence in the Dominican Republic, it is considered (by most Dominicans) to be Haitian rather than Haitian Dominican. See Davis, "Music and Black Ethnicity," 129.

57. Ibid., 145.

58. Hannah Gill, "From Margins to Mainstream: Palo and Bachata Music," in "Breaking the Rules: The Impact of Transnational Migration on Music, Religion, and Occupation," Ph.D. diss., Oxford University, 2004.

59. Ibid.

60. Interview with Giovanni Savino, August 2003; see also Deborah Pacini Hernandez, "Bridging the Digital Divide: An Interview with Giovanni Savino," *Journal of Popular Music Studies* 16, no. 1 (2004): 92–101.

61. Gill, "From Margins to Mainstream."

62. Kinito Mendez, *A Palo Limpio* (Sony International 84676, 2001).

63. Jose Itzigsohn and Carlos Dore-Cabral, "Competing Identities? Race, Ethnicity and Panethnicity among Dominicans in the United States," *Sociological Forum* 15, no. 2 (2000): 237.

64. Gill, "From Margins to Mainstream."

65. The Boston-based groups observed by Gill were Palos Peravia, Palos San Miguel, and Palos Santa Elena. Ibid.

66. According to Raquel Z. Rivera, who performs with one such group (the all-female Yaya), at least eight New York–based groups were playing palo in 2007, either exclusively or as part of broader Afro-Dominican or Afro-Caribbean repertoires: Asa-Difé, Francia Reyes, Claudio Fortunato y Sus Guedeses, Palo Mayor, Ilu Aye, Palo Monte, La 21 División, and Yaya. E-mail communication, November 4, 2007.

67. For more on the performance of traditional Dominican musics in New York, see van Buren and Dominguez, "Transnational Music and Dance in Dominican New York," 253–260.

68. Ramona Hernández and Francisco L. Rivera-Batiz, *Dominicans in the United States: A Socioeconomic Profile*, Dominican Research Monographs, CUNY Dominican Studies Institute, New York, October 6, 2003.

69. Jeanette Luna, interview by the author and Raquel Z. Rivera, May 7, 2005.

70. Giselle Roig, interview by the author and Raquel Z. Rivera, May 7, 2005.

71. For more on the topic of second-generation identity among Dominicans, see Itzigsohn and Dore-Cabral, "Competing Identities?" 225–247.

72. Itzigsohn and Dore-Cabral, for example, found that 46.7 percent of the Dominicans in their sample identified as "Hispanos," and another 16.7 percent as Latinos; ibid., 236.

73. An earlier, longer version of this section on the role of Dominicans in reggaeton appears in Deborah Pacini Hernandez, "Dominicans in the Mix: Reflections on Dominican Identity, Race and Reggaeton," in *Reggaeton,* ed. Raquel Z. Rivera, Wayne Marshall, and Deborah Pacini Hernandez (Durham, NC: Duke University Press, 2009), 135–164.

74. Jorge Duany, who has conducted extensive studies of Dominicans in Puerto Rico, notes that the 2000 U.S. Census Bureau's report of 61,455 residents of Dominican birth in Puerto Rico was clearly an undercount and guesstimates that, as of 2006, at least 100,000 Dominicans were living in Puerto Rico. Email communication, August 10, 2006.

75. Duany, "Reconstructing Racial Identity," 163.

76. Jorge Duany, "Dominican Migration to Puerto Rico: A Transnational Perspective," *Centro Journal* 17, no. 1 (2005): 258.

77. Jorge Oquendo, telephone interview by the author, July 23, 2006.

78. "Merenrap" (Ariola 3277-2-RL, 1991).

79. The role of meren-rap in the evolution of reggaeton is subject to interpretation: For some, it was a parallel development that had no direct influence on reggaeton; others, including Oquendo, see it as part of the musical and cultural stew that produced reggaeton. As Oquendo asserted in his interview, "First rap and merengue, then rap and reggaeton, then the three of them mix. . . . Meren-rap is the foundation of reggaeton, the essence, reggaeton comes out of it." This explanation of reggaeton's musical origins is hopelessly simplistic, and clearly Oquendo has a vested interest in promoting a history of reggaeton in which his record label played a central role, but it is significant in that it acknowledges the often-overlooked presence and importance of Dominican musicians and styles constituting the complex cultural matrix from which reggaeton emerged.

80. Tego Calderón, *El Abayarde* (RCA International 53021, 2003).

81. *Mas Flow* (Flow Music Productions 409429, 2003). It is important to note that Luny Tunes' mentor, DJ Nelson, was the first to introduce Dominican aesthetics into reggaeton—although the timing of the simultaneous ascent of Luny Tunes and Dominican aesthetics in reggaeton underscores the production duo's influential role in this development.

82. The term "boricua," a commonly used vernacular term for Puerto Rican people and culture, derives from *Borinquén*, the native Taíno name for their island.

83. When I conducted fieldwork in Puerto Rico in 2006, I found such highly nationalistic perceptions of reggaeton to be quite common; more recently, reggaeton is more likely to be celebrated as a pan-national style, particularly in the wake of work by reggaeton artists such as Tego Calderón and Calle 13, who have deliberately and conspicuously incorporated other Latin American styles and references to pan-Latino issues, such as immigration.

84. *The Chosen Few* (Emerald Entertainment 300102, 2008). *The Chosen Few*'s success in disseminating reggaeton and its associated images, spaces, fashions, and cultural ideologies did for reggaeton what the films *Wild Style* accomplished for hip-hop in 1983 and *Our Latin Thing* for salsa in 1972.

85. Examples include Eddie Dee, Baby Ranks (both parents Dominican), Nicky Jam (Puerto Rican father, Dominican mother, born in the Dominican Republic), OG Black, and Javia. It is important to note, however, that the artists' bios posted on Internet sites are often unreliable, because they are written by fans. On the other hand, such sites are often the only source of information on artists whose record labels do not provide authorized biographies. In the case of Eddie Dee, his Dominican background was mentioned by several of the individuals I interviewed, including no less of an authority than Boy Wonder—himself of Dominican extraction—but I could find no mention of Eddie Dee's Dominican heritage on the Internet.

CHAPTER 6

1. The earliest reference I could find to the term "cosmopolatino" was an Internet posting describing a 2004 Hispanic Heritage Month "Cosmopolatino Tour," which featured a "Latin neo-soul blend of music that is fresh and daring." "Omar Alexander and Sense Kick off Cosmopolatino Tour in Celebration of Hispanic Heritage Month," available at http://www.allbusiness.com/entertainment-arts/broadcasting-industry-radio-broadcast/5546787-1.html (accessed January 23, 2009).

2. Gervase de Wilde, "Why the World Is Catching On to Cumbia: The Infectious Music of Colombia Is Spreading across the Globe," *Daily Telegraph,* January 12, 2008.

3. "NYMosaico," available at http://calabashmusic.com/world/publisher/profile/action/viewbio?item_id=32827 (accessed February 2009).

4. Leila Cobo, "New Latin Grammy?" *Billboard* 118, no. 16 (April 22, 2006): 59, available at http://www.grammy.com/Latin/News/Default.aspx?newsID=2211&newsCategoryID=2 (accessed February 2009). In 2006, four of the five nominees were vallenato groups: Binomio de Oro de America, Jorge Celedón y Jimmy Zambrano, Los Hermanos Zuleta (the winner), and Iván Ovalle. The sole "cumbia" in the category, entitled "Yo bailo cumbia," was by the big band Alfa 8, which had begun as a salsa group before moving into merengue and other tropical genres. The winner in 2007 was also a vallenato group.

5. Scholars have long noted the importance of regional differences in Colombia and their effects on the development of Colombian cultural and national identity. Héctor Fernández L'Hoeste, for example, has observed that "regional differences are very marked, more so than in the average Latin American context, and they are profoundly reflected in local and national culture. The *patria chica* (small homeland), the sense of affiliation to a region . . . is a very important aspect of identity in Colombia and, in many cases, compensates for the deficiencies in the construct of the Colombian nation." See Fernández L'Hoeste, "On How Bloque de Búsqueda Lost Part of Its Name: The Predicament of Colombian Rock in the U.S. Market," in *Rockin' Las Américas: The Global Politics of Rock in Latin/o America,* ed. Deborah Pacini Hernandez, Eric Zolov, and Héctor Fernández L'Hoeste (Pittsburgh: University of Pittsburgh Press, 2004), 180.

6. Indigenous communities inhabit the Guajira peninsula and the highlands of the Sierra Nevada de Santa Marta mountain range on Colombia's eastern coast; and, to the west, the rain forests of the Chocó and the Sinú River basin.

7. As Fernández L'Hoeste has noted, "The attitude of the white-skinned elites was supported by cultural productions like the nineteenth-century texts by José María Samper, which proposed a pyramidal model for the development of the population, with the white elite of the interior at the top (literally, top of the mountains) and the barbaric savages of African descent from the Costa at the bottom." Personal e-mail communication, August 2007.

8. Regarding bambuco's strong Hispanic characteristics, William J. Gradante notes, "Little evidence of indigenous influence in the modern bambuco has come to light, and only when one analyzes the bambuco's less-commercialized, unpolished rustic cousins (such as the *rajaleña*) do African traits become obvious." Gradante, "Colombia," in *The Garland Encyclopedia of World Music: South America, Mexico, Central America, and the Caribbean,* ed. Dale A. Olsen and Daniel E. Sheehy (New York: Garland Publishing, 1998), 386.

9. Peter Wade, *Music, Race, and Nation: Música Tropical in Colombia* (Chicago: University of Chicago Press, 2000), 47–52.

10. In the early 1990s, world beat record companies tried to market various Colombian regional musics in the United States and internationally, but without great success. See Deborah Pacini Hernandez, "Review of *Cumbia Cumbia: A Selection of Colombian Cumbia Recordings; Peregoyo y Su Combo Vacana: Tropicalísimo; Joe Arroyo y La Verdad: Rebelion; Diómedes Díaz and Nicolas 'Colacho' Mendoza: Cantándo!* and *The Meriño Brothers: Vallenato Dynamos!*" *Ethnomusicology* 36, no. 2 (Spring–Summer 1992): 288–296.

11. Like its Mexican antecedent *música ranchera,* carrilera is sung by male or female duos or trios singing in close thirds and accompanied by guitars and is associated, like ranchera, with the low-class mestizo sectors of Colombian society. See Wade, *Music, Race, and Nation,* 115; and Deborah Pacini Hernandez, *Bachata: A Social History of a Dominican Popular Music* (Philadelphia: Temple University Press, 1995), 232–234. Although carrilera's primary audiences have been working-class mestizos from the highland interior of Colombia, it has spread, along with mestizo colonists, to Amazonian regions. When I was in Bogotá in the early 1980s, I was introduced to members of an indigenous group from the Amazon who had just returned from the *mercado* (working-class market), where they had been purchasing supplies to take back their communities; along with predictable items such as batteries, they had purchased a number of carrilera recordings.

12. Cumbia's origins are said to reach back into the colonial period, although Wade insists that no historical documentation directly links pre-nineteenth-century practices to early-twentieth-century cumbia ensembles. See *Music, Race, and Nation,* 60–61.

13. In describing coastal Colombian genres, I use the commonplace terms "flutes," "drums," and "shakers/rattles" rather than the more technical terms for these (categories of) instruments, "audiophones," "membranophones," and "ideophones," respectively.

14. Wade, *Music, Race, and Nation,* 7–11.

15. Ibid.

16. Drums used in traditional cumbia include the *llamador* (held at the knee), *bombo* (two-headed drum), *tambor mayor* (held by the legs), and *caja* (single- or double-headed).

17. Wade, *Music, Race and Nation,* 139–140.

18. Héctor Fernández L'Hoeste, "All Cumbias, the Cumbia: The Latin Americanization of a Tropical Genre," in *Imagining Our Americas,* ed. Sandhya Shukla and Heidi Tinsman (Durham, NC: Duke University Press, 2007), 339.

19. Fernández L'Hoeste suggests the *caña de millo* is a modification of a clarinet-like flute from what is now the Sudan. See "All Cumbias, the Cumbia," 339.

20. Wade, *Music, Race, and Nation,* 106–143.

21. Ibid.,124

22. These record companies did not begin pressing their own records until the mid-1940s.

23. Wade, *Music, Race, and Nation,* 118–122.

24. Jorge Arévalo, personal telephone communication, December 13, 2007.

25. Interestingly, Matilde Díaz claimed to be Mexican in order to escape the social stigma attached to female singers, who were believed to be of loose morals because they inhabited men's leisure spaces. Wade, *Music, Race and Nation,* 105.

26. Fernández L'Hoeste points out that although the term "música tropical" indexed coastal music in Colombia, it acquired different meanings elsewhere in Latin America; see "All Cumbias, the Cumbia," 340.

27. Wade, *Music, Race and Nation,* 100.

28. Valledupar is located at the southern end of the tetrahedron-shaped Sierra Nevada de Santa Marta mountain range, which is still home to various intact if struggling indigenous groups, such as Kogis, Aruacos, and Ika.

29. In this regard, vallenato's development parallels the way Texas border styles coalesced into a distinct conjunto format after they began to be recorded commercially; see Manuel Peña, *Música Tejana: The Cultural Economy of Artistic Transformation* (College Station: Texas A&M University Press, 1999), 93–94.

30. Jorge Arévalo, "The Colombian Costeño Musicians of the New York Metropolitan Region: A Manifestation of Urban Vallenato," master's thesis, Hunter College, City University of New York, 1998, 38–40.

31. Wade, *Music, Race, and Nation,* 88.

32. Lawrence J. Apps, "Afro-Colombian Traditions," in *The Garland Encyclopedia of World Music: South America, Mexico, Central America, and the Caribbean,* ed. Dale A. Olsen and Daniel E. Sheehy (New York: Garland Publishing, 1998), 409.

33. Quoted in Wade, *Music, Race, and Nation,* 164.

34. Ibid., 160–166.

35. La Sonora Dinamita was a studio band first established by Fuentes in 1960 that subsequently became so popular abroad, especially in Mexico, that "clones" (different bands using the same name) were created in order to tour simultaneously; see Pacini Hernandez, "Review of *Cumbia Cumbia,*" 292.

36. See Deborah Pacini Hernandez, Eric Zolov, and Héctor Fernández L'Hoeste, "Mapping Rock Music Cultures across the Americas," in *Rockin' Las Américas: The Global Politics of Rock in Latin/o America,* ed. Deborah Pacini Hernandez, Eric Zolov, and Héctor Fernández L'Hoeste (Pittsburgh: University of Pittsburgh Press, 2004), 1–21.

37. The term *"música gallega"* literally translated, would be "cumbias from Galicia," referring to a historically poor province of Spain from which thousands of impoverished people migrated to the Spanish Caribbean around the turn of the twentieth century. A more accurate, if loose, translation would render the term closer to "honky cumbias," as the idea being expressed is that they lacked rhythmic complexity.

38. See Lise A. Waxer, *The City of Musical Memory: Salsa, Record Grooves, and Popular Culture in Cali, Colombia* (Middletown, CT: Wesleyan University Press, 2002).

39. JGPalomino, "El Binomio de Oro de America," available at http://home.swip-net.se/~w-41164/historia.htm (accessed January 2009).

40. The first chicha groups are said to have emerged from urbanizing areas in the Peruvian Amazon; others emerged from the capital city of Lima. See Olivier Conan, liner notes to *The Roots of Chicha: Psychedelic Cumbias from Peru* (Barbés Records BR0016, 2007).

41. For more on cumbia in Peru, including another variant called *cumbia selvática,* which mixed cumbia with Amazonian indigenous aesthetics, see Wilfredo Hurtado Suarez, *Chicha Peruana: Música de los nuevos migrantes* (Lima, Peru: Grupo de Investigaciones Económicas ECO, 1995); and José Antonio Lloréns Amico, *Música popular en Lima: Criollos y andinos* (Lima, Peru: Instituto de Estudios Peruanos, 1983).

42. Fernández L'Hoeste, "All Cumbias, the Cumbia."

43. While in Mexico, Bermúdez was invited to record for RCA Victor with musicians from Pérez Prado's band (then resident in Mexico), and Pérez Prado covered one of Bermúdez's biggest international hits, "Pachito Eché," with legendary Cuban singer Beny Moré on vocals. See Wade, *Music, Race, and Nation*, 119.

44. José Juan Olvera, "Al norte del corazón: Evoluciones e hibridaciones musicales del noreste Mexicano y sureste de los Estados Unidos con sabor a cumbia," proceedings of the third annual meeting of the Latin American branch of the International Association for the Study of Popular Music, Bogota, 2000, 3, available at http://www.hist.puc.cl/historia/iaspm/pdf/Olvera.pdf (accessed February 2009).

45. Ibid. (translation mine).

46. Alissa Simon, "From Candles to Strobe Lights: Identifying Commercial Cumbia" (unpublished manuscript, 1998). The Mexican two-step, it should be noted, is basically danced to a polka rhythm.

47. Olvera, "Al norte del corazón," 6.

48. Ibid. Note that the term "tejano" is the Spanish modifier for anything or anybody Texas Mexican, as in tejano cuisine.

49. See Eric Zolov, "La Onda Chicana: Mexico's Forgotten Rock Counterculture," in *Rockin' Las Américas: The Global Politics of Rock in Latin/o America*, ed. Deborah Pacini Hernandez, Eric Zolov, and Héctor Fernández L'Hoeste (Pittsburgh: University of Pittsburgh Press, 2004), 22–42.

50. AllMusic Guide Online, available at http://wm03.allmusic.com/cg/amg.dll?p=amg&sql=11:jzfixq95ld0e. Laure's bio on this site also includes the statement that Laure's rhythm was referred to as "chunchaca." Olvera notes that the Mexicanized chunchaca rhythm was disavowed by Colombians; "Al norte del corazón," 4.

51. Helena Simonett, "Música Grupera," in *Encyclopedia of Latin American Popular Music*, ed. Krist Ward and George Torres (Westport, CT: Greenwood Press, forthcoming).

52. In the 1990s, gruperos came back in style and were referred to as "onda grupera": The word "onda" (wave, or groove) linguistically indexed gruperos' roots in 1960s rock 'n' roll, when the term "onda" was in fashion. See Ramiro Burr, "Los Temerarios: Mexico's Superstars of Melody and Romance," *Billboard*, July 9, 2005.

53. Olvera asserts that gruperos originated in Monterrey; "Al norte del corazón," 6. Simonett, in contrast, believes they first developed elsewhere in Mexico, but that Monterrey subsequently became "the hub for the grupo movement." Simonett, "Música Grupera."

54. See Gene Fowler and Bill Crawford, *Border Radio: Quacks, Yodelers, Pitchmen, Psychics, and Other Amazing Broadcasters of the American Airwaves* (Austin: University of Texas Press, 2002).

55. U.S. Census Bureau, available at http://www.census.gov/prod/2001pubs/c2kbr01-3.pdf (accessed February 2009).

56. Olvera, "Al norte del corazón," 9–11.

57. Juan Tejeda, "*Conjunto! Estilo y Clase*: Interview with Narciso Martínez," in *Puro Conjunto: An Album in Words and Pictures*, ed. Juan Tejeda and Avelardo Valdez (Austin: Center for Mexican American Studies, University of Texas, 2001), 336.

58. Manuel Peña, *The Texas-Mexican Conjunto: History of a Working Class Music* (Austin: University of Texas Press, 1958), 107.

59. Peña, *Música Tejana*, 197.

60. Simonett, personal e-mail communication, July 15, 2008.

61. See Helena Simonett, *Banda: Mexican Musical Life across Borders* (Middletown, CT: Wesleyan University Press, 2001), esp. 169, 256–259.

62. Olvera, "Al norte del corazón, 5."

63. Ibid.

64. Celso Piña, *Barrio Bravo* (WEA Latina 87454, 2001).

65. In terms of their sheer size and associated paraphernalia, such as light and smoke systems, sonidero sound systems might be compared to Jamaican sound systems as well as the *picó* sound systems I have described elsewhere ("Sound Systems, World Beat and Diasporan Identity in Cartagena, Colombia," *Diaspora: A Journal of Transnational Studies* 5, no. 3 (1996): 429–466), but the musical genres associated with these Afro-Caribbean sound system events (dancehall reggae and *champeta* [coastal Colombian versions of various Afro-pop styles], respectively, as opposed to Mexican cumbia) are quite distinct.

66. Cathy Ragland, "Mexican Deejays and the Transnational Space of Youth Dances in New York and New Jersey," *Ethnomusicology* 47, no. 3 (Fall 2003): 347; Helena Simonett, "Quest for the Local: Building Musical Ties between Mexico and the United States," in *Postnational Musical Identities: Cultural Production, Distribution, and Consumption in a Globalized Scenario,* ed. Ignacio Corona and Alejandro Madrid (Lanham, MD: Lexington Books, 2007), 119–136.

67. Simonett, "Quest for the Local."

68. The transnational dimensions of the sonidero event observed by Ragland and Simonett are worth noting. In addition to playing music, DJs read aloud announcements and greetings passed to them by audience members, typically dedicated to family members back in Mexico. Since DJs record their performances and duplicate them on the spot, those attending the dance, whose personalized greetings are embedded within the soundtrack of the larger event, can purchase these recordings and send them back to Mexico. (Or, if the event takes place at a sonidero in Mexico, they can be sent to the United States) Sonidero events are thus enriched by an oral dimension with deep cultural resonances that effectively (and affectively) link listeners on both sides of the border. Simonett, for example, notes that "by engaging in the shows, emotional ties with the homeland remain rich and potent. The club is a space where migrants simultaneously live in the old country and in the new." Simonett, "Quest for the Local," 124. Ragland similarly notes that these events serve to literally reposition their listeners by "evok[ing] a newly constructed landscape of social life in New York that is built on a shifting of location, sounds, and images in which the Mexican immigrant youth lives and creates his own cultural and personal reality." Ragland, "Mexican Deejays," 347.

69. Ragland, "Mexican Deejays," 342.

70. Simonett, personal e-mail communication, October 20, 2007.

71. Maria Antonia Vélez, "Narcocorridos, Ballads for Illegal Heroes in Colombia," paper delivered at Harvard University Department of Music Colloquium, 2001 (photocopy).

72. Fernández L'Hoeste, "All Cumbias, the Cumbia," 355–366.

73. See the Web site of one of the companies that produces Colombian narcocorridos: Corridos Prohibidos, available at http://www.corridosprohibidos.net (accessed February 2009).

74. In the early decades of the twentieth century, Colombians were among New York City's diverse immigrants of Latin American origin, but their numbers were initially

too small to make a mark on the city's Latin music landscape. Virginia E. Sánchez Korrol, for example, lists Hispanic organizations located in Manhattan in 1926 and 1927 that include a Club Colombia; the South American Sporting Club might also have had Colombian members. See Virginia E. Sánchez Korrol, *From Colonia to Community: The History of Puerto Ricans in New York City* (1983; repr. Berkeley: University of California Press, 1994), 144–145.

75. Data cited in María Elena Cepeda, "The Colombian Connection: Popular Music, Transnational Identity, and the Political Moment," Ph.D. diss., University of Michigan, 2003, 23; revised version published as *Musical Imagi/Nation: U.S. Colombians in the Latin(o) Music "Boom"* (New York: New York University Press, 2009).

76. Luis Eduardo Guarnizo, Arturo Ignacio Sánchez, and Elizabeth M. Roach, "Mistrust, Fragmented Solidarity, and Transnational Migration: Colombians in New York City and Los Angeles," *Ethnic and Racial Studies* 22, no. 2 (March 1999): 371.

77. Michael W. Collier and Eduardo A. Gamarra, *The Colombian Diaspora in South Florida*, Working Papers Series, Latin American and Caribbean Center, Florida International University, Miami, Florida, May 2001, available at http://lacc.fiu.edu/research_publications/working_papers/WPS_001.pdf (accessed January 27, 2009).

78. Guarnizo, Sánchez, and Roach, "Mistrust, Fragmented Solidarity, and Transnational Migration," 372.

79. Collier and Gamarra, "The Colombian Diaspora in South Florida."

80. Ibid.

81. The 2007 American Community Survey reported 777,554 Colombians in the United States (available at http://www.census.gov/acs/www/index.html [accessed February 2009]).

82. See Peggy Levitt and Mary C. Waters, eds., *The Changing Face of Home: The Transnational Lives of the Second Generation* (New York: Russell Sage Foundation, 2002), 8–9.

83. Cepeda, "The Colombian Connection," 62.

84. Arévalo, "The Colombian Costeño Musicians of the New York Metropolitan Region," 89, 48.

85. They also incorporated instruments such as congas, timbales, güiros, and güiras that are characteristic of other Spanish Caribbean musics. Ibid., 31.

86. Ibid., 82.

87. Carlos Vives, *Clásicos de la Provincia* (Phillips 314-518884-2, 1994).

88. Fernández L'Hoeste, "All Cumbias, the Cumbia," 343.

89. Arévalo, "The Colombian Costeño Musicians of the New York Metropolitan Region," 77.

90. Ibid., 76.

91. Cepeda, "The Colombian Connection," 179.

92. Collier and Gamarra, "The Colombian Diaspora in South Florida."

93. As Guarnizo, Sánchez, and Roach observe, "The socio-demographic profile of Colombians in the United States is unlike that of Latin American immigrants in general and puts them closer to mainstream Americans—and affluent Cubans—than to more numerous and poorer Mexicans, Dominicans and Salvadorans." "Mistrust, Fragmented Solidarity, and Transnational Migration," 372.

94. Carlos Vives, *El Amor de Mi Tierra* (EMI International 22854, 1999).

95. Cepeda, "The Colombian Connection," 61.

96. Gloria Estefan, *Abriendo Puertas* (Epic 67284, 1995).

97. Ibid., 60–62. Santander subsequently broke with Estefan and established his own Santander Music Group. Another example of a Colombian musician who found work with Estefan is the Cali-born, Berklee College of Music–trained jazz musician-composer-engineer Juan Vicente Zambrano, who participated in Vives's *El Amor de Mi Tierra,* playing keyboards and assisting in the production.

98. Santaolalla, who moved to Los Angeles in 1978, is better known for contributing soundtracks for film and television—e.g., *Brokeback Mountain* and *Deadwood*—but he has also been credited with being the most important contributor to the development and commercial ascent of contemporary *rock en español,* not only in Latin America but also in the United States.

99. Juanes, *Fíjate Bien* (Universal Latino 159563, 2000); *Un Día Normal* (Universal Latino 017532, 2002); *Mi Sangre* (Universal Latino 000347502, 2004).

100. Agustin Garza, "Culture Mix: Nowadays, Juanes Loves L.A.: The Colombian Star Returns to the City That Launched His Career, Shooting a Video for a Powerful New Album," *Los Angeles Times,* August 18, 2007.

101. Jace Clayton, "Slow Burn: A Century of Cumbia," *Fader,* no. 55 (July–August 2008), available at http://thefader.cachefly.net/thefader_issue55.pdf (accessed February 2009).

102. See http://www.myspace.com/samim23 (accessed February 2009).

103. DJ Samim's "Heater" video on Youtube, available at http://www.youtube.com/watch?v=NZ806mlFoMY (accessed February 2009).

104. Shaggy featuring Trix and Flix, "Feel the Rush," posted video/MP3 on blog page "The Heat Wave," available at http://www.theheatwave.co.uk/blog/item/shaggy-feat-trix-flix-feel-the-rush (accessed February 2009).

105. DJ Rupture, comments on Wayne Marshall's blog "WayneandWax," March 8, 2008, available at http://wayneandwax.com/?p=304 (accessed January 27, 2008).

106. *King Chango* (Luaka Bop/Warner Brothers 9 46288-2, 1996).

107. Translation: "[Un] evento uniendo amistad, música y nuevos experimentos, y que se atreve a olvidar las leyes de la industria del disco." The festival was subsequently held in other locations, including Argentina and Holland (see the First Festival of Cumbias Experimatales, August 3–11, 1996, La Ceiba, Honduras, available at http://www.periferico.org/festicumex/engels/main3.html [accessed February 2009]).

108. See, for example, Susana Asensio, "The Nortec Edge: Border Traditions and 'Electronica' in Tijuana," in *Rockin' Las Américas: The Global Politics of Rock in Latin/o America,* ed. Deborah Pacini Hernandez, Eric Zolov, and Héctor Fernández L'Hoeste (Pittsburgh: University of Pittsburgh Press, 2004), 312–331; and Ignacio Corona and Alejandro L. Madrid, eds., "Ideology, Flux, and Identity in Tijuana's Nor-tec Music," in *Postnational Musical Identities: Cultural Production, Distribution, and Consumption in a Globalized Scenario* (Lanham, MD: Lexington Books, 2008), 99–117.

109. Clayton, "Slow Burn." For more on cumbia villera, see Fernández L'Hoeste, "All Cumbias, the Cumbia," 346–351.

110. Chapin [no first name], "Lost in MySpace: La Nueva Cumbia," "La Onda Tropical: An Exotic Musical Revolution," available at http://laondatropical.blogspot.com/2008/01/lost-in-myspace-la-nueva-cumbia.html (accessed February 2009).

111. Ibid.

112. Richard Gehr, "Chicha Libre and the Brooklyn-Peru Connection: Bringing Lima's Trippy Underground Sound to Park Slope," *Village Voice,* March 25, 2008, avail-

able at http://www.villagevoice.com/2008-03-25/music/the-brooklyn-peru-connection/2 (accessed May 2009).

113. Quoted in Peter Wade, "Rethinking Mestizaje: Ideology and Lived Experience," *Journal of Latin American Studies* 37, no. 2 (May 2005); also in Wade, *Music, Race, and Nation,* 196.

114. Wade, "Rethinking Mestizaje."

115. See, for example, Conan, *The Roots of Chicha,* and Clayton, "Slow Burn."

CHAPTER 7

1. "RIAA Releases Benchmark Study of Hispanic Consumers of Pre-Recorded Music," RIAA News Room, December 1, 1999, available at http://www.riaa.com/newsitem.php?id=9D438995-0F74-BCF4-63F8-5C3920048218&searchterms=Benchmark%20study%20hispanics&-terminclude=&termexact (accessed January 29, 2009).

2. For a fuller discussion of the differences between the terms "Latin," "Latino," and "Latin American," see Deborah Pacini Hernandez, "The Name Game: Locating Latinas/os, Latins, and Latin Americans in the US Popular Music Landscape," in *A Companion to Latina/o Studies,* ed. Juan Flores and Renato Rosaldo (Malden, MA: Blackwell Publishers, 2007), 49–59.

3. Leila Cobo, "Trends and Potential," *Billboard,* December 25, 2004, 35.

4. For more on the intersections of U.S. Latinos with world beat, see Deborah Pacini Hernandez, "A View from the South: Spanish Caribbean Perspectives on World Beat," *World of Music* 35, no. 2 (1993): 40–69.

5. Because musics of Mexican origin popular in Texas, California, and other parts of the Southwest had few, if any, African-derived aesthetics, they were not suitable candidates for the world beat industry either. Some conjunto music, however, made it into the more folk music–oriented world music circuits. A notable example is the 1998 recording *Los Super Seven,* a collection of songs performed by a mix of seven traditional and contemporary Mexican American musicians, including country and western/rock 'n' roller Freddy Fender (born Baldemar Huerta), David Hidalgo of Los Lobos, and conjunto accordionist Flaco Jiménez (RCA 07863-67689-2, 1998).

6. For musical examples, see *Vaya!!!! R & B Groups Go Latin* (Relic 7098, 1995) and relevant commentary in the liner notes by Donn Fileti.

7. Northern world beat consumers proved to be highly receptive to Cuban music of all sorts, from folkloric groups, such as Los Muñequitos de Matanzas, to contemporary dance bands, such as NG La Banda, and even rock-oriented groups, such as Mezcla and Síntesis. For more on the intersections of Cuban music and world beat, see Deborah Pacini Hernandez, "Dancing with the Enemy: World Beat and the Politics of Race and Authenticity in Cuban Popular Music," *Latin American Perspectives* 25, no. 3 (1998): 110–125. Ariana Hernández-Reguant has also explored this topic in her unpublished manuscript "World Music Producers and the Cuban Frontier."

8. *Buena Vista Social Club* (AMG 366880, 1997).

9. Guerra, for example, released a song, "A Pedir Su Mano," that was a merengue version of the Congolese soukous musician Lea Lignazi's "Dede Priscilla."

10. Alisa Valdes, "The Berry Gordy of Tropical Latin Music," *Boston Globe,* June 21, 1998.

11. Ibid.

12. The Twenty-fourth Annual New York Salsa Festival in 1999, for example, included Dominican *merengueros* Sergio Vargas, Puerto Rican merenguero Elvis Crespo, and New York Dominican *merenguera* Millie Quezada. See Ben Ratliff, "Flash and Discipline in the Art of Salsa," *New York Times,* September 14, 1999.

13. Peter Watrous, "A Producer Who Infuses Salsa's Beat with the Soul of the Streets," *New York Times,* February 9, 1998.

14. Valdes, "The Berry Gordy of Tropical Latin Music."

15. Ibid.

16. Leila Cobo, "Salsa Champion May Sell Part of Record Company," *Miami Herald,* April 8, 1998.

17. See Stephen Holden, "Mambo Kings and Queens," *New York Times,* September 13, 1997.

18. Juan A. Moreno-Velázquez, "Ralph Mercado se declara en bancarrota," *El Diario/La Prensa,* November 20, 2000.

19. See Mireya Navarro, "For Sale: A Latin Music Legacy," *New York Times,* June 7, 2001; and "Universal Music Group Acquires RMM Records' Assets," available at http://forums.allaboutjazz.com/showthread.php?t=1908&page=3 (accessed January 29, 2009).

20. Leila Cobo, "Emusica Buys Fania Holdings," *Billboard,* August 27, 2005, 15.

21. As mentioned in Chapter 6, readers should be aware that the adjective "tejano" refers generically to anything of Texas Mexican derivation, but capitalized "Tejano" refers specifically to the more eclectic and pop-oriented commercial musical popular in Texas.

22. Abel Salas, "Record Label Abandons Tejano Experiment," *Hispanic* (September 1998): 14.

23. Ramiro Burr, "Regional Mexican Music Dances through a Changing Landscape," *Billboard,* July 19, 1997, 41, 44, 52.

24. Ramiro Burr, "Tejano Market Hits a Lull: Dip Opens Doors for Mexican Genre," *Billboard,* December 13, 1997, 5, 86.

25. Ibid.

26. Valdes, "The Berry Gordy of Tropical Latin Music."

27. John Lannert, "Exploding Regional-Mexican Market Attracts 'Major' Attention," *Billboard,* August 17, 1996, 35, 42.

28. Ibid.

29. Burr, "Tejano Market Hits a Lull."

30. Lannert, "Exploding Regional-Mexican Market Attracts 'Major' Attention."

31. "Fonovisa: A Mexican Record Company Expanding in the US," *Music and Copyright,* April 31, 1996.

32. Leila Cobo, "Acquisition of Fonovisa Makes UMG a Latin Music Mammoth," *Billboard,* April 27, 2002,10.

33. Phil Hardy, "UMG Becomes Market Leader in Mexico and in the US Latin Music Market with Fonovisa Distribution Deal," *Music and Copyright,* January 22, 2003.

34. Ramiro Burr, "Hats Off to the Music of Regional Mexico," *Billboard,* July 25, 1998, 49, 55.

35. Quoted in Josh Kun, "A Good Beat, and You Can Protest to It," *New York Times,* May 14, 2006.

36. "Freddie Martinez," available at http://www.freddierecords.com/biography.html (accessed January 29, 2009).

37. Ramiro Burr, "Regional Mexican: Independents on the Rise," *Billboard*, June 26, 2004, 29.

38. Jewish American salsa pianist and bandleader Larry Harlow was one of the primary organizers of the protest. See Jim Melanson, "NARAS Trustees Hear Latinos," *Billboard*, May 3, 1975, 8.

39. As a 1983 article in *Billboard* explains, "The new Latin Grammys will honor excellence in all the *major* groupings of Latin music listened to by U.S. Latins [*sic*], the fruit of the labor of this country's Latin record industry." Enrique Fernández, "NARAS Takes a Welcome Step," *Billboard*, June 18, 1983, 59.

40. This is not to suggest that all *rock en español* is the same, but rather that the rock traditions from different Latin American nations are categorized collectively.

41. Keith Negus, "La cultura, la industria y la matriz de la salsa: El negocio de la música en los Estados Unidos y la producción de la música Latina" (Culture, Industry and the Salsa Matrix: The Music Business in the United States and the Production of Latin Music), *Revista de Ciencias Sociales* 4 (1998): 27–52. See also Keith Negus, *Music Genres and Corporate Cultures* (London: Routledge, 1999).

42. Ramiro Burr, "Musicians Want Pact's Benefits," *Express News* (San Antonio, Texas), May 11, 1999.

43. Negus, "Culture, Industry and the Salsa Matrix."

44. Rob Patterson, "Tejano Blues and Union Dues Support Tejano Advancement in Recording Campaign," *San Antonio Current*, 1999.

45. Suzanne Gamboa, "Caucus Probes Latino Musician Pay Gap," *Boston Globe*, September 1, 2001.

46. The term "Latin Academy of Recording Arts and Sciences" illuminates the inherent absurdity of employing the vestigial term "Latin" to describe the extraordinary range of musics from throughout the Spanish- and Portuguese-speaking worlds.

47. John Lannert, "LARAS Makes Its Mark on NARAS," *Billboard*, February 5, 2000, 15.

48. Direct competition between U.S. Latinos and major Latin American stars is not limited to the sales of recordings: Miami-based Latino artists seeking performance gigs also find it hard to compete with major Latin American stars passing through Miami; see Jose Davila, "You Got Your Reggaetón in My Hip-Hop: Crunkiao and 'Spanish Music' in the Miami Urban Scene," in *Reggaeton*, ed. Raquel Z. Rivera, Wayne Marshall, and Deborah Pacini Hernandez (Durham, NC: Duke University Press, 2009), 200–212.

49. Fernando González, "Latin Grammies: An Idea Whose Time Has Come?" *Miami Herald*, May 24, 1996.

50. Mireya Navarro, "Latin Grammys Border Skirmish," *New York Times*, September 13, 2000.

51. For more on Miami's transformation into the center of the Latin/o American music and culture industries, see George Yúdice, *The Expediency of Culture: Uses of Culture in the Global Era* (Durham, NC: Duke University Press, 2003); and Daniel Party, "The *Miamization* of Latin-American Pop Music," in *Postnational Musical Identities: Cultural Production, Distribution, and Consumption in a Globalized Scenario*, ed. Ignacio Corona and Alejandro L. Madrid (New York: Lexington Books, 2008), 65–80.

52. Martin Polon, "The Gateway to the South," *One to One,* September 1997, 73.

53. Criticism of the Latin music construct has come from Latin American sources as well. Colombian musicologist and professional musician Jairo Moreno, for example, has argued that the concept of Latin music, which originates in the United States, not Latin America, reflects "the process of imagining Latin America from the particular perspective afforded and dictated by [the] condition [of being] an immigrant to the U.S." The term, he goes on to say, is an artifact of "a discursive community that enjoys the perspective (e.g., socio-economical advantages, information access, opportunities for traveling, mechanisms of production) made possible by living in the U.S." Interestingly, Moreno states this in the context of arguing that, in the 1970s, U.S.-based companies, particularly Fania and its mostly Puerto Rican participants, were responsible for defining the concept of "Latin music" and designating New York–based Afro-Cuban salsa as the quintessential symbol of Latin American identity, then exporting it back into Latin America for consumption. Moreno notes that, during this period, other Latin American musics were not similarly deployed by the U.S.-based Latin music labels as hemispheric symbols of Latin unity and solidarity. See Moreno, "Tropical Discourses: Community, History, and Sentiment in Rubén Blades's Latin Music(s)," *Journal of Popular Music Studies* 13, no. 2 (2001): 133–163.

54. Given the ambiguities of the term *"Latinos,"* it is unclear if Colón is referring to U.S. Latinos or all Latin/o Americans. The original Spanish reads as follows: "La nueva moda era redefinir todo lo latino como cubano. . . . Por el derecho de poder controlar todo lo que sea Latino, una vez mas nos han convertido en botín para la mafia de Miami." "Willie Colón dice que los Estefan son 'la punta de lanza de la mafia cubana,'" Associated Press, September 16, 2001 (translation mine).

55. Cobo, "Acquisition of Fonovisa."

56. Leila Cobo, "Latin Grammys a Hit," *Billboard,* November 19, 2005, 12.

57. As Leila Cobo notes, few Tejano recordings were being released at the time; so, if reduced production and sales were ostensibly the reasons for the category changes, in principle the Tejano category should have been eliminated as well. See Cobo, "Latin Notas: Grammys Shift Categories," *Billboard,* August 12, 2006, 70.

58. Arlene Dávila, *Latinos Inc.: The Marketing and Making of a People* (Berkeley: University of California Press, 2001), 70–73.

59. Randall Roberts, "Hitsville: The Year in Music, by the Numbers," *LA Weekly's* Music Blogs, December 17, 2008, available at http://blogs.laweekly.com/play/poped/the-year-in-music-by-the-numbe (accessed January 29, 2009).

60. In 2007, for example, Latin music accounted for only 6.4 percent of reported album sales. Leila Cobo, "Digital Dilemma, Online Sales Remain Inconsistent for Latin Market," *Billboard,* April 26, 2008, 20.

61. The precise figures reported by the 2007 American Community Survey are 44,019,880 Latinos out of a total population of 298,757,310 (available at http://www.census.gov/acs/www/index.html [accessed February 2009]).

62. Leila Cobo, "CC Bows 'Hurban' Format," *Billboard,* November 27, 2004, 8.

63. Daddy Yankee, *Barrio Fino* (V.I. Music 450639, 2004).

64. Leila Cobo, "Reggaeton Broke Out but Regional Mexican Acts Drove Latin Biz," *Billboard,* December 24, 2005, 20.

65. Leila Cobo, "Latin Albums Surge amid Industry Declines," *Billboard,* July 30, 2005, 7–8.

66. Ibid.

67. Leila Cobo, "Radio Flips for Reggaetón," *Billboard,* September 10, 2005, 47.

68. Javier Andrade, "Mas Gasolina?" *Hispanic* (May 2006).

69. Leila Cobo, "Reggaetón Boosts Latin Sales," *Billboard,* April 29, 2006, 12.

70. Leila Cobo, "Latin Notas: What the Numbers Tell Us; Latin Retail: Not as Rosy, or Maybe not as Dire, as You Think," *Billboard,* January 20, 2007, 12.

71. Cobo, "Latin Albums Surge," 7–8.

72. Negus, *Music Genres and Corporate Cultures,* 14–30.

Selected Bibliography

Acosta-Belén, Edna, and Carlos E. Santiago. *Puerto Ricans in the United States: A Contemporary Portrait.* Boulder, CO: Lynne Reiner Publishers, 2006.

Alvarez, Luis. "From Zoot Suits to Hip Hop: Towards a Relational Chicano/a Studies." *Latino Studies* 5 (2007): 53–75.

Andrews, George Reid. *Afro-Latin America.* New York: Oxford University Press, 2004.

Aparicio, Frances R. *Listening to Salsa: Gender, Latin American Music, and Puerto Rican Cultures.* Middletown, CT: Wesleyan University Press, 1998.

Aparicio, Frances R., and Cándida Jáquez, with María Elena Cepeda, eds. *Musical Migrations: Transnationalism and Cultural Hybridity in Latin/o America* (New York: Palgrave Macmillan, 2003).

Arévalo, Jorge. "The Colombian Costeño Musicians of the New York Metropolitan Region: A Manifestation of Urban Vallenato." Master's thesis, Hunter College, City University of New York, 1998.

Asensio, Susana. "The Nortec Edge: Border Traditions and 'Electronica' in Tijuana." In *Rockin' Las Américas: The Global Politics of Rock in Latin/o America,* edited by Deborah Pacini Hernandez, Eric Zolov, and Héctor Fernández L'Hoeste, 312–331. Pittsburgh: University of Pittsburgh Press, 2004.

Audinet, Jacques. *The Human Face of Globalization: From Multicultural to Mestizaje.* Lanham, MD: Rowman and Littlefield, 1999.

Austerlitz, Paul. *Merengue: Dominican Music and Dominican Identity.* Philadelphia: Temple University Press, 1997.

———. "From Transplant to Transnational Circuit: Merengue in New York." In *Island Sounds in the Global City: Caribbean Popular Music and Identity in New York,* edited by Ray Allen and Lois Wilken, 44–60. New York: New York Folklore Society and the Institute for Studies in American Music, Brooklyn College, 1998.

Avant-Mier, Roberto. "Latinos in the Garage: A Genealogical Exploration of Latino/a Influence in Garage Rock, Rock and Pop Music." *Popular Music and Society* 31, no. 5 (2008): 555–574.

Ayala, César J., and Rafael Bernabé. *Puerto Rico in the American Century: A History since 1898.* Chapel Hill: University of North Carolina Press, 2007.

Bilby, Kenneth M. "The Caribbean as a Musical Region." In *Caribbean Contours,* edited by Sidney W. Mintz and Sally Price, 181–218. Baltimore: Johns Hopkins University Press, 1985.

Boggs, Vernon W., ed. *Salsiology: Afro-Cuban Music and the Evolution of Salsa in New York City.* New York: Excelsior Music Publishing, 1992.

Cepeda, María Elena. "The Colombian Connection: Popular Music, Transnational Identity, and the Political Moment." Ph.D. diss., University of Michigan, 2003. Revised version published as *Musical Imagi/Nation: U.S. Colombians in the Latin(o) Music "Boom."* New York: New York University Press, 2009.

Collier, Michael W., and Eduardo A. Gamarra. "The Colombian Diaspora in South Florida." Latin American and Caribbean Center, Florida International University, Miami, Florida, May 2001.

Corona, Ignacio, and Alejandro L. Madrid, eds. "Ideology, Flux, and Identity in Tijuana's Nor-tec Music." In *Postnational Musical Identities: Cultural Production, Distribution, and Consumption in a Globalized Scenario,* 99–117. Lanham, MD: Lexington Books, 2008.

Dávila, Arlene. *Latinos, Inc.: The Marketing and Making of a People.* Berkeley: University of California Press, 2001.

Davila, Jose. "You Got Your Reggaetón in My Hip-Hop: Crunkiao and 'Spanish Music' in the Miami Urban Scene." In *Reggaeton,* edited by Raquel Z. Rivera, Wayne Marshall, and Deborah Pacini Hernandez, 200–212. Durham, NC: Duke University Press, 2009.

Davis, Martha Ellen. "Music and Black Ethnicity in the Dominican Republic." In *Music and Black Ethnicity: The Caribbean and South America,* edited by Gerard H. Béhague, 119–155. New Brunswick, NJ: Transaction Publishers, 1994.

Delgado, Richard, and Jean Stephanic, eds. *The Latino/a Condition: A Critical Reader.* New York: New York University Press, 1998.

Duany, Jorge. "Dominican Migration to Puerto Rico: A Transnational Perspective." *Centro Journal* 17, no. 1 (2005): 243–269.

———. "Reconstructing Racial Identity: Ethnicity, Color and Class among Dominicans in the United States and Puerto Rico." *Latin American Perspectives* 25, no. 3 (May 1998): 147–172.

Dzidzienyo, Anani, and Suzanne Oboler, eds. *Neither Enemies nor Friends: Latinos, Blacks and Afro-Latins.* New York: Palgrave, 2005.

Fernández L'Hoeste, Héctor. "All Cumbias, the Cumbia: The Latin Americanization of a Tropical Genre." In *Imagining Our Americas,* edited by Sandhya Shukla and Heidi Tinsman, 338–364. Durham, NC: Duke University Press, 2007.

Flores, Juan. "'Cha Cha with a Backbeat': Songs and Stories of Latin Boogaloo." In *From Bomba to Hip-Hop: Puerto Rican Culture and Latino Identity,* 79–112. New York: Columbia University Press, 2000.

———. *From Bomba to Hip-Hop: Puerto Rican Culture and Latino Identity.* New York: Columbia University Press, 2000.

———. "'Puerto Rican and Proud, Boyee!' Rap, Roots and Amnesia." *Boletín del Centro de Estudios Puertorriqueños* 5, no. 1 (1992–1993): 22–31.

———. "Wild Style and Filming Hip-Hop." *Areito* 10, no. 37 (1984): 36–39.

Flores, Juan, ed. "'Qué Assimilated, Brother, Yo Soy Assimilao': The Structuring of Puerto Rican Identity." In *Divided Borders: Essays on Puerto Rican Identity,* 183–195. Houston: Arte Público Press, 1993.

Flores, Juan, and Renato Rosaldo, eds. *A Companion to Latina/o Studies.* Malden, MA: Blackwell Publishing, 2007.

Garcia, Matt. "The 'Chicano' Dance Hall: Remapping Public Space in Post–World War II Greater Los Angeles." In *Sound Identities: Popular Music and the Cultural Politics of Education,* edited by Cameron McCarthy, Glenn Hudak, Shawn Miklauic, and Paula Saukko, 317–341. New York: Peter Lang Publishing, 1999.

Garofalo, Reebee. *Rockin' Out: Popular Music in the U.S.A.* Saddle River, NJ: Pearson/Prentiss Hall, 1997.

Gill, Hannah. "From Margins to Mainstream: Palo and Bachata Music." In "Breaking the Rules: The Impact of Transnational Migration on Music, Religion, and Occupation." Ph.D. diss., Oxford University, 2004.

Giovannetti, Jorge L. "Popular Music and Culture in Puerto Rico: Jamaican and Rap Music as Cross-Cultural Symbols." In *Musical Migrations: Transnationalism and Cultural Hybridity in Latin/o America,* edited by Frances R. Aparicio and Cándida F. Jáquez, 81–98. New York: Palgrave Macmillan, 2003.

Glasser, Ruth. *My Music Is My Flag: Puerto Rican Musicians and Their New York Communities, 1917–1940.* Berkeley: University of California Press, 1995.

Glick Schiller, Nina, Linda Basch, and Cristina Blanc-Szanton, eds. "Transnationalism: A New Analytic Framework for Understanding Migration." In *Towards a Transnational Perspective on Migration: Race, Class, Ethnicity, and Nationalism Reconsidered,* 1–24. New York: New York Academy of Sciences, 1992.

Gronow, Pekka. "Ethnic Recordings: An Introduction." In *Ethnic Recordings in America: A Neglected Heritage,* 1–49. Washington, DC: American Folklife Center, 1982.

Guarnizo, Luis Eduardo, Arturo Ignacio Sánchez, and Elizabeth M. Roach. "Mistrust, Fragmented Solidarity, and Transnational Migration: Colombians in New York City and Los Angeles." *Ethnic and Racial Studies* 22, no. 2 (March 1999): 367–396.

Guevara, Rubén. "The View from the Sixth Street Bridge: The History of Chicano Rock." In *The Rock History Reader,* edited by Theo Cateforis, 37–42. New York: Routledge, 2007.

Habell-Pallán, Michelle. *Loca Motion: The Travels of Chicana and Latina Popular Culture.* New York: New York University Press, 2005.

Haney Lopez, Ian F. "Colorblind to the Reality of Race in America." *Chronicle of Higher Education* 53, no. 11 (November 3, 2006).

Hannerz, Ulf. *Transnational Connections: People, Cultures, Places.* London: Routledge, 1996.

Haslip-Viera, Gabriel. "The Evolution of the Latino Community in the New York Metropolitan Area, 1810 to the Present." In *Latinos in New York: Communities in Transition,* edited by Gabriel Haslip-Viera and Sherri Baver, 3–29. Notre Dame, IN: Notre Dame University Press, 1996.

Hernández, Ramona, and Francisco L. Rivera-Batiz. *Dominicans in the United States: A Socioeconomic Profile.* Dominican Research Monographs, City University of New York Dominican Studies Institute, New York. October 6, 2003.

Hernández-Reguant, Ariana. "World Music Producers and the Cuban Frontier." Unpublished manuscript.

Hutchinson, Sydney. "*Merengue Típico* in Santiago and New York: Transnational Regionalism in a Neo-Traditional Dominican Music." *Ethnomusicology* 50, no. 1 (Winter 2006): 37–72.

Itzigsohn, Jose, and Carlos Dore-Cabral. "Competing Identities? Race, Ethnicity and Panethnicity among Dominicans in the United States." *Sociological Forum* 15, no. 2 (2000): 225–247.

Jiménez Román, Miriam. "Looking at That Middle Ground: Racial Mixture as Panacea?" In *A Companion to Latina/o Studies,* edited by Juan Flores and Renato Rosaldo, 325–336. Malden, MA: Blackwell Publishing, 2007.

Jones, Alan, and Jussi Kantonen. *Saturday Night Forever: The History of Disco.* Edinburgh, UK: Mainstream Publishers, 1999.

Kasinitz, Phillip, John H. Mollenkopf, Mary C. Waters, and Jennifer Holdway. *Inheriting the City: The Children of Immigrants Come of Age.* Cambridge, MA: Harvard University Press, 2008; New York: Russell Sage Foundation, 2008.

Keil, Charles. "People's Music Comparatively: Style and Stereotypes, Class and Hegemony." *Dialectical Anthropology* 10 (1985): 119–130.

Kun, Josh. "Bagels, Bongos, and Yiddishe Mambos, or the Other History of Jews in America." *Shofar* 23, no. 4 (Summer 2005): 50–68.

Lawrence, Tim. *Love Saves the Day: A History of American Dance Music Culture.* Durham, NC: Duke University Press, 2003.

Levitt, Peggy. *Transnational Villagers.* Berkeley: University of California Press, 2001.

Levitt, Peggy, and Nina Glick Schiller, eds. "Conceptualizing Simultaneity: A Transnational Social Field Perspective on Society." *International Migration Review* 38, no. 3 (Fall 2004): 1002–1039.

Levitt, Peggy, and Mary C. Waters. *The Changing Face of Home: The Transnational Lives of the Second Generation.* New York: Russell Sage Foundation, 2002.

Lipsitz, George. "Cruising around the Historical Bloc: Postmodernism and Popular Music in East Los Angeles." *Cultural Critique* 5 (Winter 1986–1987): 157–177.

———. *Dangerous Crossroads: Popular Music, Postmodernism and the Poetics of Place.* New York: Verso, 1994.

———. *Footsteps in the Dark: The Hidden Histories of Popular Music.* Minneapolis: University of Minnesota Press, 2007.

———. "Land of a Thousand Dances: Youth, Minorities, and the Rise of Rock and Roll." In *Recasting America: Culture and Politics in the Age of Cold War,* edited by Larry May, 267–283. Chicago: University of Chicago Press, 1989.

Loza, Steven. *Barrio Rhythms: Mexican American Music in Los Angeles.* Urbana: University of Illinois Press, 1993.

———. *Tito Puente and the Making of Latin Music.* Urbana: University of Illinois Press, 1999.

Manuel, Peter. *Popular Musics of the Non-Western World.* New York: Oxford University Press, 1988.

———. "Representations of New York City in Latin Music." In *Island Sounds in the Global City,* edited by Ray Allen and Lois Wilken, 23–43. New York: New York Folklore Society and the Institute for Studies in American Music, Brooklyn College, 1998.

Marshall, Wayne. "Dembow, Dem Bow, Dembo: Translation and Transnation in Reggaeton." *Song and Popular Culture* 52 (2008): 131–151.

———. "From Música Negra to Reggaeton Latino: The Cultural Politics of Nation, Migration, and Commercialization." In *Reggaeton,* edited by Raquel Z. Rivera, Wayne Marshall, and Deborah Pacini Hernandez, 19–76. Durham, NC: Duke University Press, 2009.

———. "Routes, Rap, Reggae: Hearing the Histories of Hip-Hop and Reggae Together." Ph.D. diss., University of Wisconsin, Madison, 2007.

Martínez-Echazábal, Lourdes. "Mestizaje and the Discourse of National/Cultural Identity in Latin America, 1845–1959." *Latin American Perspectives* 25, no. 3 (May 1998): 21–42.

McCarthy, Jim, with Ron Sansoe. *Voices of Latin Rock: The People and Events That Created This Sound.* Milwaukee: Hal Leonard Corporation, 2004.

Menchaca, Martha. "Latinas/os and the *Mestizo* Racial Heritage of Mexican Americans." In *A Companion to Latina/o Studies,* edited by Juan Flores and Renato Rosaldo, 313–324. Malden, MA: Blackwell Publishing, 2007.

Meraz, Gerard. "An Oral History of East Los Angeles DJ Culture." Master's thesis, California State University, Northridge, December 2004.

Morales, Ed. *The Latin Beat: The Rhythm and Roots of Latin Music from Bossa Nova to Salsa and Beyond.* Boston: DaCapo Press, 1999.

Moreno, Jairo. "Tropical Discourses: Community, History, and Sentiment in Rubén Blades's Latin Music(s)." *Journal of Popular Music Studies* 13, no. 2 (2001): 133–163.

Negus, Keith. "La cultura, la industria y la matriz de la salsa: El negocio de la música en los Estados Unidos y la producción de la música Latina" [Culture, Industry and the Salsa Matrix: The Music Business in the United States and the Production of Latin Music]. *Revista de Ciencias Sociales* 4 (1998): 27–52.

———. *Music Genres and Corporate Cultures.* London: Routledge, 1999.

Olvera, José Juan. "Al norte del corazón: Evoluciones e hibridaciones musicales del noreste mexicano y sureste de los Estados Unidos con sabor a cumbia." Proceedings of the third annual meetings of the Latin American branch of the International Association for the Study of Popular Music, Bogota, 2000. Available at http://www.hist.puc.cl/historia/iaspm/pdf/Olvera.pdf (accessed September 17, 2007).

Pacini Hernandez, Deborah. *Bachata: A Social History of a Dominican Popular Music.* Philadelphia: Temple University Press, 1995.

———. "Dancing with the Enemy: World Beat and the Politics of Race and Authenticity in Cuban Popular Music." *Latin American Perspectives* 25, no. 3 (1998): 110–125.

———. "Dominicans in the Mix: Reflections on Dominican Identity, Race and Reggaeton." In *Reggaeton,* edited by Raquel Z. Rivera, Wayne Marshall, and Deborah Pacini Hernandez, 135–164. Durham, NC: Duke University Press, 2009.

———. "The Name Game: Locating Latinas/os, Latins, and Latin Americans in the US Popular Music Landscape." In *A Companion to Latino Studies,* edited by Juan Flores and Renato Rosaldo, 49–59. Malden, MA: Blackwell Publishing, 2007.

———. "Review of *Cumbia Cumbia: A Selection of Colombian Cumbia Recordings*; *Peregoyo y Su Combo Vacana: Tropicalísimo*; *Joe Arroyo y La Verdad: Rebelion*; *Diómedes Díaz and Nicolas 'Colacho' Mendoza: Cantándo!* and *The Meriño Brothers: Vallenato Dynamos!" Ethnomusicology* 36, no. 2 (Spring–Summer 1992): 288–296.

———. "Sound Systems, World Beat and Diasporan Identity in Cartagena, Colombia." *Diaspora: A Journal of Transnational Studies* 5, no. 3 (1996): 429–466.

———. "A View from the South: Spanish Caribbean Perspectives on World Beat." *World of Music* 35, no. 2 (1993): 40–69.

Pacini Hernandez, Deborah, and Reebee Garofalo. "Between Rock and a Hard Place: Negotiating Rock in Revolutionary Cuba, 1960–1980." In *Rockin' Las Américas: The Global Politics of Rock in Latin/o America,* edited by Deborah Pacini Hernandez, Eric Zolov, and Héctor Fernández L'Hoeste, 43–67. Pittsburgh: University of Pittsburgh Press, 2004.

Pacini Hernandez, Deborah, Eric Zolov, and Héctor Fernández L'Hoeste. "Mapping Rock Music Cultures across the Americas." In *Rockin' Las Américas: The Global Politics of Rock in Latin/o America,* edited by Deborah Pacini Hernandez, Eric Zolov, and Héctor Fernández L'Hoeste, 1–21. Pittsburgh: University of Pittsburgh Press, 2004.

———. *Rockin' Las Américas: The Global Politics of Rock in Latin/o America,* edited by Deborah Pacini Hernandez, Eric Zolov, and Héctor Fernández L'Hoeste. Pittsburgh: University of Pittsburgh Press, 2004.

Party, Daniel. "The *Miamization* of Latin-American Pop Music." In *Postnational Musical Identities: Cultural Production, Distribution, and Consumption in a Globalized Scenario,* edited by Ignacio Corona and Alejandro L. Madrid, 65–80. New York: Lexington Books, 2008.

Peña, Manuel. *Música Tejana: The Cultural Economy of Artistic Transformation.* College Station: Texas A&M University Press, 1999.

———. *The Texas-Mexican Conjunto: History of a Working Class Music.* Austin: University of Texas Press, 1958.

Pérez Firmat, Gustavo. "Latunes: An Introduction." *Latin American Research Review* 43, no. 2 (2008): 180–203.

———. *Life on the Hyphen: The Cuban-American Way.* Austin: University of Texas Press, 1994.

Portes, Alejandro. "Introduction: The Debates and Significance of Immigrant Transnationalism." *Global Networks* 1, no. 3 (2001): 181–193.

Portes, Alejandro, Luis Guarnizo, and Patricia Landholt. "The Study of Transnationalism: Pitfalls and Promise of an Emergent Research Field." *Ethnic and Racial Studies* 22, no. 2 (March 1999): 217–237.

Portes, Alejandro, and Rubén G. Rumbaut. *Immigrant America: A Portrait.* Berkeley: University of California Press, 1990.

Quintero Rivera, Ángel. *Salsa, sabor y control! Sociología de la música "tropical."* Havana, Cuba: Casa de las Américas, 1998.

Ragland, Cathy. "Mexican Deejays and the Transnational Space of Youth Dances in New York and New Jersey." *Ethnomusicology* 47, no. 3 (Fall 2003): 338–354.

Reyes, David, and Tom Waldman. *Land of a Thousand Dances: Chicano Rock 'n' Roll from Southern California.* Albuquerque: University of New Mexico Press, 1998.

Rivera, Raquel Z. "Between Blackness and Latinidad in the Hip Hop Zone." In *A Companion to Latino Studies,* edited by Juan Flores and Renato Rosaldo, 351–362. Malden, MA: Blackwell Publishing, 2007.

———. "Boricuas from the Hip Hop Zone: Notes on Race and Ethnic Relations in New York City." *Boletín del Centro de Estudios Puertorriqueños* 8, nos. 1–2 (1996): 202–215.

———. *New York Ricans from the Hip Hop Zone.* New York: Palgrave Macmillan, 2003.

———. "Policing Morality, *Mano Duro Stylee*: The Case of Underground Rap and Reggae in Puerto Rico in the Mid-1990s." In *Reggaeton,* edited by Raquel Z. Rivera, Wayne Marshall, and Deborah Pacini Hernandez, 111–134. Durham, NC: Duke University Press, 2009.

Rivera, Raquel Z., Wayne Marshall, and Deborah Pacini Hernandez, eds. *Reggaeton.* Durham, NC: Duke University Press, 2009.

Roberts, John Storm. *The Latin Tinge: The Impact of Latin American Music on the United States.* New York: Oxford University Press, 1999. First published 1979.

Romo, Ricardo. *East Los Angeles: History of a Barrio.* Austin: University of Texas Press, 1983.

Rondón, César Miguel. *The Book of Salsa: A Chronicle of Urban Music from the Caribbean to New York City.* Chapel Hill: University of North Carolina Press, 2008. Translated by Frances R. Aparicio, with Jackie White, from the original *El libro de la salsa: Crónica de la música del Caribe urbano* (Caracas, Venezuela: Editorial Arte, 1980).

Rosales, Arturo F. *Chicano! The History of the Mexican American Civil Rights Movement.* Houston: Arte Público Press, 1997.

Safa, Helen. "Challenging *Mestizaje*: A Gender Perspective on Indigenous and Afrodescendant Movements in Latin America." *Critique of Anthropology* 25, no. 3 (2005): 307–330.

Salazar, Max. "Afro-American Latinized Rhythms." In *Salsiology: Afro-Cuban Music and the Evolution of Salsa in New York City,* edited by Vernon W. Boggs, 239–248. New York: Excelsior Music Publishing, 1992.

———. *Mambo Kingdom: Latin Music in New York.* New York: Schirmer Trade Books, 2002.

Sánchez, George. *Becoming Mexican American: Ethnicity, Culture and Identity in Chicano Los Angeles, 1900–1945.* New York: Oxford University Press, 1993.

Sánchez Korrol, Virginia E. *From Colonia to Community: The History of Puerto Ricans in New York City.* Berkeley: University of California Press, 1994. First published 1983.

Santiago, Javier. *Nueva ola portoricensis: La revolución musical que vivió Puerto Rico en la década del 60.* Santurce, Puerto Rico: Editorial del Patio, 1994.

Shapiro, Peter. *Turn the Beat Around: The Secret History of Disco.* New York: Faber and Faber, 2005.

Simon, Alissa. "From Candles to Strobe Lights: Identifying Commercial Cumbia." Unpublished manuscript, 1998.

Simonett, Helena. *Banda: Mexican Musical Life across Borders.* Middletown, CT: Wesleyan University Press, 2001.

———. "Música Grupera." In *Encyclopedia of Latin American Popular Music,* edited by Krist Ward and George Torres (forthcoming).

———. "Quest for the Local: Building Musical Ties between Mexico and the United States." In *Postnational Musical Identities: Cultural Production, Distribution, and Consumption in a Globalized Scenario,* edited by Ignacio Corona and Alejandro Madrid, 119–136. Lanham, MD: Lexington Books, 2007.

Singer, Roberta L. "Tradition and Innovation in Contemporary Latin Popular Music in New York City." *Latin American Music Review* 4, no. 2 (1983): 183–202.

Singer, Roberta L., and Elena Martinez. "A South Bronx Music Tale." *Centro Journal* 16, no.1 (Spring 2004): 177–201.

Spottswood, Richard K. "Commercial Ethnic Recordings in the United States." In *Ethnic Recordings in America: A Neglected Heritage,* 51–66. Washington, DC: American Folklife Center, 1982.

Strachwitz, Chris, with James Nicolopulos. *Lydia Mendoza: A Family Autobiography.* Houston: Arte Público Press, 1993.

Suro, Robert, and Jeffrey Passel. *The Rise of the Second Generation: Changing Patterns in Hispanic Population Growth.* Report published by the Pew Hispanic Center, Washington, D.C., October 14, 2004.

Tallaj, Anjelina. "'A Country That Ain't Really Belong to Me': *Dominicanyorks,* Identity and Popular Music." *Phoebe* 18, no. 2 (Fall 2006): 1–14.

Tejeda, Juan, and Avelardo Valdez. *Puro Conjunto: An Album in Words and Pictures.* Austin: Center for Mexican American Studies, University of Texas, 2001.

Torres-Saillant, Silvio, and Ramona Hernández. *The Dominican Americans.* Westport, CT: Greenwood Press, 1998.

Van Buren, Thomas, and Leonardo Ivan Dominguez. "Transnational Music and Dance in Dominican New York." In *Dominican Migration: Transnational Perspectives,* edited by Ernesto Sagas and Sintia E. Molina, 244–273. Gainesville: University Press of Florida, 2004.

Vázques, Blanca, Juan Flores, and Pablo Figueroa. "Interview with KMX Assault: The Puerto Rican Roots of Rap." *Boletín del Centro de Estudios Puertorriqueños* 1, no. 1 (1992–1993): 39–51.

Wade, Peter. *Music, Race, and Nation: Música Tropical in Colombia.* Chicago: University of Chicago Press, 2000.

———. "Rethinking Mestizaje: Ideology and Lived Experience." *Journal of Latin American Studies* 37, no. 2 (May 2005): 239–257.

Washburne, Christopher. *Sounding Salsa: Performing Latin Music in New York City.* Philadelphia: Temple University Press, 2008.

Waxer, Lise A. *The City of Musical Memory: Salsa, Record Grooves, and Popular Culture in Cali, Colombia.* Middletown, CT: Wesleyan University Press, 2002.

Zolov, Eric. "La Onda Chicana: Mexico's Forgotten Rock Counterculture." In *Rockin' Las Américas: The Global Politics of Rock in Latin/o America,* edited by Deborah Pacini Hernandez, Eric Zolov, and Héctor Fernández L'Hoeste, 22–42. Pittsburgh: University of Pittsburgh Press, 2004.

———. *Refried Elvis: The Rise of the Mexican Counterculture.* Berkeley: University of California Press, 1999.

Index

Deborah Pacini Hernandez is Associate Professor, Anthropology and American Studies, Tufts University. She is the author of *Bachata: A Social History of a Dominican Popular Music* (Temple) and the coeditor of *Reggaeton* and *Rockin' Las Américas: The Global Politics of Rock in Latin/o America.*

Oye Como Va!

Deborah Pacini Hernandez

Oye Como Va!

*Hybridity and Identity in
Latino Popular Music*

TEMPLE UNIVERSITY PRESS
Philadelphia

Temple University Press
1601 North Broad Street
Philadelphia PA 19122
www.temple.edu/tempress

Copyright © 2010 by Deborah Pacini Hernandez
All rights reserved
Published 2010
Printed in the United States of America

♾ The paper used in this publication meets the requirements of the
American National Standard for Information Sciences—Permanence of
Paper for Printed Library Materials, ANSI Z39.48-1992

Library of Congress Cataloging-in-Publication Data

Pacini Hernandez, Deborah.
  Oye como va! : hybridity and identity in Latino popular music /
  Deborah Pacini Hernandez.
    p. cm.
  Includes bibliographical references and index.
  ISBN 978-1-4399-0089-5 (cloth : alk. paper) — ISBN 978-1-4399-0090-1
(pbk. : alk. paper)
  1. Hispanic Americans—Music—Social aspects.   2. Popular music—Social
aspects—United States.   I. Title.
  ML3917.U6P33 2009
  781.64089'68073—dc22   2009012832

2 4 6 8 9 7 5 3 1

Contents

Preface

B ecause hybridity—the mixture of two or more dissimilar elements—produces objects or people that are in between and out of place, it is often considered dangerous, inferior, or contaminating. My dual-region ancestry, set down in two areas widely and erroneously perceived to be racially and culturally distinct (Latin America and the United States), has been the source of tensions and anxieties associated with feeling in between and out of place. My father, who was born in Barranquilla, Colombia, was himself of mixed ancestry: the child of a Colombian mother and a third-generation Italian Colombian father, whose extended Colombian-born Italian Colombian family members kept their ties to and identification with the "old country" as active as they could in the days before means of transportation and communication made it easy to do so. Indeed, my paternal grandfather had broken with his parents' generation's standing practice of returning to Italy to find a bride when he married my grandmother, a local Colombian woman, who, family lore has it, may have been of Sephardic ancestry. My mother, who was born and raised in the United States, has maternal ancestors who have resided in the mid-Atlantic and northeastern part of the country for generations. But her father was an immigrant from Canada, the child of German immigrants to the province of Kitchener, who came to the United States as a young man to practice his chosen profession as a Presbyterian minister.

Complicating my ancestral mix is the fact that I lack strong cultural roots in any one place. Because my father's quixotic and peripatetic nature impelled my family to move repeatedly among New York State, Colombia, and various other parts of Latin America, my childhood—and, hence, my deepest sense of self—was indelibly imprinted with the rhythms, sounds, and sights of multiple locations. As an adult, I have spent several years, on and off, in the northern coastal region of Colombia (known locally as *la costa*), where I lived as a child. My first marriage was to a *barranquillero* (whose indigenous ancestry was unclaimed but phenotypically visible), who turned out to be as unstable as my father; thus, for the seven years of our marriage, I continued moving back and forth between Colombia and the United States. As a result, my daughter, Radha, was born in coastal Cartagena, and my son, Tai, was born in New York, and neither one has lived in the place where he or she was born for more than a few months. After I became an anthropologist, I spent several seasons in Colombia doing fieldwork, but now the years I have lived in the United States far outnumber the years I have lived in Colombia. My vivid memories of and family connections and personal attachments to Colombia nevertheless remain integral features of my psyche, alongside those—equally powerful—that I have developed in the United States. Despite my ambiguous identity and the instability connected with my lack of deep roots in a single location, I am grateful for my life of multiplicities and movement. These are the life experiences that have, among other things, honed my sensitivity to hybridity (and its discontents) whenever and wherever I have encountered or observed it.

This book—which explores the simultaneously powerful, vexing, and stimulating relationships between hybridity, music, and identity—grew out of my personal realization of the dangers (as George Lipsitz has phrased it) of living at the crossroads.[1] Growing up with English- *and* Spanish-speaking relatives and friends, listening to rock 'n' roll *and cumbias,* loving corn flakes *and* Colombia's corn *arepas,* I identified with both the United States and Colombia but never felt that I belonged completely in, or to, either one. As a child, I was unsure how to answer when people asked where I was from, and when I got older, I was confounded by the identity boxes on official forms. In the 1980s, I claimed the term "Latina" as a better alternative than "My father is from Colombia, and my mother is from the United States." Even so, I often found myself excluded from the "Latina" category because my profile did not conform to widespread expectations of what that identifier was supposed to encompass: My background included Latin American ancestry and residence, but my parents were both college-educated and middle-class (despite the economically precarious situations we often found ourselves in as a result of my father's instability). Moreover, because of my light skin and its concomitant privileges, I was not a target of the overt racism experienced by darker-skinned Latinos. But since I did not conform to prevailing ideas of who or what it was to be "American" either, I found myself in between and out of place.

In my adolescence, a time when group identity is so important to a young person's developing sense of self, I did not have one. Now, having spent decades as a researcher and educator exploring the diversity of U.S. Latino experiences, I know that many other Latinos and Latinas with mixed ancestries and multiple geographic roots have also had to defend themselves against charges of fraudulently claiming an identity—be it white, black, Puerto Rican, American, Latino, or any other presumably bounded category. Indeed, the effects of ambiguity and dislocation produced by hybridity and border crossings have been well articulated in a vibrant body of literature pioneered by Latino and Latina writers such as Piri Thomas, Gloria Anzaldúa, Cherríe Moraga, and Frances Negrón-Muntaner and subsequently developed further by many others who have similarly experienced the alienation of feeling out of place. Given the pervasiveness of essentialist notions of fixed and unambiguous boundaries (among Latinos and non-Latinos alike), it is perhaps more accurate to locate myself and other similarly hybrid individuals as living not only at the crossroads but also in the crosshairs of U.S. identity politics.

If many Latinos have themselves been quite conscious of their hybridity, in the U.S. popular imagination the styles of music associated with Latinos have often been imagined as the "natural" expressions of communities defined ethnically or racially, as if they were unmixed and disconnected from other musics or, if mixed at all, mixed only with proximate cultures rather than with broader cultural developments on the national (and international) stage. The corollary has been that Latinos who listened to rock 'n' roll, disco, and other contemporary styles of rock and hip-hop were somehow cultural traitors for having abandoned their ancestral identity and culture in order to get ahead by passing as something they were not. Some scholars, in contrast, have demonstrated the analytical power and possibilities of more inclusive approaches to U.S. Latino musical practices—such as Juan Flores in his pioneering work comparing New York Puerto Rican and Chicano identities and exploring the complicated roots of New York Puerto Rican boogaloo, George Lipsitz in his essays on merengue and *banda* in *Footsteps in the Dark,* and Luis Alvarez in his recent call for "relational" Latino studies.[2]

Oye Como Va![3] builds on and extends such comparative, cross-cultural work by placing hybridity itself at the center, examining and validating Latino music making and identity formation that have always taken place at the intersections of (presumably) dissimilar categories. Latinos' relationship to their hybridity has not been unproblematic, as it has often conflicted with equally powerful and valid desires to maintain a cultural identity uncomplicated by mixture or references to other genealogies. Central to the premise of this book, however, is the idea that far from being something abnormal or problematic, hybridity, whether racial, ethnic, cultural, or a combination of these, is one of the signature characteristics of the Latino experience: It is not a question of "either/or," but rather, like hybridity itself, of "both/and." *Oye Como Va!* brings to the surface and into focus the many ways that Latino musicians and their fans have refused to permit prevailing, often essentialist constructions of individual and group identity (no matter who espouses them) to limit their ability to define themselves.

As we move further into the new millennium, all sorts of border crossings have become easier and more commonplace, and even expected. Taking note of these developments, the eclectic, thoroughly transnational Latin Grammy–nominated musician Kevin Johansen—who grew up in and now performs his unique blend of Latin American and U.S. styles in both his mother's Argentina and his father's United States—announces on his Web site, "Mixture is the future."[4] In validating and valorizing Latino hybridity, however, it is important to emphasize that I am aware of the distinctions between cultural and racial hybridity and that I do not confuse racial hybridity with the concept of color-blindness, *blanqueamiento* (whitening), or other similarly veiled ways of erasing and denying the persistence of racial disparities and inequalities, which I discuss at length in Chapter 1.

My approach to the subject of hybridity and identity in Latino popular music is comparative and connective. I draw data from multiple sources in order to contrast the numerous inter- and intracultural strategies for negotiating hybridity (whether personal or musical) adopted over the past century and into the new millennium by Latinos from different ethnic, racial, and national backgrounds in different regions of the United States. Included are the musical practices of the foundational U.S. Latino communities: New York Puerto Ricans and Mexican Americans in California and the Southwest. Because globalization and the multiple diasporas it has set in motion have complicated the U.S. Latino music landscape, however, I add to the analytical mix examples of the musical blendings and layerings being produced by Dominicans and Colombians, recent immigrants whose identities, in a globalizing context, have proven to be even more complex than those of their predecessors. Still, this book is not intended to be comprehensive; some important groups, locations, and styles receive little or no attention. For example, Cuban music and Cuban Americans in the United States (whose locations and trajectories have not been the same) are mentioned but are not central within my narrative.[5] Other significant "urban borderlands" in the U.S. interior, such as Chicago, where the new musical hybrid *duranguense* appeared, are not covered here either. It is my hope that this book will serve as a template and road map for future comparative research into the layerings and mixings that have always characterized the United States and that have been intensified by newer immigrant flows.

My methodology is also hybrid. I draw extensively on my many years of fieldwork in the Spanish Caribbean and among Spanish Caribbean Latinos, but this is not an ethnography. My primary goals are to connect dots, to reveal patterns, and to interpret them through the theoretical lenses of hybridity and identity—or, more precisely, identities: what happens at the intersections of race, class, ethnic, national, gender, and generational identity formation. It is noteworthy that my work would not have been possible as recently as fifteen years ago, since most of the groundbreaking ethnographies and cultural histories of particular Latino communities and their musics had not yet been published. Today, I can see and interpret "the big picture" only because I can stand on the shoulders of Frances Aparicio, Juan Flores, Ruth Glasser, George Lipsitz, Manuel Peña, Raquel Z. Rivera, Helena Simonett, Peter Wade, Lise Waxer, and other scholars too numerous to mention. I am grateful to and thank them all.

Many others contributed to this book more directly by reading and commenting on drafts, answering particular queries, sharing their own work, or leading me to the work of others. They include (in alphabetical order—and my apologies for inadvertent omissions) Jorge Arévalo Mateus, Paul Austerlitz, Boy Wonder (Manuel Alejandro Ruiz), Christian Capellan, Maria Elena Cepeda, Marti Cuevas, Benjamin de Menil, Jorge Duany, Héctor Fernández L'Hoeste, Kai Fikentscher, Juan Flores, Hannah Gill, Jorge Giovanetti, Rubén Guevara, Peggy Levitt, Jeanette Luna, Peter Manuel, Wayne Marshall, Gerard Meraz, Carmen Oquendo, Jorge Oquendo, Juan Otero, Edilio Paredes, Cathy Ragland, Raquel Z. Rivera, Marisol Rodriguez, Giselle Roig, Helen Safa, Dave Sanjek, Helena Simonett, Roberta Singer, Chuy Varela, and Elijah Wald. I also thank the anonymous manuscript readers, whose insightful and knowledgeable comments were extremely helpful. Others contributed to this book in more practical ways: Aldo Marin from Cutting Records, Marika Pavlis from Rhino/Warner Brothers, and Gerard Meraz, who assisted with images and permissions; the deans at Tufts University, who gave me time off from teaching to work on the manuscript; Tufts University's FRAC Committee, which provided publication support; and Paige Johnson, Lynn Wiles, and Susan Ulbrich in the Anthropology Department and Kathy Spagnoli and Lauren Coy in American Studies, who helped in myriad small but important ways. Many thanks also go to those who assisted in the production process: Leslie Cohen, who helped format the original manuscript; Heather Wilcox, who provided copyediting; Carleen Loper, who assisted with proofreading; and Jan Williams, who did the indexing. Last but not least, I want to thank the Editorial, Production, and Marketing staff at Temple University Press, especially Janet Francendese, Joan Vidal, and Gary Kramer.

My most constant and valued source of support, however, has been my husband, best friend, and partner for life, Reebee Garofalo, whose unfaltering love and sense of humor carried me through some truly difficult moments and made the rest of them just plain fun. He also generously shared his extensive knowledge of U.S. popular music while I was thinking through material that intersected with his own work, making connections that I might not have discerned myself and referring me to additional sources. I am particularly grateful to him for reading many drafts of chapters for which—although he was not always familiar with the subject matter—he managed to provide me with a critical (if gentle) eye that greatly strengthened this book. Reebee's genealogy and upbringing, by the way, could not be more different from mine. To begin with, he is 100 percent southern Italian, as were his parents and his grandparents and his close-knit extended family, who still preface their Thanksgiving turkey dinner with a lasagna. (Luckily I had an Italian surname when I first met the family!) In addition, Reebee has spent all but a few years of his life in the northeastern region of the United States—in New Haven, where he grew up, and in Boston, where he has spent nearly forty years putting his interests in popular music and political activism together in socially productive ways. The almost two decades that I have spent with Reebee in the Boston area—after a childhood and young adulthood spent moving every few years—have given me a stability I had not known previously. I am deeply grateful to Reebee for the gift of roots.

I was also fortunate to be surrounded by a warm and generous circle of family and friends whose support deserves acknowledgment. I am particularly grateful to my mother, Betsey Pacini, whose natural curiosity and ability to savor new places and things taught me to make the best of growing up nomadic. Janine, Murray, and Zamawa in Somerville and Boston enriched my social and intellectual life while the book was in progress. I was also fortunate to be on the sidelines of, but close enough to be inspired by, the activities of Reebee's marching band, the Second Line Social Aid and Pleasure Society Brass Band, and the amazing Honk! Festival of activist marching bands they organize every October in Somerville. Most of the book, however, was written not in my adopted hometown, Somerville, but in our cottage on Broad Cove in Onset, on the south shore of Massachusetts, where we spend our summers and as many weekends as we can. My ability to raise my eyes from my computer screen and look out onto Broad Cove's constantly changing colors and textures and its passing wildlife helped me stay centered and sane during the intensely focused work of writing. More importantly, Carleen, Jim, Elliott, Irena, Dan, Rhonda, Dale, Mike, Bridget, Austin, Randy, Doug, Rocky, and Debby welcomed us into the kind of caring neighborhood community that I did not believe still existed.

Developing roots in Boston and southeastern Massachusetts has been made even easier by the blessing of living in close proximity to my daughter, Radha, and my son, Tai (now grown since I acknowledged them in my first book on *bachata* back in 1995), and their respective partners, Doug and Tiffany. I have had the additional joy of being able to bask regularly in that lovely stream of sunshine provided by Radha's daughter, Soleil. Undoubtedly, I delayed working on the manuscript to grab every opportunity to have Soleil stay with us overnight and on weekends, but I know the book is better for it because her youthful energy and insatiable curiosity about the world she is growing up in are contagious and invigorating. Soleil, I should note, whose father is a black Dominican born in Puerto Rico and raised in Cambridge, Massachusetts, has an even more complicated racial, ethnic, and cultural genealogy than mine. But I am confident that she is growing up in a world where she can celebrate and enjoy her hybridity as an asset and a source of strength. Soleil, this book is dedicated to you and to others like you.